LIFE SPACES

LIFE SPACES
Gender, Household, Employment

edited by
Caroline Andrew
and
Beth Moore Milroy

UBCPress
Vancouver

ISBN 0-7748-0295-2 (hardcover)
ISBN 0-7748-0408-4 (paperback)

Canadian Cataloguing in Publication Data

Main entry under title:
Life spaces : gender, household, employment

Bibiliography: p. 187
ISBN 0-7748-0408-4

  1. Women and city planning — Canada.
2. Cities and towns — Canada. 3. Feminism.
4. Women — Employment — Canada. 5. Sociology.
Urban — Canada. I. Andrews, Caroline, 1942-
II. Milroy, Beth Moore, 1940-
~~HT127.L54~~ ~~1988~~   307.7'6'0971   C88-091278-2

This book has been published with the help of a grant
from the Social Science Federation of Canada, using funds
provided by the Social Sciences and Humanities Research
Council of Canada.

UBC Press
University of British Columbia
6344 Memorial Rd.
Vancouver, BC V6T 1Z2
(604) 822-3259
Fax: (604) 822-6083

Contents

Notes on Contributors

CAROLINE ANDREW, Department of Political Science, University of Ottawa.

FRAN KLODAWSKY, Status of Women Office, Carleton University, Ottawa.

SUZANNE MACKENZIE, Department of Geography, Carleton University, Ottawa.

WILLIAM MICHELSON, Department of Sociology and Centre for Urban and Community Studies, University of Toronto.

BETH MOORE MILROY, School of Urban and Regional Planning, University of Waterloo.

DENISE PICHÉ, Ecole d'architecture, Université Laval, Québec.

DAMARIS ROSE, Institut national de recherche scientifique—Urbanisation, Université du Québec, Montréal.

ARON SPECTOR, Ark Research Associates, Ottawa.

GRACE STRACHAN, Community Renewal Branch, Ministry of Municipal Affairs of Ontario, Toronto.

PAUL VILLENEUVE, Département de Géographie, Université Laval, Québec.

GERDA R. WEKERLE, Faculty of Environmental Studies, York University, Toronto.

JEANNE M. WOLFE, School of Urban Planning, McGill University, Montreal.

Introduction

CAROLINE ANDREW and BETH MOORE MILROY

Existing theories about urban structure make no allowance for the fact that women's and men's experiences of cities are different or that women's activities shape and are shaped by urban structure and processes. Current analyses tend to wash out all distinctions between women and men in the name of a genderless humanity. Implicitly, if unintentionally, male experience has become the societal norm, and changes in gender relations have been ignored. Eliminating women as a distinct category of urban actors leads to inaccurate descriptions, explanations, and prescriptions for our cities.

This book explores the inter-relationship between gender and urban structure; it is concerned with feminist analyses of how and why urban areas are structured as they are. Gender—which signifies socially created as opposed to biologically based differences between women and men—is relevant to the analysis of urban structure. Just as Marxist scholarship has made researchers aware of the importance of class as a factor in analyzing social phenomena, so feminist scholarship has helped illustrate the centrality of gender.

This collection is a tribute to the vitality and excitement of the research being done into gender and urban structure in Canada. The authors come from a variety of disciplines and use various approaches in their common concern to explore the ways in which gender relations operate in Canadian urban environments. The collection originated in a day-long session at a conference organized by the Institute of Urban Studies of the University of Winnipeg in August 1985. The object of the session was to bring together people interested in the analysis of gender relations in an urban context and to present an overview of the state of research in this area.

By using the term "gender" rather than "sex," one is insisting on the social construction of differences between females and males and, therefore, focusing on the role of social institutions and social processes in moulding patterns of behaviour and thought. It is not biological differences (which may be denoted by "sex") that are the focus of attention; rather, it is the way in which elements of the social structure, and specifically those elements germane to urban life, create differences in what females and males do and are expected to do in a particular society. Our knowledge about urban life is overwhelmingly androcentric, or male-centred, and yet it is created without explicit reference to either sex. Gender-based studies are explicit about whether women or men are under scrutiny as well as about the social conventions within which the behaviour occurs (Eichler and Lapointe, 1985).

The authors whose studies appear here all work in areas at the junction between physical urban structure and the socioeconomic practices that shape it and spring from it. In this collection, "urban structure" connotes the way everyday life spaces are laid out and made more or less accessible to women and men and express their interests as they conduct their daily lives. This book presents a uniquely Canadian perspective on the question of gender and urban environment, with certain general themes reappearing throughout the chapters.

The study of gender relations through an examination of urban structure and process is a relatively recent activity which can be best understood within the context of the evolution of feminist thought. In what can be called the first wave of contemporary feminist thought—characterized by Simone de Beauvoir's *The Second Sex*—the solution to the inferior position of women was seen to lie in their entrance to the paid labour force. Research focused on the labour force and on the work place as its physical location. A second phase of feminist thought, focusing not so much on the equality of women but on their specificity, examined the dual roles of women participating in market labour and continuing to be largely responsible for the care of children and the maintenance of households. The physical setting was no longer either the work place or the home; it was an interrelationship of the two. The city, in particular, can be seen as the physical stage on which the multiple aspects of women's lives are acted out. The feminist emphasis on the "personal as political" encouraged women to treat the environment of daily life as a lens for understanding their experience. As Robin Morgan perceived, women were not dealing with idiosyncractic, but widespread, experience:

> Women's liberation is the first radical movement to base its politics—in fact, create its politics—out of concrete personal experiences. We've learned that those experiences are *not* our private hang-ups. They are shared by every woman, and are therefore political. (1970, p. xvii)

Access, equality of treatment, dominance, power—all these vital questions can be raised through an examination of the institutions governing social relations in the modern urban environment.

CANADIAN PERSPECTIVES

This book differs from others that deal with gender and environment in that it takes a Canadian perspective; all the articles deal specifically with Canada and aspects of the Canadian urban experience. The Canadian experience of gender and environment differs from other countries in three ways: 1) Canadian cities are different from those in other countries; 2) the Canadian institutional and policy framework is unique, and 3) there are specifically Canadian elements to the theoretical material used to understand the development of urban structures. In the research process, that is, the process of moving back and forth between practice and theory, all these factors become important.

The history, geography, demography, and culture of Canada mean that our cities have a specificity of their own. Although large Canadian cities share many characteristics common to North American cities, they are not identical to those of the United States. This argument has been developed in detail by Michael A. Goldberg and John Mercer in their book, *The Myth of the North American City*: "Canada and the United States are distinct and distinguishable places and societies. Moreover, and in keeping with our thrust that cities are tightly integrated into the societies of which they form an important part, Canadian and American cities differ markedly and across well-defined dimensions" (1986, p. 246).

Some of these differences are central to the study of gender relations in the urban environment. To take one significant example, Canadian inner cities are less devastated than are their American counterparts; they still retain a viable residential component relatively close to the core, and they are less dangerous places to visit or to live in. For this reason, a higher percentage of families with children are found in Canadian cities, as compared to American ones. These factors obviously affect the lives of the women and men living in these cities and therefore will influence the analysis of gender relations and the urban environment. One might even speculate on the relationship between this Canadian characteristic of liveable cities and the fact that the articles in this volume treat women as playing a variety of roles, both as actors in and as victims of the structuring of urban space, rather than treating women almost exclusively as submitting to unfavourable urban conditions created by others. As Canadian cities are seen to be places in which families, and therefore women, can choose to live, it has been easier to conceptualize the relationship between urban structure and women as involving both influence on women and influence by women.

Another Canadian feature has been our long tradition with resource towns and with the particular form of urban planning associated with this kind of community. In the early period, the creation of the resource town was very much the responsibility of the private company interested in exploiting the resources. What little planning took place was done by the company. However, more recently, governments have taken a much more active role in the development of resource towns, and the planning has increasingly introduced a wider variety of aspects, such as recreational and social dimensions. Some of the particular features of resource towns—a narrow range of employment possibilities, usually dominated by traditionally male occupations; a social hierarchy tightly focused on one's place in the work force of the major company; a high level of social problems—are of obvious import to a study of gender relations. The impact on gender relations of this particular form of development has been one focus for studies of resource towns (Women's Research Centre, 1977; Luxton, 1980).

Another difference in the Canadian urban reality comes from the particular institutional and policy framework that exists in Canada. Existing governmental structures, intergovernmental relations, and policy directions shape the direction of urban governance and the directions of urban research. The fact that there has been greater public intervention in social and economic questions in Canada, as compared to the United States, once again makes the Canadian urban experience unique. At all levels, the state has played a more active role in the development of the urban structure. An indication of this public sector activity can be seen from the fact that much of the early impetus to study gender and the urban environment in Canada stems from government initiatives, notably from the federal government. The National Capital Commission, emphasizing its Canada-wide responsibility for developing model urban environments, organized a national workshop in 1975 on the concerns of women in shaping the urban environment. The Ministry of State for Urban Affairs, whose brief existence was the high point of federal concern for urban policy, sponsored a series of studies in 1975 on the place of women in various cities across Canada. In both cases these activities were part of the federal government programme for International Women's Year. It may be that the federal government was more interested in fulfilling its international obligations than in looking seriously at questions of gender relationships but its activities clearly sparked interest in this area.

Not only has Canadian urban development been influenced by the relatively interventionist role of the government as a whole, but it is also clearly influenced by the particular division of responsibilities within the public sector. The Canadian federation is, comparatively speaking, decentralized, and the provincial governments have been quite conscious of their constitutional responsibility for municipal institutions. Compared to the United States, Canada's provincial governments have been stronger and the municipalities weaker. This has led, among other results, to much greater success in creating regional governments in Canada because provincial governments have been better able to impose regional structures.

The nature of the overall governmental system obviously influences the kinds of programmes available and the capacity of different groups to make use of them. Our analysis of social housing programmes, for instance, is influenced by the fact that the recent trend in Canada has been towards a greater provincial role in this policy area, changing the political strategies involved. For example, the organization involved in promoting housing programmes specifically for women differs depending upon whether the initiative is provincial or federal.

But research does not only stem from the observation of reality; it is also influenced by theory. The area of gender and environment has been influenced by a great many fields of study, as the references in these articles witness. Urban sociology, geography, urban studies, women's studies, not to mention the work done on gender and environment itself—all these disciplines and perspectives have helped mould the way Canadian researchers have examined the relations between gender and our urban environment. A great number of these theoretical influences are international, but some of them are Canadian. For instance, the metropolitan thesis in Canadian history emphasizes the role of cities and the importance of the urban influence throughout Canadian development (Careless, 1967; Davis, 1985). Development has taken place through linkages between metropolitan centres and through urban influences penetrating the surrounding hinterland. Economic, social, and cultural progress has come from the urban centres and has spread to the areas controlled by these centres. This tradition of historical research interprets the role of cities in a more positive light than the rather more anti-urban tradition associated with the frontier thesis in the United States. The strength of the metropolitan thesis in Canada may help to reinforce the characteristic of the research done in Canada that we noted earlier, that of seeing women in a wide variety of roles, rather than simply as victims of a hostile urban environment.

The Canadian perspective on the study of the relations between gender and environment emerged from the interplay of practice and theory. The Canadian urban experience influenced researchers and practitioners, and this practical understanding was clarified by reference to the different bodies of scholarship. Certain early federal initiatives have already been mentioned, such as the NCC Conference and the studies undertaken by the Ministry of state for Urban Affairs. The centre of this emerging research area in Canada has been York University. Particularly important is the work of Gerda Wekerle, who was instrumental in creating *Women and Environments*, a periodical which acts as an information exchange and a link between urban practice and theory.¹ One of the co-editors of *New Space for Women* (Wekerle *et al.*, 1980), Gerda Wekerle has not only been active in promoting research in Canada but has also acted as a link between Canadian and international scholars interested in the study of gender and environments.

KEY THEMES

The articles in this book share the sense of urgency common to much of modern feminist scholarship that argues the vital importance—both practical and theoretical—of understanding gender relations. The authors recognize that Canadian cities, like those elsewhere, are currently undergoing processes of economic restructuring that are profoundly affecting both urban structure and gender relations. The contributors believe that the better the understanding of these major changes, the more able one is to work for desirable outcomes or to prevent harmful consequences.

One way to understand the impact of these processes of economic restructuring on gender relations is to analyze the inter-relation of the processes of production and reproduction.

Gender relations in any particular society can be understood by examining the relations between the organization of 1) the production of goods and services and 2) the way in which the society goes about maintaining and reproducing the labour force outside the labour process itself. In effect, all societies produce goods and services and must also maintain the conditions necessary to continue that production. This process of reproducing the society may involve education, health services, child care, emotional support, and so on. The extent to which these are carried out within or beyond the home and the extent to which they form part of "family responsibilities" or are socialized vary; they must be examined for specific societies at specific times.

This approach exists in mainstream theorizing about urban systems, notably in the Marxist perspective. The feminist research using this approach differs from the Marxist by emphasizing gender as a theoretical construct and set of social relations not reducible to class. This concern with gender has led to a clear appreciation of the intricacy of the inter-relations between production and reproduction.

In her article, Suzanne Mackenzie explores the impact of changes in production and in reproduction not only on gender roles but also on the way urban form is structured. She selects two periods both marked by an "urban crisis" and a "woman crisis." The late 1800's and the mid-1900's were both transition periods in which significant economic restructuring occurred. Mackenzie discusses the shifts in the organization of production and reproduction that took place in both periods and identifies how cities were restructured and gender roles altered. The beginning of the twentieth century saw the transition to industrial capitalism in Canada, accompanied by an urban pattern of reproduction isolated in private homes away from spheres of production. This had obvious repercussions for urban structure—with the creation of residential suburban neighbourhoods—and for gender roles—with the full-time housewife in a nuclear family supported in the suburban home by the income of her husband.

Changes in the organization of production in the middle and late twentieth century include massive entry of women into the paid work force (Armstrong, 1984). The increasing use of female labour brings about modifications in the form and locus of reproductive activities: for instance, demands for child care outside the home. Changes in production and reproduction are beginning to influence both urban structure and gender relations. In the case of urban structure, for example, the logic of bedroom suburbs is being questioned, leading to a reinvestment in central residential areas. The pattern of gender relations is also changing, in part because working mothers present a challenge to the household division of labour.

The article by Damaris Rose and Paul Villeneuve shares the same general perspective of the impact of economic restructuring on gender roles, although it deals specifically with the contemporary period. It has a double mission: 1) to investigate how city structure changes with restructuring in the labour market, and 2) to examine how residential patterns are linked to the spatial restructuring of the labour market. Major shifts at the present time include the feminization of the labour force and an increasing bipolarization of jobs into professional and unskilled categories as the proportion of traditional middle-class jobs shrinks. With these shifts in the labour market, the pattern of residential location changes. And residential location is a key element in how reproduction is structured.

Rose and Villeneuve examine the extent to which inner-city Montreal neighbourhoods have been socially transformed as a result of both labour market changes and gender relations. In certain neighbourhoods, a large number of new residents are professional women who share with the long-resident working-class women a need for social services and support systems. In these circumstances, class differences may be mitigated by similar gender needs, allowing socially mixed neighbourhoods to develop. Once again urban form and gender relations are linked with production and reproduction.

Jeanne M. Wolfe and Grace Strachan's article also deals with the impact of economic changes on urban structure, in a case study of late nineteenth-century Montreal and the role played by Julia Drummond in the Montreal Parks and Recreation Association. The urban reform movement can be understood as a reaction to the social problems created by industrialization and immigration, and Wolfe and Strachan argue that insufficient attention has been given to the role of women in the urban reform movement. Women, largely of the upper middle class, organized to push for better services in order to improve the living conditions of the urban poor and, therefore, mitigate the social costs of industrialization. They were concerned with improving the living conditions of women, almost exclusively in terms of their role as mothers: better parks and playgrounds would allow for healthier, happier, and eventually more productive children.

Wolfe and Strachan look closely at the organizational methods used by these women activists. They used their husbands' positions, which combined the resources of social respectability and wealth, with their own energy and networks, creating organizations and activities that have had enduring impacts on urban structure. This study underlines, as does that of Rose and Villeneuve, the importance of understanding both the impact of economic restructuring and the influence of community organizing on gender roles and urban structure. The restructuring of relations of production and reproduction in urban settings has transformed gender roles. However, women have not been merely passive victims of these changes; they have also acted to redirect, channel, and control processes of urban change.

William Michelson's article is also directly concerned with understanding the impact of major economic changes on the lives of women in the urban community and how these women have experienced these changes. He looks at the impact of the trend towards increasing paid employment for women and concludes that although there is some convergence between the apparent uses of time and space by women and men working outside the home, there are important differences in their experiences. For instance, while the amount of daily travel time for employed women and men is similar, the experience of the time spent differs considerably. For women, the commute is tension-producing because they are in transition between responsibilities at both ends of the travel. Michelson's conclusions emphasize the difficulties felt by working mothers in reconciling their dual roles in the home and at work. Michelson is concerned about elements of urban structure that act either to facilitate or to hinder the lives of working women; his policy recommendations call for planning that more fully physically integrates the different spheres of activity. "Creating more mixed, integrated land uses" would be a concrete step in linking work and home so that groups in the population, such as working mothers, encounter fewer difficulties in their daily struggle to bridge these different realms. However, this is never imagined to be either a panacea or a sufficient change. Indeed, running throughout this collection is an understanding of the tension between the need to make minor adjustments so that mothers can better handle a double-load and the wish to alter attitudes towards home and child care in more fundamental ways.

The article by Gerda Wekerle continues the policy thrust developed by Michelson. She examines the origins and evolution of women's housing cooperatives developed in Canada. Her conclusion is that they have been successful in creating supportive communities for women and in creating opportunities to participate in decisions about their own environment. This has not been automatic: with respect to physical design, for example, Wekerle analyzes the struggles of various cooperatives to try to adapt government programmes and procedures to desired ends. On the whole, however, housing cooperatives are seen as an attractive solution to the particular problems many women face in housing markets.

Fran Klodawsky and Aron Spector also pursue the relationship between women and housing, focusing their attention on single-parent families. If the problems are primarily economic in nature for this predominantly female group, the authors argue that the solutions must be sought more broadly—through financial assistance in some cases but also the provision of community facilities, the possibility of job training, and the general development of a supportive urban environment. Once again, the analysis of women's needs and women's experiences illuminates linkages between a broad variety of areas rather than the segmentation of the urban environment.

Piché's article is based on the early stages of a project using action research. Her central concern is how to bring women into the planning process: how to ensure that they participate in decisions and that their concerns are recognized. But these are not simple objectives to attain and Piche' reflects on the difficulties involved. The women she studies have been so socialized by their gender and class affiliations that it is not easy for them to articulate their needs. When asked what leisure activities they wanted, their first answers were in terms of activities entirely related to their role within the family; their imaginations have been so constrained that they can only think in terms of furthering the role they play in serving others. Only after extensive discussion and as they gain confidence in articulating their needs and aspirations do they begin to make timid claims on the public realm: for example, expressing their desire for collective space that they can control. Gaining a sense of women's real needs and desires for urban spaces requires research techniques capable of cutting through their initial responses, so tenaciously anchored in notions of women's needs as secondary and subordinate to those of children and men.

Throughout this book runs the theme of the relationship between understanding situations and changing them. This is one of the major themes in recent feminist thought: how can we build understanding that simultaneously escapes sexism and recognizes the need to change current affairs? Much of feminist methodological literature attempts to deal with this problem of designing methodologies that are non-sexist and that can deal with what should be and not only with what is. As Jill McCalla Vickers has expressed it:

> It is important to realize that most of our thought is still conditioned, constrained and limited by the fact that we first learned to think using tools and categories devised by men to understand their reality, not ours. As some women become culture-makers and as we communicate with our own students in a new idiom, we must create new tools of thinking and establish new norms for feminist research and action. Probably the most important *political* value of feminist research at this stage is its capacity to challenge, however implicitly, the ontological underpinnings of male-stream thought and of patriarchal symbol systems. (1982, p. 44)

In the urban context, this theme has obvious practical implications. How can interventions in urban structure and processes be planned and developed in order to create a non-sexist city when all the people involved in the planning and intervention are themselves products of a sexist society and a sexist urban structure? It is Piché's text that deals most explicitly with this methodological problem; she addresses the question of planning for the real needs of women and female adolescents through the participation of those people concerned. How does one go beyond the first articulations of expressed needs, which often reflect the patterns of socialization of the society, and allow for the articulation of the real needs? In her article, Piché outlines the kind of action research that she feels can lead to democratic planning processes. Through group interviews with women and female adolescents, research can be a consciousness-raising activity rather than a manipulative process. Planning can be done with the participation of those most affected by it, but proper attention must be paid to the question of methodology. As Piché shows, women's first answers about their needs were in terms of helping others—the traditional female role. It was only with discussion that women were able, and willing, to put forward their own needs in relation to leisure activities and therefore begin to understand the present situation in such a way as to be able to transform it.

Michelson's methodology also addresses this question. The research has important implications for public policy because the findings indicate that something that might be seen as genderless—travel patterns of working women and men—in fact involves two very different kinds of experience. This finding would not have been possible with all data-gathering methods. By using time-budgets and by interviewing for subjective evaluations of behaviour, researchers were able to differentiate between superficially similar patterns of behaviour.

Wekerle's method represents yet another way to connect the process of understanding reality with that of changing it. By conducting case studies of admittedly unrepresentative but innovative projects, the author hopes to understand the processes of change in our society. There may be very few housing cooperatives for women in Canada, and so it can be argued that understanding the processes that create them is not relevant to understanding Canadian society. However, if they are examples of new developments in our society, then understanding them helps us understand and act on future directions and changes. Once again, what has traditionally been labelled the subjective element becomes important: the choice of subject is not determined by its objective importance but because it is felt to represent the working out of specific problems and to contain the germ of things to come.

This shared preoccupation with the relationship between understanding and changing reality emerges clearly in the articles in this book. It is for this reason that policy recommendations are so much a part of the arguments presented—if reality is to be understood so it can be changed, then it is necessary to explain the kinds of changes that should be introduced. This policy thrust leads to a constant tension between what is seen as feasible and what is seen as desirable. Housing programmes should be altered or zoning modified, but at the same time fundamental changes are needed in the basic structure of our society.

From the major points of view in this book—the importance of the processes of production and reproduction and the relationship between understanding situations and changing them—emerge the book's triple foci on theory, research, and policy. These three elements are seen as indissolubly tied together: it is necessary to theorize, to observe, and to act. In organizing this book we have chosen to recognize the importance of these questions by discussing them more fully in a concluding chapter dealing with gender-specific approaches to theory and method. We have also chosen to emphasize research and methodological aspects by including a bibliography on Canadian materials relating to women and environments. We hope that the inclusion of this bibliography will encourage more research and will reinforce the integration of theory, research, and policy.

NOTE

1. *Women and Environments* is published three times a year and is available from the Centre for Urban and Community Studies, University of Toronto, 455 Spadina Avenue, Room 426, Toronto, Ontario, M5S 2G8, Canada.

REFERENCES

Armstrong, Pat (1984). *Labour Pains*. Toronto: Women's Press.

Canada. Ministry of State for Urban Affairs (1975). *Metropolitan Canada: Women's Views of Urban Problems*. Ottawa: Ministry of State for Urban Affairs.

Careless, J. M. S. (1967). "Frontierism, Metropolitanism and Canadian Historians." In Carl Berger (Ed.), *Approaches to Canadian History* (pp. 63-83). Toronto: University of Toronto Press.

Davis, Donald E. (1985). "The 'Metropolitan Thesis' and the Writing of Canadian Urban History." *Urban History Review,* 14 (2), pp. 95-113.

Eichler, Margrit, and Lapointe, Jeanne (1985). *On the Treatment of the Sexes in Research*. Ottawa: Social Sciences and Humanities Research Council of Canada.

Goldberg, Michael A., and Mercer, John (1986). *The Myth of the North American City*. Vancouver: University of British Columbia Press.

Luxton, Meg, (1980). *More than a Labour of Love*. Toronto: Women's Press.

Morgan, Robin (Ed.) (1970). *Sisterhood Is Powerful*. New York: Random House.

National Capital Commission (1975). *Women in the Urban Environment*. Ottawa: National Capital Commission.

Vickers, Jill McCalla (1982). "Memoirs of an Ontological Exile: The Methodological Rebellions of Feminist Research." In Angela Miles and Geraldine Finn (Eds.), *Feminism in Canada* (pp. 27-46). Montreal: Black Rose Books.

Wekerle, Gerda, Peterson, R., and Morley, D. (Eds.) (1980). *New Space for Women*. Boulder: Westview.

Women's Research Centre (1977). *Northern British Columbia Women's Task Force Report on Single Industry Resource Communities*. Vancouver: Women's Research Centre.

1

Building Women, Building Cities: Toward Gender Sensitive Theory in the Environmental Disciplines

SUZANNE MACKENZIE

Twice in the last hundred years, the "woman question" has assumed a central social importance: first at the turn of the century, and again within the last two decades. And twice within the last hundred years, Canadians have experienced, or at least been assured they were experiencing, an "urban crisis": first at the turn of the century, and again within the last two decades. In both periods, some alert though not always discriminating observers drew some connections, suggesting that women were largely responsible for problems in the city. More sensitive observers pointed out that women's activities appeared to be in a process of transition and that this transition appeared to threaten the social and environmental norms of urban life.

Nellie McClung said at the beginning of this century: "At the present time there are many people seriously alarmed at the discontent among women. They say women are no longer content with woman's work and woman's sphere. Many people believe that women are deserting the sacred sphere of home-making and rearing of children: in short, women are losing their usefulness" (n.d., p. 228). Almost eighty years later, a French urban sociologist, Manuel Castells, wrote:

> The feminist movement is threatening the very logic of urban structure, for it is the subordinate role of women which enables the minimal "maintenance" of its housing, transport and public facilities. In the end, if the system still "works" it is because women guarantee unpaid transportation . . . because they repair their homes, because they make meals when there are no canteens, because they spend more time

shopping around, because they look after others' children when there are no nurseries, and because they offer "free entertainment" to the producers where there is a social vacuum and an absence of cultural creativity. . . . The subversive nature of the feminist movement is not due to its demand for more nurseries, but to the refusal henceforth onwards to look after anything at all! (1978, pp. 177-78)

The parallels are startling. Both McClung and Castells emphasize that the activities of women are specific to and well defined by their gender: bearing and educating children and caring for adults is woman's work. Both emphasize that these activities are centred in a specific place—the home—which is women's primary work place. Both emphasize that this work is useful and in fact essential to society as a whole; but while society could not exist without it, this work is somehow separate from society. And both emphasize that women are resisting this role, doing different and often unexpected things, and organizing to demand and create the social and environmental prerequisites for extending these new activities.

What is not so obvious as these parallels are the connections between these two periods of unruly, discontented women and urban crisis. How did the discontent of McClung and her contemporaries become absorbed into the "logic of urban structure"? And how has this laid the basis for a new discontent, a new feminist movement which threatens that urban logic?

This paper is about these connections, both the historical connection between the two periods and the more general, theoretical connections between women's lives and urban change. These are traced by examining how women's activities and protests relate to the restructuring of urban process and city form, looking at the emergence of the woman question and urban question in Canadian cities between the 1880's and 1910's, its apparent resolution, and the subsequent development of new problems and protests in the late twentieth century. This discussion will lead to some conclusions about the relations between gender change and changes in cities. In order to do this, however, it is first necessary to outline some basic concepts which underlie the historical discussion and which are presupposed in the theoretical conclusions.

GENDER AND ENVIRONMENT

The connections between women's activities and urban problems are part of the more general question of the relationship between gender and environment, a question of growing concern in the environmental disciplines as a whole[1]. The attention it has received has made it evident that this question requires more than the grafting of a new empirical object of study onto existing disciplinary discourses. It requires, rather, a re-examination and reformulation of our understanding of gender and the development of concepts for urban analysis which are sensitive to a socially constructed idea of gender.

This reformulation begins where feminist analysis as a whole does, with the disaggregation of the ahistorical category "woman" (and by implication "man"). As feminism developed, the concept of "woman" altered. Women became social actors, and as they acted, consciously and collectively, to change their conditions of life, feminism developed a far-reaching and comprehensive analysis which recognized that women's and men's patterns of activity, and the constituents of femininity and masculinity are historically constructed and changed. Any attempt to understand women's position in society had to begin not with an ahistorical and biologically determined category "woman" but with the question: what social processes throughout history structured women's lives and, thereby, the gender category "woman"? Feminists are reanalyzing the whole of contemporary and historical social life from the perspective of its influence on gender relations. The aim of this analysis is to identify and then strategically to alter the processes and institutions which restrict women's use of social resources.

Feminists have identified the relations between the production of social goods and services and the reproduction of people as the major conditions structuring gender relations. These two kinds of work are ahistorically and universally necessary for the maintenance of a society, but their specific content and the relations between them vary historically, in an inter-related manner. Feminists argue, from anthropological and historical evidence, that women's biological capacity to reproduce was socially translated into a primary responsibility for child care and, in many societies, a responsibility for other aspects of social reproduction, such as the care and maintenance of adults and a household. Some responsibility for reproduction of people was a consistent feature of women's roles and structured their access to resources and participation in productive work. However, the circumstances in which reproduction went on, the social meaning of this work, and thus the social status of women has varied over history. Women's role is seen as a social construction, and its variation is largely a function of the way in which production and reproduction have been organized and related to each other.

At certain periods of history, when the relations of production and reproduction were changing, gender roles would also undergo transition. The activities of women and men would alter, calling into question the social definition of what was appropriate behaviour for men and women and what the nature of "woman" and "man" was. Periods of social transition in production and reproduction were therefore accompanied by a concomitant "gender question."[2]

At such times of transition, the change of gender roles could become a publicly contested "woman question," if women acted to control the processes of this change. Such was the period in which McClung wrote, and such is the period in which we now live: periods of transition in the way we produce social goods and services and the way we reproduce ourselves as individuals and as a community, a transition in which gender role change is an integral feature.

In order to understand the importance of changing gender roles to the constitution and change of city form and urban process, we must examine the city from the perspective of the relations between production and reproduction. A gender sensitive understanding of cities begins by looking at cities as concrete but mutable systems which provide resources for production and reproduction.[3] Using the relations of production and reproduction as an organizational skeleton, we can trace how changes in these essential activities affected not only women's and men's activities and gender roles but also city form and urban process.

The following sections of this paper utilize such a framework. As industrialization changed social and economic life in turn-of-the-century Canadian cities, there was a crisis in women's social position, one both articulated in and partially resolved by the transformation of urban morphology. Women living in this altered city created new patterns of activity which came into conflict with the previous resolution, giving rise to a new woman question.

THE RISE AND DEMISE OF THE FIRST WOMAN QUESTION

The first publicly recognized woman question in Canadian cities arose with the transition to an industrially based monopoly capitalist society. Although actual processes varied regionally, the colonial nature of the Canadian economy meant that for all Canadian cities, industrialization was not a gradual development but was imposed in a relatively short period stretching over the three decades between the 1880's and the First World War.[4]

The pre-industrial economy of Canadian cities was primarily commercial. Cities were largely trade and transportation centres, where kinship-based patronage structured the elite. Throughout the pre-industrial period, the expanding scale and specialization of production led to its growing spatial and functional separation from the activities of reproduction. The family, which in pre-capitalist and early capitalist rural economies had been the basic unit of both production and reproduction, became more exclusively concerned with reproducing workers and class relationships.

The degree of separation and insularity varied in different urban classes and was reinforced by changes in the social landscape of the city. The emerging commercial bourgeoisie developed specialized and territorially discrete productive and reproductive districts. The latter was built around the "ideal" family centred on an "ideal"woman, and complemented by educational and social services. Bourgeois women, who were largely removed from productive activity, were concerned with bringing up and maintaining the city's leadership. Artisanal families, producing commodities for local markets, retained closer spatial and functional integration of workshop and home. Women in these families were part of a household productive unit, combining the production of goods and services for sale with the care of the family and household. The home and workshop were one: a woman doing the household accounts was doing the business bookkeeping at the same time. The commercial export-oriented economy offered little steady, socially valued work to unskilled workers whose families experienced considerable friction between their spatially and socially unconnected working lives and home lives. Women in these families had especially conflicting dual roles.

Thus the definition of what was appropriate behaviour and attributes for women varied over classes. But while Bliss Carman's "Protectress of the immortal seed . . . restricted to the cradle and the hearth . . . skipping the valley of reason" (Bliss Carman Papers, n.d., quoted in Cook and Mitchinson, 1976, p. 80), may have been the bourgeois ideal for the feminine gender, the records we have of the lives of non-elite women indicate that most women were more family partners, albeit junior ones.

Cities in this period had few specialized areas. Transportation and commercial activities tended to be concentrated in a warehouse/office district, but most of the city, with the exception of the few elite residential districts, was a heterogeneous collection of homes, shops, and small workshops: compact, dense, and undifferentiated.

Between about 1880 and 1910, people's activities and the urban landscape changed beyond recognition. Large-scale factory production based on machine technology—which had been replacing artisanal craft manufacture in the U.S. and Britain for some time—was introduced into Canadian cities, often in the form of American branch plants. This led to a growing concentration of people in cities, increased competition for urban space, and heightened demands on urban resources, and thus to scarcities and the crowding of housing, streets, utilities, schools, and markets.

Large-scale machine manufacture also finally shattered the unity of home and work, which had been weakening in the late commercial period. As production became concentrated in the factory or retail firm, family members no longer worked together but went off, as individuals, to wage jobs. The household became a separate and private sphere, where people pooled their wages to maintain themselves and where they lived: carrying out essential leisure time functions such as eating, resting, learning, loving, and expressing feeling. These many home activities became seen as secondary to work; their timing, their form, their quality and quantity became increasingly dependent on the relations family members had with the public wage sphere.

The separation of life into two spheres created not only a new (and universally contested) kind of life for the majority of people but also a new urban problem. Value was now produced in the manufacture of commodities, a process which required a healthy, relatively literate, and disciplined labour force, available in the requisite industrial divisions and willing to work for a given number of hours every day. The viability of new enterprises presupposed that an industrial labour force could be created out of a pre-industrial one, one which was generally self-trained and self-regulated, accustomed to relative independence and to the integration of their living and working times and places.

Throughout the 1880's, it became more and more evident that the working-class family, in its present form, was unable to reproduce this new kind of industrial labour unaided. People were unskilled and unused to machine work. Many were ill-fed and unhealthy; many—including children— were homeless, more and more seemed threateningly angry. The family had neither the skills nor the resources to reproduce labour alone.

Increasingly, private charities and local governments intervened to help the family. The reproduction of labour became a social question. A leading activist in the Toronto Children's Aid Society, J. J. Kelso, summed up the situation in 1894, saying:

> The governing power must come to regard the child as a future citizen and must see that it has opportunities for development along the lines of education and morality. A child's education begins from its earliest infancy and the State has a right to insist that its training shall be such as to fit it ultimately for the proper discharge of its duties and responsibilities. (quoted in Rutherford, 1974, pp. 212-13)

As Kelso implies, there was simultaneous need for new services to educate and maintain the labour force and for a new kind of family, one centred on producing good workers and citizens. But these needs appeared to be contradictory. And the contradiction arose from the adjustments which women were making to these new industrial conditions.

As more and more elements of family service—such as education or health care—and of household manufacture—such as raising and processing food or making clothing—were transferred from the family unit to the factory and from homes to public institutions, women brought their traditional activities into the wage sector. By 1891, women had followed these activities to such an extent that they numerically dominated the new public sectors of nursing, teaching young children, and, in an unpaid capacity, organizing charity. A less privileged group of women formed the majority of workers in the factories producing consumer goods. And as factory work was displacing traditional (male) craft manufacture, and as women's service work replaced male clerks and charity administrators, women were seen to be displacing male workers.

Even more menacing, women in the now-public wage and charitable sector were seen as a threat to the family. The public sectors into which most women moved were providing substitutes for household goods and family services. Women's entry into wage work and other areas of public life both reflected and reinforced the erosion of the household. And at the same time, growing numbers of bourgeois women, claiming that government and commerce "have ursurped what used to be our responsibility" (Leathes, 1914, p. 78), were leaving their own families to organize for voting rights, higher education, and professional careers.

All of this, in conjunction with declining marriage and fertility rates, raised the spectre of the decline of the family. A letter to the Toronto *Star* in 1892, signed by a "working girl," gives voice to the ultimate fear when it says: "Women are gradually declaring and proving their ability and willingness to bear the burden of their own support. These days, marriage isn't all that attractive to the average girl" (quoted in Klein and Roberts, 1974, p. 227).

The "new woman," resisting or delaying marriage, working in public, bearing fewer children, and demanding some economic and political equality, was seen as a threat both to the bourgeois ideal family and to the working-class family. The responses women made to new industrial conditions appeared not only to create the problems of factory production but also to undermine the family. And despite its eroded productive role in the face of extended socialization of reproduction, the family was still a necessary institution. It reproduced the future and current industrial labour force, provided a refuge from the increasingly intensive and dehumanized work processes in the public wage sphere, and offered a market for the new manufactured household goods. There was no institution to replace the family and no viable model to act as alternative to the bourgeois ideal family. The family needed to be supported, restructured, and improved.

Providing services for a new industrial labour force while at the same time strengthening the family and maintaining women in (or, more accurately, confining them to) an unwaged, private, but essential domestic role became an important urban question. Contemporary reformers saw the city, and especially the slums, as leading to "drunkenness in parents; to delinquency in children; to disorderly conduct; to wife and family desertion . . . to immorality in the growing generation" (Kelso, quoted in Rutherford, 1974, p. 167); they warned that "the city has destroyed the home" (Woodsworth, 1911, p. 23; see also Rutherford, 1974 and Stelter and Artibise, 1977).

The separation between "work" and "life" which had created this problem and given rise to the woman question also suggested a solution. This solution was based on an extension of the separation, through reorganizing the urban landscape into a city of separate spheres: on the one hand, suburban residential neighbourhoods which provided single family homes complemented by a range of appropriate services to assist the family; on the other, central industrial/commercial areas where the public work of the city could be carried out, complemented by appropriate infrastructure and support services and unhampered by reminders of private life—hungry children, church bells, or courting couples.

The new urban-suburban landscape reflected both the operation of market forces—the speculation in urban land as a means of profit accumulation—and the coordination and facilitation of these market processes by local governments. Between the 1880's and the First World War, urban governments extended and rationalized the ongoing process of suburbanization, extending city boundaries or providing trunk sewers, gaslights, and street car lines, for example. Gradually, urban cores became more exclusively commercial and industrial, while suburban housing developments expanded with increasing numbers of shops, schools, and other services to complement them. This process was not entirely a planned solution, but it helped to alleviate both the issue of creating a new industrial labour force and the "woman problem." And the rhetoric of the solution and the problem took on strong overtones of environmental determinism.

Single-family homes in suburban neighbourhoods separated women and children from the temptations of the city, temptations like wage jobs and, in the words of a contemporary reformer, " 'communistic modes of thought' and sexual promiscuity" (quoted in Wright, 1975, p. 42). But they did more than keep women from displacing male workers and threatening the stability of the family. They also provided the basis for a new role: the full-time housewife, a role which developed with the proliferation of new household commodities and the emergence of the new science of home economics.

The home economics movement in the late nineteenth century extended the principals of business and science into the household, giving women a scientific and social mission with which to absorb their potentially dangerous energies. Women's ordering of the household—fighting against newly discovered germs and applying newly discovered psychology to children and husbands—became an essential part of ordering the social world. The goods, methods, and expertise of the market were thus extended into the household, making it in many ways a healthier and more comfortable place for women to work and everyone to live. But it was a contradictory change. On the one hand, it tied women's household work ever more firmly to the market, replacing their traditional skills and control over manufacture and service with purchased goods and magazine images of families and homes to be emulated. On the other hand, it reinforced the separation between home and wage work place, between public and private times and spaces, so that women were bound ever closer to an increasingly specialized, spatially separated, and single gender world (see Cross, 1977; MacMurchy, 1919; and National Council of Women of Canada, 1900).

The woman question was resolved by defining women's nature and activities in terms of the home and neighbourhood, which became the focus of private life, offering rest from work (and passivity), time for emotion (and illogic), and a place for sexual expression (and its confinement). And women, who actively maintained the home and neighbourhood, themselves became associated with all these things. Women came to be seen as private, passive, non-working, emotional, illogical, and sexually confined. They were bounded by the home, they filled up the home, and they tied up the bundle of its associated values. And these values soon came to be seen as defining women's nature.

THE NEW PROBLEMS OF WOMEN AND THE CITY

Throughout the twentieth century, most Canadian women have lived and worked within these bounds. They have been no more passive than their publicly active mothers and grandmothers. They campaigned vigorously to improve their working conditions; they organized Women's Institutes to educate themselves; they pressed for family allowances and better schools; they offered each other time, money, and advice. But all of this went on "at home"; it was private and, somehow, thereby both "natural" in the sense of being women's activity, and invisible.

The bounds extended spatially, into more distant suburbs, with larger houses, larger shops, and more sophisticated services. Caring for the home required new kinds of work and new machines and products; most especially, reaching the shops and services required a car. Domestic work and raising a family became more and more expensive, while the increased need for homes, schools, hospitals, and other services required more and more workers, leading to the recruitment of women for wage jobs.

By the 1950's, these push and pull factors caused more and more women to enter the labour force. Their priorities had not changed; most still saw themselves primarily as mothers and wives responsible for ensuring the best and most comfortable life for their families. But it was now more advantageous, often necessary, to earn some money as well as work at home. Once again, women adjusted their organization of time and their use of space to maintain their families. But, as in the earlier period, this was not easy.

The primary source of problems is the dual role. Most women, whether married or single mothers, have to work at wage earning jobs while retaining most or all of the responsibility of caring for children, other adults, and a home and neighbourhood. This dual role problem is in large part a result of the solution to the earlier woman question.

While the nineteenth-century urban question had focused on inadequate conditions for reproduction in the central cities, the solution to the problem—the extensive, distant, and expensive suburbs separated from wage work places—became the mid-twentieth-century urban problem. It is especially acute for that growing proportion of the labour force who also care for their home and family. Work in the home, the place associated with leisure, is not seen as real work, nor are the home and neighbourhood designed to be work places. What women do in these places is invisible in the public sphere (as it was meant to be), so employers make few concessions to the fact that women have other jobs (except perhaps to pay them less and fire them more readily because they are assumed to have other means of support). Transit companies make few concessions to women's different working hours and the fact they must travel not only to work but also to shopping areas and day care. And because it is assumed that women are caring for children in the home, child care is not a public priority. Even if a woman is fortunate enough to find adequate, affordable child care, it is unlikely to be where she wants it or available when she requires it. At the end of a long day, after getting the family off to school, child care, work, travelling to a wage job herself, to shop or to meet with a child's doctor or teacher, she comes home again to a domestic work place which requires hours of hard work and complex planning to keep running.[5]

Just as the initiation of the "suburban solution," based on the spatial, temporal, and functional separation of home and work, depended upon the separate housewife role for women, so the maintenance of this complex and expensive separation now depends upon women's dual roles. And just as the suburban solution resulted in a woman who confined herself to the activities of nurture, so this new dual role gives us "super woman": shorn perhaps of an overwhelming maternal instinct which guided her to cook, clean, and bear unrestricted numbers of children but newly endowed with abilities to pursue a career and earn her own money; while efficiently raising a clever, companionate family.

These super women, while based in real changes in gender relations and women's activities are no more representative than the total mother had been. The conflicts in women's dual roles gave rise to a new woman question and women's movement in the late 1960's, resulting in women defining themselves at least in part as political actors. These problems are also giving rise to new solutions created by women themselves, solutions which are helping to restructure the city.

Women are once again readjusting their use of space and time and breaking down the temporal and functional separation of home and work. Because many women work both at home and in the wage sector, they are organizing services at the interface. Community day care centres, health advice centres, and alternative consumer services structure women's domestic working conditions, provide time for wage work, and create employment. Women are creating their own jobs—looking after each other's children, sewing each other's drapes—jobs which are socially necessary to reproduce a family but are also remunerative and located at the intersection of the private home and the public wage economy.[6] Women are redesigning, or redesignating, homes and neighbourhoods: sharing houses with other single parents, turning basements into workshops, or reoccupying and revitalizing inner cities (see Holcomb, 1981; Rose, 1984).

These changes are neither adequate, easy, nor straightforward practical solutions. They often create as many problems as they solve, both practically and analytically. But it is essential that we understand these changes as the ongoing and simultaneous creation of new cities and new women.

BUILDING WOMEN, BUILDING CITIES: METHOD AND PROSPECTS

As can be seen above, focusing on changes in the relations between production of goods and services and reproduction of people provides an analytic framework within which to study gender change in the urban environment and the reason why a woman question arose coterminously with periods of urban crisis twice within the last hundred years. The two benchmarks examined in this paper—the-turn-of-the-century women's movement and contemporary feminism—have both been periods when appropriate female roles and the very nature of "woman" have come into question. These changes in gender roles have been the result of changes in the activities which women and men were performing in order to produce society's goods and services and reproduce people. In both periods, a fundamental element of this transition has been the development of new modes of environmental appropriation, the creation of new urban forms, and the new use of old forms.

It is not a simple coincidence that periods of urban transition happen simultaneously with periods of gender role alteration. Women in part create the urban crisis. Their actions are responses to both the kinds of cities in which they live and work and the resources their living and working environments provide for them. Changes in the city and in women's activities are inextricably linked. Neither the role of housewife-mother nor those of the children and men who formed her primary concern would have been created in its early twentieth-century form without the separated city. Nor would the suburbs have developed without the housewife-mother, her children, and her breadwinner husband. The transformation of the city was partly a process of creating and reinforcing a new feminine activity pattern. And while this new role animated and expanded the suburbs, maintaining them has caused women to take on dual roles as homemakers and wage workers, which has made the suburbs in some measure obsolete and is forcing the creation of new urban forms and spaces.

The historical discussion suggests, therefore, that gender and urban environments are constructed interdependently. Gender is an essential parameter of city development and change, neither of which can be fully understood unless our concept of the people who occupy cities and act in them is an androgynous one. Similarly, the urban environment is a factor in the way women (and men) work, organize, and change.

But the history of women's activities in Canadian cities has revealed more than a historical link between gender and environment. It has indicated how this link is created: through the day-to-day, often apparently insignificant and disconnected actions of women in cities. These activities are at the centre of the reciprocal relation between women and cities.

Women have moved the boundaries and rearranged the content of analytic categories as they have moved the location and timing of their activity. Understanding women and cities therefore requires not only a new set of concepts structured around the relations of production and reproduction but also a new methodology which permits one to examine how daily activities alter and adapt these analytic constructions.

Production and reproduction remain useful because the activities encompassed within them are universal, trans-historical necessities. For any society to survive, its members must reproduce themselves as biological and social entities and produce the goods and services for their needs. But production and the reproduction of people are complex, and while some form of production and reproduction is always necessary, there is no established way in which these things must be done.

These categories, therefore, offer only an analytic starting point. Continuing the analysis, we must focus on the historically specific and mutable content and relations of these categories, by focusing on human actions in time and space as these actions alter these categories.[7]

Time and space are useful concepts with which to guide empirical examination. They not only form the context of human environmental relations, but they also shape and are shaped by human interaction; they illuminate the process and shifting boundaries of production and the reproduction of people. The boundaries are breaks in space and time: changing behaviour, clothing, companions, locations, and rhythms of activity as people move from home to wage work place and public to private. The boundaries shift as changes occur in where people live and work, in the extension or contraction of the number of areas in which they do things associated with living or working, or in the curtailment or extension of time available or necessary for various aspects of life and work.

Space and time are categories which allow us to collect the multitude of activities which make up people's lives while at the same time retaining the conceptual fluidity to see changes in these lives. They give form and substance to human action; they allow the bundling together of various aspects of human action into what Raymond Williams calls "practical continuities" which guide and legitimate action (1979, p. 116).

We have seen above how the various components of production and reproduction of people are separated in time and space and how this temporal-spatial separation confirms their social separateness and even opposition. Conversely, the dimensions on either side of this permeable division are associated in time and space, and this temporal-spatial association confirms their interdependence. For example, home and family places and times are also places and times for private, non-market, emotional, and sexual relations, all of which converge in the constitution of "woman" and are confirmed by the presence in and activities around the home. The work-place becomes "non-woman," confirmed by her relative or apparent absence from productive places and times.

But space and time not only provide the basis of routine, tradition, and social reproduction; they are also powerful agents of change and the basis of new patterns of activity. This process of change alters both the patterns of people's lives and the constituents of gender categories. In the late nineteenth century, women adjusted their space and time to industrial factory production, moving from the household-workshop into the public wage sphere, thereby gaining resources in the form of wages rather than solely through home manufacture and service. In the early to mid-twentieth-century, women reallocated their time to domestic work, providing resources within the private and non-productive space of the home and community. The separate sphere of home-community, and women's activity there, implied a definition of women as passive and nurturant. And the maintenance of this separate sphere assumed women carried out this socially invisible but essential work. In the late twentieth century, both the suburban solution and this gender definition began to break down as women once again readjusted their space and time to provide resources in monetary form as well as in kind, both within the wage sphere and increasingly within the community or even the home.

There is a pattern, a repetitive rhythm, to this readjustment of women's space and time. The achievement of one set of objectives always seems to throw up a series of new problems. This stems largely from the fact that women live, work, and organize from a contradictory position. Women are defined in terms of, and in many cases are primarily occupied with, essential social work—mothering and caring for adults—in a society where power, planning priorities, and even language and analytic categories derive from the public sphere of producing goods and services. Whether or not they directly act in public space and time, domestic workers must accommodate themselves and their activities to it—to their husbands' wages (and their own) or to the kinds of goods, housing, or education provided by this public sphere.

Throughout the capitalist period, women's organization has been constrained by the need to balance the requirements of reproduction—the bearing and education of children and the maintenance of adults—with the need to produce society's goods and services. Therefore, women in the period under discussion are always functioning at the interface of productive and reproductive resources and spaces, in a society which separates these resources and spaces both concretely and analytically.

And yet, the monotonous and frustrating rhythm of solutions leading to new problems which is engendered by this contradictory position is also an indication of women's efficacy. The achievement of objectives creates new problems precisely because these achievements alter the urban environment. As women adjust and accommodate, they also alter their own working and living environment, rendering previous solutions obsolete and opening up new possibilities. By extending the resources available to full-time domestic workers, women helped to create the preconditions of their own dual roles. The birth of this dual role in the 1940's and the 1950's, and its extension in the following decades, demarcates a new adjustment in the relations between production and reproduction, one where the city of separate spheres is animated, tied together, and contradicted by the lives of women who work in both spheres. And in responding to the problems of their dual roles, women are breaking down, shifting, and redesignating the boundaries between home and work.

The shifting of activities and social definitions which bemused, disrupted, and angered nineteenth-century urban dwellers is now visible to us as the transition toward a new relation between production and reproduction, a different city, and new activity patterns. However, it is not so easy to explain these diverse and apparently disconnected activities and changes in our own period. It is certainly not easy to see into the future to predict the outcomes of the changes in urban form which women and men are now creating, nor to foresee their implications for gender roles. What is evident, however, is that the process of gender constitution and the process of constituting urban environments are inextricably linked; the historically creative as well as the analytic link must be sought in the way in which real men and women act to ensure their survival as individuals and as a community.

NOTES

1. Within the past ten years, an international and interdisciplinary literature concerned with women and environments has grown up. See for example, Keller (1981), Stimpson, *et al.* (1981), Wekerle, *et al.* (1980). For a review of the geographic literature, see Zelinsky, Monk and Hanson (1982). Also see the journal *Women and Environments*.

2. These concepts are based on a modification of Engels's work on *The Origin of the Family, Private Property and the State*. Some other classic works in this area include Clark (1968), Pinchbeck (1930), Reiter (1975), and Rowbotham (1974).

3. Although some non-feminists have also made an argument for viewing the city as a system in which production and reproduction interact, most urban analysts still see the city primarily in terms of a productive system or, as Manuel Castells has done, as an arena for reproduction (1977). As noted below, working from the intersection is analytically difficult. Both "common sense" (pre-feminist common sense) and analytic language tend to slide to one side or the other.

4. A more detailed discussion of the first "woman question" is found in Mackenzie (1980). The discussion of pre-industrial and early industrial cities draws upon Cross (1974), Glazebrook (1968), Goheen (1970), Kealey (1973), Masters (1947), Naylor (1975), and Woodsworth (1911). Although most of these works take some note of women's role, the primary sources for discussion of the "woman question" are Canadian Women's Educational Press Collective (1974), Cook and Mitchinson (1976), Griffiths (1976), McClung (1915), and the National Council of Women of Canada (1900).

5. These problems have been well documented in the literature on gender and environment. See references in Note 1 and the article by William Michelson in this volume.

6. Similar kinds of alterations have been discussed in the emerging literature on post-industrial society. While much of this literature remains pre-feminist and tends to see informal, home-based solutions in industrialized societies as temporary or peripheral, some international feminist-informed analysis has

begun to assess the implications of these alterations. See for example, Oppong (1983), Redclift (1985), and Roldan (1985). This is also true of some work emerging out of the Locality Studies initiative in Britain. See Cooke (1986). Canadian contributions include Mackenzie (1986, 1987), Ross and Usher (1986), and Nicholls and Dyson (1983).

7. Geographers and those in related disciplines have recently begun to reconsider the concepts of time and space within the context of exploring humanist and historical materialist frameworks. One of the more influential non-geographic discussions, which has engaged both humanists and historical materialists, is that of Anthony Giddens, especially Giddens (1981).

REFERENCES

Canadian Women's Educational Press Collective (1974). *Women at Work: Ontario, 1850-1930*. Toronto: Canadian Women's Educational Press.

Castells, Manuel (1977). *The Urban Question: A Marxist Approach*. London: Edward Arnold.

Castells, Manuel (1978). *City, Class and Power*. London: Macmillan.

Clark, Alice (1968). *Working Life of Women in the Seventeenth Century*. London: Frank Cass.

Cook, Ramsay and Mitchinson, Wendy (Eds.) (1976). *The Proper Sphere: Women's Place in Canadian Society*. Toronto: Oxford University Press.

Cooke, Philip (Ed.) (1986). *Global Restructuring: Local Response*. London: Economic and Social Research Council.

Cross, D. Suzanne (1977). "The Neglected Majority: The Changing Role of Women in Nineteenth-Century Montreal." In G. Stelter and A. Artibise (Eds.), *The Canadian City: Essays in Urban History* (pp. 255-81). Toronto, Carleton Library, McClelland and Stewart.

Cross, Michael (Ed.) (1974). *The Workingman in the Nineteenth Century*. Toronto: Oxford University Press.

Engels, Friedrich (1973). *The Origin of the Family, Private Property, and the State*. New York: Pathfinder Press.

Giddens, Anthony (1981). *A Contemporary Critique of Historical Materialism. Volume I: Power, Property and the State*. Berkeley: University of California Press.

Glazebrook, G.P. (1968). *Life in Ontario: A Social History*. Toronto: University of Toronto Press.

Goheen, Peter (1970). *Victorian Toronto, 1850-1900: Pattern and Process of Growth*. Department of Geography Research Paper 127, Chicago: University of Chicago.

Griffiths, N. (1976). *Penelope's Web: Some Perspectives on Women in European and Canadian Society*. Toronto: Oxford University Press.

Holcomb, Briavel (1981). "Women's Roles in Distressing and Revitalizing Cities." *Transition, 11*(2), pp. 1-6.

Kealey, Greg (1973). *Canada Investigates Industrialism: The Royal Commission on* the Relations of Labor and Capital, 1889. Toronto: University of Toronto Press.

Keller, Suzanne (Ed.) (1981). *Building for Women*. Lexington: Lexington Books.

Klein, Alice and Roberts, Wayne (1974). "Besieged Innocence: The 'Problem' and Problems of Working Women, Toronto, 1896-1914." In Canadian Women's Educational Press Collective (Eds.), *Women at Work, Ontario, 1850-1930* (pp. 211-60). Toronto: Canadian Women's Educational Press Collective.

Leathes, Sonia (1914). "Votes for Women: Speech Given to the National Council of Women of Canada, Montreal." *University Magazine, 13,* pp. 68-78.

Mackenzie, Suzanne (1980). *Women and the Reproduction of Labour Power in the Industrial City: A Case Study.* Urban and Regional Studies Working Paper 23, University of Sussex, Brighton, England.

Mackenzie, Suzanne (1986). "Women's Responses to Economic Restructuring: Changing Gender, Changing Spaces". In Roberta Hamilton and Michelle Barrett (Eds.), *The Political Diversity: Feminism, Marxism, and Canadian Society* (pp. 81-100). London: Verso.

Mackenzie, Suzanne (1987). "Neglected Spaces in Peripheral Places: Home-Workers and the Creation of a New Economic Centre." *Cahiers de géographie du Québec 13*(83), pp. 247-60.

MacMurchy, M. (1919). "The Canadian Girl at Work." In R. Cook and W. Mitchinson (Eds.), *The Proper Sphere: Women's Place in Canadian Society* (pp. 195-97). Toronto: Oxford University Press.

Masters, D. C. (1947). *The Rise of Toronto.* Toronto: University of Toronto Press.

McClung, Nellie (1915). *In Times Like These.* Toronto: University of Toronto Press, reprint 1972.

McClung, Nellie, (n.d.) "The New Citizenship: Political Equality League of Manitoba." In R. Cook and W. Mitchinson (Eds.), *The Proper Sphere: Women's Place in Canadian Society* (pp. 287-93). Toronto: Oxford University Press, 1976.

National Council of Women of Canada (1900). *Women Of Canada: Their Life and Work.* Ottawa: National Council of Women of Canada, reprint 1975.

Naylor, Tom (1975). *The History of Canadian Business: 1867-1914,* Vols. 1 and 2. Toronto: James Lorimer.

Nicholls, William and Dyson, William (1983). *The Informal Economy: Where People Are the Bottom Line.* Ottawa: Vanier Institute for the Family.

Oppong, Christine (1983). "Women's Roles and Conjugal Family Systems in Ghana." In E. Lupri (Ed.) *The Changing Position of Women in Family and Society: A Cross-National Comparison* (pp. 331-43). Leiden: E. J. Brill.

Pinchbeck, Ivy (1930). *Women Workers and the Industrial Revolution, 1750-1850.* London: Frank Cass.

Redclift, Nanneke (1985). "The Contested Domain: Gender, Accumulation and the Labour Process." In N. Redclift and E. Mingione (Eds.) *Beyond Employment: Household, Gender and Subsistence* (pp. 92-125). London: Basil Blackwell.

Reiter, Rayna (Ed.) (1975). *Toward an Anthropology of Women.* New York: Monthly Review.

Roldan, Martha (1985). "Industrial Outworking, Struggles for the Reproduction of Working-class Families and Gender Subordination." In N. Redclift and E. Mingione (Eds.), *Beyond Employment: Household, Gender and Subsistence* (pp. 248-85). London: Basil Blackwell.

Rose, Damaris (1984). "Rethinking Gentrification: Beyond the Uneven Development of Marxist Urban Theory." *Environment and Planning D: Society and Space 1*(2), pp. 47-74.

Ross, David and Usher, Peter (1986). *From the Roots Up: Economic Development as if Community Mattered.* Toronto: Lorimer.

Rowbotham, Sheila (1974). *Women, Resistance and Revolution.* Harmondsworth: Penguin.

Rutherford, Paul (Ed.) (1974). *Saving the Canadian City: The First Phase 1880-1920.* Toronto: University of Toronto Press.

Stelter, Gilbert and Artibise, Alan (Eds.) (1977). *The Canadian City: Essays in Urban History.* Toronto: Carleton Library, McClelland & Stewart.

Stimpson, Catharine, Dixler, Elsa, Nelson, Martha, and Yatrakis, Kathryn (Eds.) (1981). *Women and the American City.* Chicago: University of Chicago Press.

Wekerle, Gerda, Peterson, Rebecca, and Morley, David (Eds.) (1980). *New Space for Women.* Boulder: Westview.

Williams, Raymond (1979). *Politics and Letters.* London: Verso.

Woodsworth, James S. (1911). *My Neighbour: A Study of City Conditions.* Toronto: University of Toronto Press, reprint 1972.

Wright, Gwendolyn (1975). "Sweet and Clean: The Domestic Landscape in the Progressive Era." *Landscape 20*(1), pp. 38-43.

Zelinsky, Wilbur, Monk, Janice, and Hanson, Susan (1982). "Women and Geography: A Review and Prospectus." *Progress in Human Geography 6*(3), pp. 317-66.

2

Women Workers and the Inner City: Some Implications of Labour Force Restructuring in Montreal, 1971-81

DAMARIS ROSE and PAUL VILLENEUVE,
with the collaboration of
FIONA COLGAN

INTRODUCTION

This chapter deals with changes in the occupational and sexual division of labour within a Canadian metropolitan city, Montreal, during the 1970s, a period of major economic restructuring during which women entered the labour force in ever greater numbers.[1] The article is based in a perspective which sees changes both in women's roles in employment and in the kinds of households in which women live as important to an understanding of labour force restructuring and its social implications, particularly at the neighbourhood level. This perspective is broadly situated within neo-Marxist approaches to spatial divisions of labour and urban restructuring (see, for example, Massey, 1984; Williams, 1986), but unlike much of this work (for example, Smith, 1986), it refuses to accept "second billing" at the conceptual level for transformations occurring in modes of reproduction of labour and social relations. Furthermore, in trying to explore in a Canadian, and specifically a Quebec context, theoretical arguments and issues developed largely on the basis of American experiences, we have been forced to question some commonly held assumptions about the effects of the current round of labour force restructuring at the neighbourhood level.

FEMINIZATION AND BIPOLARIZATION OF THE WORK FORCE: INTERLINKED TENDENCIES

There is an inter-relationship between two widely noted tendencies in the present phase of economic restructuring: the widespread process of *feminization* of the work force, and an increasing tendency for *bipolarization*[2] or bifurcation of the work force. Bipolarization refers to the redistribution of the labour force along the spectrum of occupational types: at one pole, there is an increase in managerial, professional, and supervisory occupations; at the other pole is a concentration of non-specialized white-collar and low-level service and sales occupations. These two extremes are both growing more rapidly than the middle layer of white-collar workers (Weiss, 1985, p. 84). In the United States the relative decline of the skilled blue-collar work force combined with falling real incomes of large fractions of the middle class has prompted a flurry of concern (Ehrenreich, 1986; Wessel, 1986). Canadian analysts have also expressed concern about such tendencies, particularly with respect to white-collar jobs undergoing transformations associated with the introduction of new technology (Bradbury, 1985, p. 41; Payeur, 1985). Both of these processes have been linked to the growing numbers of tertiary sector jobs. Some of the key growth sectors within the service industries are known to exhibit a more bifurcated distribution of occupations than traditional manufacturing industry, a bifurcation whose amplitude is reinforced by the fact that it is, by and large, low-paid women who occupy these new lower-level jobs (Smith, 1984).

The feminization tendency is widespread, common to many countries and found across almost all economic sectors in Canada (see, for example, Armstrong, 1984; Labour Canada Women's Bureau, 1983). The increased availability of employment for women has been closely linked to the expansion of white-collar office work and the personal, public, and commercial services sectors—a process which began in the 1950's (see, for example, Mackenzie, 1983). Not only has such employment grown massively in absolute terms, but in Canada and Quebec most of it also became increasingly feminized in the 1970's (Armstrong, 1984; Messier, 1984). In the Montreal Census Metropolitan Area (CMA) between 1971 and 1981, the largest single contributor to female job creation was the group of sectors which we have designated "distributive services" (that is, transportation, warehousing, utilities, wholesale and retail trade). In this area, 52,755 female jobs were created, amounting to more than a quarter of the increase in female employment over the decade. Just over half of these jobs were non-specialized white-collar and service positions. Inferring from published data available by detailed sector (Statistics Canada, 1981, cat. 93-965), most of these new positions were in retail sales. In general, since feminization is particularly noticeable in the sectors of retail trade, accommodation and food services, recreational services, public administration, finance, and services to business management (Armstrong, 1984), one would expect to see strong expressions of this tendency in metropolitan cities where these functions have experienced rapid growth.

With respect to manufacturing, there is now a fairly well-developed literature in regional geography which has documented how the deindustrialization of traditional heavy industries (employing mainly men) in peripheral regions has often gone hand in hand with the growth of light assembly manufacturing (employing mainly women), largely because of the availability of new and malleable work forces (see, for example, Aydalot, 1981; Massey, 1984). Within the manufacturing sector in the province of Quebec, the existence of an overall feminization trend in the division of labour is open to question, however, because a very high proportion of manufacturing consists of labour-intensive industry that has traditionally employed large numbers of women (such as clothing, shoes). This type of production has been undergoing large-scale deindustrialization, while the type of manufacturing that is prospering is based on high-technology engineering, in which few women have been able to gain a foothold. We shall return to these developments and their implications in the Montreal context; what is important for now is that, with manufacturing, feminization seems to be associated with those branches that are being "deskilled."

The notion of *bipolarization* is both theoretically controversial and empirically difficult to research. Still, it is a more satisfactory way of conceptualizing the overall tendencies in the current round of employment restructuring, than to argue, as has been the tendency until recently, that there is currently either an overall deskilling or an overall reskilling of employment, depending on one's point of view (see Lipietz, 1986; Villeneuve and Rose, 1985). Bipolarization is integrally connected with changes in the technical division of labour, which involve a greater functional separation of the activities of production from those of control over both manual and clerical tasks. Control functions can be increasingly concentrated and routine operations more easily fragmented—a process facilitated by the introduction of computerized technology (Menzies, 1982a, 1982b, 1985a, 1985b). The introduction of technological change tends to produce situations where, on the one hand, a higher proportion of the work force are in positions of control over others (such as managers or supervisors) while on the other hand, previously skilled jobs are deskilled or routinized. Evidently some economic sectors are more prone to technology-influenced bifurcation than others (Villeneuve and Rose, 1985): finance, insurance and postal services are areas where this has been well-documented for Canada (Menzies, 1982a; 1985b; Payeur, 1985). Furthermore, within manufacturing, a distinction should be drawn between specialized production requiring highly skilled workers and "deskilled execution and assembly" (Lipietz, 1986, p. 30).

The expression of such tendencies is far from constant over space. As

economic geographers have pointed out, functional fragmentation combined with enhanced control technologies often lead to increased geographical separation of the activities of major corporations (Pred, 1978, pp.
107-20). The regional political economy perspective has since gone further:
Lipietz argues, for instance, that work tasks can be fragmented and
delocalized, to the extent that "labour pools differentiated mainly by skills
and social conditions" occupy different regions (1986, p. 31). The effects of
bipolarization may thus vary greatly between localities (Harrison, 1982),
depending on the pre-existing configurations and characteristics of labour
pools, which will influence the types of employment restructuring carried
out (Massey, 1984).

To this aspect of bipolarization, linked to the importance of technological
change to cheapen the costs of producing goods and information, should be
added two other aspects. The growth of service sector jobs in food services
and personal and recreation services, and the fact that these sectors make up
an increasing proportion of the *total* labour force, itself increases
bifurcation of the work force. Jobs created in this sector are either
managerial and supervisory or low-paying white-collar and service jobs:
there is very little employment in the middle levels.

A third, more recent aspect, less noted by researchers, is that pressures
resulting from budgetary cuts and the current ideological climate are leading
to an increasing marginalization and downgrading of jobs in the middle of
the spectrum. In Canada over the past few years a number of bitter labour
disputes in the public and parapublic sectors have centred on this issue; in
Montreal it is particularly apparent in the continuing crisis in health care
funding (Armstrong, 1984, Ch. 3; Maroney, 1983; Rose and Villeneuve,
1985).

In order to appreciate fully what is entailed in bipolarization processes, it
is necessary to examine the restructuring of occupational structure by
gender. Feminization and bipolarization are interlinked processes. Up until
now, those sectors in which the largest number of female jobs have been
created—retailing, restaurants, and hotels—have not been particularly
affected by technological change. Yet the massive increase in such low-level
white collar and service jobs combined with the expansion of professional
and managerial employment in already highly feminized sectors such as
education, health, and social services in the 1970's, does suggest that
feminization processes seem likely to contribute to an overall bipolarization
in the employment structure of large metropolitan areas. Thus it is not
adequate to explain polarization trends only in terms of technological
change and the growth of low-level service jobs. Moreover, within
manufacturing, the split between reskilled highly specialized sectors and

routinized parts and assembly work is also likely to be strongly gender-typed. There are complex causal links between technological change, the availability of cheap labour, and the weaker position of women within the labour force. These links still require much greater theoretical specification and elaboration.

BIPOLARIZATION AND FEMINIZATION IN MONTREAL

It has been recently argued, by Ross and Trachte (1983) and by Sassen-Koob (1984), with the aid of detailed survey material, that tendencies for bipolarization of the work force are strongest in cities which have become centres of concentration in advanced services to corporations, either at the global or the regional level (Cohen, 1981). These types of services are more likely than other services to have concentrations of people in both well-and poorly paid jobs. Sassen-Koob argues moreover that "the existence of a critical mass of very high income workers provides the conditions for a rapidly expanding process of high income residential and commercial 'gentrification.' This entails . . . [a] demand for low-income workers to service the high income lifestyles" (1984, p. 157; see also Holcomb, 1984). In addition, such cities typically had a labour-intensive manufacturing sector such as the clothing industry. Despite declines in official employment levels, these sectors have largely been maintained. Thousands of jobs have gone underground in that they continue to exist but in forms very different from traditional manufacturing. The emergence of new sweatshops and industrial homeworking are ways for the small- and medium-sized companies in this sector to survive foreign competition (Ross and Trachte, 1983, pp. 407-16). The attraction to global cities of recent waves of legal and illegal Third World immigrants makes possible this emergence of a downgraded manufacturing labour force (Greater London Council, 1985; Labelle et al., 1984; Sassen-Koob, 1984).

Montreal is not a global city in the sense of being a high-level control centre for multinational corporate capital. Its financial sector has stagnated in terms of high-level national control functions (these having become increasingly concentrated in Toronto, as documented by Semple and Green, 1983). On the other hand, Montreal has become a strong corporate centre for the province of Quebec, while services to business management, including services for export, have shown a strong growth. In the 1970's the city exhibited significant differences from, for instance, Toronto, in seeing a stronger growth in public services such as education, health, and social services, and in public administration (Lamonde and Polèse, 1984).

Montreal was somewhat atypical of Canadian cities in the 1970's, in that the public sector continued to show a fairly rapid expansion; this may be owing in part to its strong role as regional centre for the province of Quebec for education and hospitals and to the strength of research and development in the medical sector, as well as to the expansion of the Quebec state apparatus. Montreal also has a high proportion of its labour force in retailing and recreation services as well as in tourism, which is seen as a means of economic revitalization. Tourism creates low-wage service jobs that are dependent on the wider economy (ibid.).

These general trends make Montreal seem a strong candidate for an increased bipolarization of the work force, in which gender has played an important role. We have already noted that retailing and recreation services are low-wage, increasingly female sectors. The public sector in general has a high proportion of professionals, managers, and supervisors and, as a result of union pressure for affirmative action, these have become much more feminized occupations. The stagnation in finance is reflected in an occupational composition that is more and more gender-typed: analysis of special compilations obtained from Statistics Canada[3] shows that this sector is increasingly polarized, with male managers on the one hand and low-level female white-collar workers on the other. (Overall, there were more men than women employed in the sector in 1971 and more women than men in 1981.) In the business services sector, both male and female professional jobs have been increasing rapidly (although men still greatly outnumber women) and there has been a substantial rise in the number of women in low-level jobs.

In the manufacturing sector, a high proportion of Montreal's labour has been in the clothing and related labour-intensive industries—much like New York or London. As alluded to earlier, restructuring in the 1970's and 1980's has involved the deindustrialization of traditional labour-intensive industries, entailing *in situ* closures and relocations to other areas. At the same time, there has been a partial conversion (Lamonde and Polèse, 1984) to capital-intensive high technology engineering industries, to which access is restricted to those with highly specialized skills. This has led to a doubly bipolarized occupational structure. In 1981, the *Census of Manufacturing* data (Statistics Canada, cat. 31-209, 1981) indicate that 16.9 per cent of all manufacturing production workers were in the clothing industry; in spite of this sector's decline, it remained an important part of manufacturing. Of these workers 73.1 per cent were female. The greatly modernized transportation equipment sector was the next most important branch of manufacturing, employing 11.9 per cent of all production workers, 93.5 per cent of them men. Women's opportunities within manufacturing are still largely restricted to precisely those sectors that are in decline: 40.3 per cent of all female production workers were in the clothing industry in 1981 (ibid.).

These figures do not, however, tell the full story. Women's employment in the clothing industry may be declining far less precipitously than official accounts suggest. An estimated 22,000 garment industry jobs in Montreal have gone underground while official unionized work has shrunk drastically (Rose and Grant, 1983). As in New York and London, female immigrant workers have been heavily used in this process. Various factors have created a sizeable pool of immigrant labour in Montreal since the mid-1970's, including the particularly liberal immigration policies of the Quebec government toward political refugees from Central America; the attraction of Haitians to Quebec for linguistic reasons, and the high number of women among such recent immigrants (Bernèche, 1983; Labelle et al., 1984). About two-thirds of these women work in manufacturing, mostly in the clothing industry (ibid.). This dequalification within the clothing industry, which has taken place at the same time as the expansion of specialized engineering industries employing highly skilled male labour, may thus be seen as adding to gender-typed bipolarizations of the work force.

Economic restructuring and the increased participation of women have affected the occupational composition and sexual division of the Montreal work force between 1971 and 1981. The statistics are summed up in Figure 1 (which, like all the data on occupations presented in this chapter, uses a seven-fold categorization of occupations).[4] All occupational categories have become increasingly feminized (overall, the change is from 34.7 per cent to 41.4 per cent), with the notable exception of skilled production occupations, in which the share of jobs held by women fell from 9.5 per cent to 9.0 per cent, presumably because of the particular nature of deindustrialization and industrial conversion that have taken place in Montreal.

SPATIAL VARIATIONS IN FEMINIZATION AND BIPOLARIZATION IN MONTREAL: THE INNER-CITY RESIDENT WORK FORCE

We are concerned about the social impacts of feminization and bipolarization, particularly inasmuch as these may be reflected in new forms of unequal competition for resources within urban neighbourhoods where people at both ends of the spectrum may be living (Rose, 1984). Although major global and regional centres tend to concentrate such tendencies within their midsts, little attention has been focused upon how these processes are differentiated *within* cities.

There is reason to suppose that a higher proportion of the labour force resident in the inner city would be female, compared to the metropolitan area as a whole, because of life-cycle factors as well as employment

Life Spaces

Figure 1

OCCUPATIONAL STRUCTURE BY GENDER

MONTREAL CMA, 1971 AND 1981

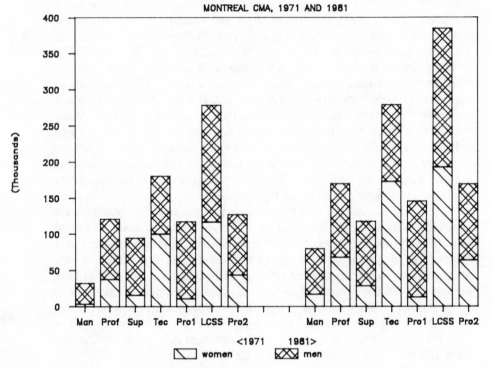

LEGEND FOR OCCUPATIONAL GROUPS*
(these abbreviations are used in all figures and tables)

Man	Managers and senior administrators
Prof	Professionals (such as liberal arts, social science, engineering)
Sup	Supervisors and forepersons
Tec	Technicians and upper-level white-collar (such as nurses, secretaries, police, real estate agents)
Pro1	Skilled production and construction workers
LCSS	Lower-level clerical, service, and sales
Pro2	Semi- and low-skilled production and construction workers

*See chapter notes for discussion of categories used.

structure. Labour force participation rates of non-married women are still much higher than those of married women, and much greater proportions of non-family households are found in inner-city areas than in the suburbs. With certain exceptions, women who live in the inner city also tend to work there (although not necessarily in the central business district—CBD— itself); this is especially true of those who live in the downtown core.[5] To the extent that single women, and those in dual-income couples, obtain substantial numbers of the new professional and managerial jobs created in the processes of growth and restructuring of white-collar jobs in the inner city, we may reasonably expect many of these women, as housing consumers, to opt for inner-city rather than suburban locations (Rose, 1984).

It also seems reasonable to suppose that within inner-city areas of Canadian cities, levels of bipolarization of the resident labour force might be higher than for metropolitan areas as a whole. Canadian inner cities are typically socially heterogeneous places, more so than their United States counterparts (Goldberg and Mercer, 1986, pp. 157-61). Montreal is no exception, having always contained wealthy neighbourhoods of substantial size, notably Upper Outremont and Westmount (zones 76 and 75 in Map 1), while at the same time, neighbourhoods of a traditionally working-class character still remain not far from the downtown core (e.g. Pointe-St-Charles, zone 81) and Centre-Sud (zone 45 and the eastern part of zone 44). The large ethnic minority concentrations in certain neighbourhoods (Saint-Louis/ Mile End, zones 70 and 71) also contribute to the lower end of the occupational spectrum, as many are employed in traditional manufacturing and low-level service occupations. During the late 1970's, the downtown fringe (zones 77, 83, 73, and 44) began to experience upscale gentrification both through redevelopment for offices and commerce and through housing renovation. More recently, gentrification has occurred on a far more modest scale in the Plateau Mont-Royal (a working- and lower middle-class district, zone 72 and part of 73 and 74) and in Saint-Louis/ Mile End. At the same time, skilled manufacturing jobs were disappearing as a result of closures and relocations accelerated by physical expansion of the downtown area (Morin, 1984). These trends would tend to increase bipolarization of the labour force, especially when coupled with the large population decline experienced in most inner-city neighbourhoods from the early 1960's to the 1980's, owing mainly to the movement to the suburbs of large numbers of middle-income blue-and white-collar households (see, for example, Mathews, 1986, pp. 107-11).

In view of these suppositions, we carried out a simple empirical analysis of bifurcation in the occupational structure in Montreal's inner-city resident work force, compared to the CMA as a whole. We present trends in

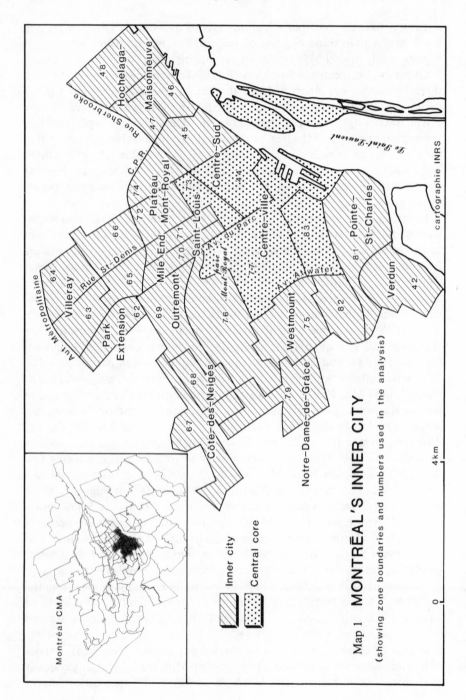

Map 1 **MONTRÉAL'S INNER CITY**

(showing zone boundaries and numbers used in the analysis)

feminization after an initial discussion of bifurcation, because, as we shall see, the gender composition of the poles sheds further light on the findings.

In order simply to measure bipolarization in Montreal, we examined the overall occupational structure of the resident labour force (without regard to sector or gender) for the Montreal CMA as a whole and for an area which we have designated as the inner city. The latter is a geographical area comprising the Island of Montreal's downtown core and the older neighbourhoods, generally built up before 1945, and other high-density neighbourhoods located within about thirty minutes of the downtown core by public transit in 1981.[6] Our definition deliberately includes two high-density areas built up in the 1960's and early 1970's, which have become important zones of settlement for new (mainly Third World) immigrants. The work force in this geographic area is probably divided between inner-city and inner-suburban manufacturing and low-level service work in the inner city and elsewhere.

Within the inner city we also designated a central core, consisting of the CBD and immediately adjacent residential and mixed-use neighbourhoods. (The map illustrates the boundaries of these zones.) The central core was singled out because it is there that economic and physical restructuring of urban space are most intertwined: we have already alluded to the eastward expansion of the CBD into a working-class neighbourhood, for example. We also operated under the assumption that the labour force living in the urban core was most directly linked to employment restructuring in the CBD; thus we expected levels of bipolarization to be highest here.

TABLE 1

Indices of bipolarization and average level in the occupational
structure of the Montreal labour force, 1971 and 1981

| | Bipolarization level | | Average level | | Change 1971-81 | |
	1971	1981	1971	1981	Bipolar.	Average
Montreal CMA	1.848	1.873	3.348	3.462	1.35%	3.41%
Inner city	1.875	1.915	3.245	3.352	2.10%	3.28%
Central core	1.852	1.904	3.104	3.205	2.81%	3.26%

Source: Computations based on Statistics Canada, Censuses of 1971 and 1981, special compilations. For explanation of calculations, see text.

Figure 2(a)   LABOUR FORCE BY OCCUPATIONS

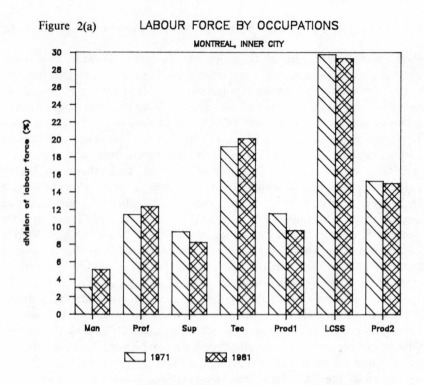

2(b)   LABOUR FORCE BY OCCUPATIONS

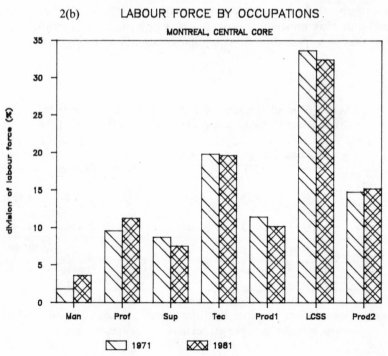

Figure 3(a)   OCCUPATIONAL STRUCTURE

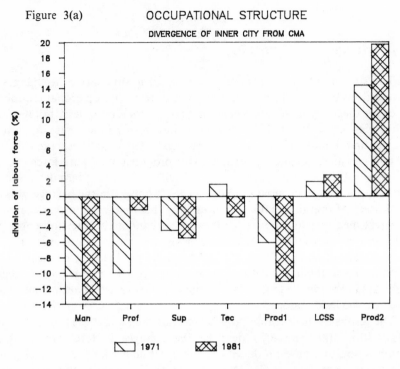

3(b)   OCCUPATIONAL STRUCTURE

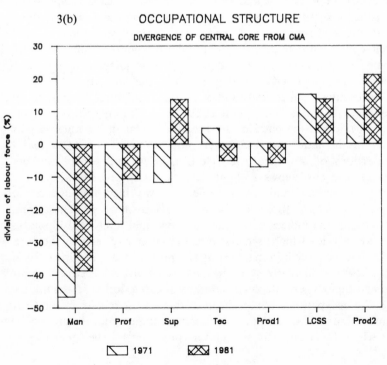

Bipolarization in the Inner City

Two simple statistics were computed in order to summarize the changes in proportions of the work force in the seven different occupational groupings used for the analysis [see the legend on Figure 1 for a brief description of the categories used]. We ranked these groupings from 7 (managers) down to 1 (semi- and low-skilled production workers). We used these rankings to obtain statistics, weighted according to the proportions of work force in each category, of the "average occupational level" and the standard deviation of distribution across occupational categories. Changes in the average give an indication of overall reskilling or deskilling (bearing in mind that these are not real measures and power levels since we cannot consider job content). Changes in the standard deviation provide a crude indicator of trends in bipolarization: an increase in the index can be produced by changes in the proportions at the top and/or at the bottom. As well, a large proportionate decrease in the middle (specialized white-collar workers and technicians) can increase the index value.[7]

The results of these computations are illustrated in Table 1, while Figures 2(a), 2(b), 3(a), and 3(b) describe the changes in total labour force composition that have produced the values tabulated for the inner city and the central core. For the CMA as a whole, the increase in bipolarization is statistically significant, but its size is muted by the fact that, during the 1970's, tens of thousands of women joined the labour force in specialized white-collar jobs—that is, in the middle of our spectrum. Most of these women were resident in suburban areas. The increase in polarization is sharper in the inner city and sharper still in the core area.

The occupational composition of the resident labour force (both sexes) in the inner city and its central core in 1971 and 1981 are shown in Figures 2(a) and 2(b). While the patterns are broadly similar in the inner city and the core, in the latter we find lower proportions of managers and higher proportions of non-specialized clerical, sales, and service workers. The central core also shows a slight decrease in specialized white-collar and technical workers and an increase in low-skilled production workers, opposite trends to those for the inner city as a whole. These trends are reflected in the indices of average occupational levels and bipolarization. The average level increased more in the inner city than in the core area, reflecting the growth in managerial and professional categories. Bipolarization, however, increased more in the core—reflecting a growth in both the top and the bottom categories, combined with a decline in the middle.

If the occupational composition of these areas relative to the CMA as a whole (Figures 3(a) and 3(b)) is examined, some major differences between the whole inner city and its central core emerge. The inner city became relatively *more* deficient in residents with managerial occupations between 1971 and 1981, while the core became relatively less deficient. The core did not lose forepersons and supervisors or skilled production workers to the same extent as the inner city as a whole: in spite of deindustrialization and redevelopment, the working-class character of some neighbourhoods in the core was retained in 1981. The increase in professionals is striking, as is the shift from an over-representation to an under-representation of specialized white-collar workers, compared to the CMA, in both the inner city as a whole and its core, owing no doubt to suburbanization of white-collar families. The representation of low-level white collar, sales, and service workers increases slightly in the inner city but decreases in the core; this could be related to displacement caused by gentrification.

With respect to the inner city as a whole, these findings are consistent with the theoretical propositions and research on global cities presented earlier. All the same, the empirical analysis presented here cannot make a direct causal link between trends regarding the *residence* of managers, professionals, and non-specialized white-collar and service workers and trends in the restructuring of *employment* along global city or regional control centre lines. To investigate such links requires detailed analysis of place of work by place of residence, which is beyond the scope of this chapter.[8]

Feminization in the Inner City

In order to appreciate more fully the social significance of these trends, we also need to examine shifts in gender composition within this increasingly bifurcated work force. This is particularly important since our indices do not take account of employment income, a crucial element mediating the "consumption power" associated with different positions in the occupational hierarchy. Since, by and large, women's earnings are only around three-fifths of those of men, the extent to which women hold occupations at either pole could possibly increase or decrease the social effects of bifurcation at the neighbourhood level (we shall return to the question of income levels later on).

The extent to which the occupational structures in the inner city and central core are feminized is depicted in Figures 4(a) and 5(a). Notably, within the non-specialized white-collar and service category—increasingly important in the inner city, as we have seen—more than 50 per cent of those living in the core were female in 1981, higher than for the inner city as a whole. All the same, as shown by Figures 4(b) and 5(b) (which show whether a category contains a greater or lower proportion of women than the same category in the CMA as a whole), this category was by 1981 less feminized than in the CMA as a whole, whereas in 1971 there was no difference. This

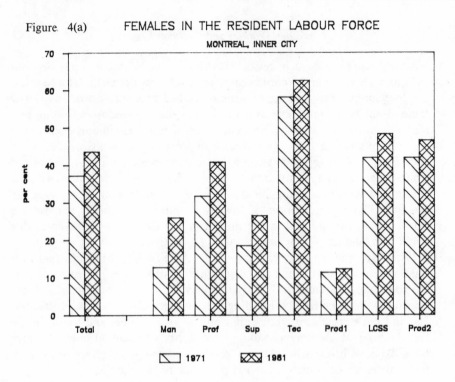

Figure 4(a)   FEMALES IN THE RESIDENT LABOUR FORCE

MONTREAL, INNER CITY

1971   1981

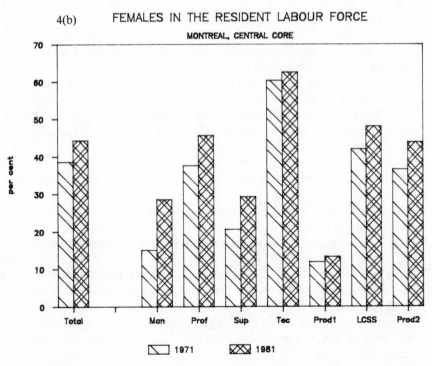

4(b)   FEMALES IN THE RESIDENT LABOUR FORCE

MONTREAL, CENTRAL CORE

1971   1981

Figure 5(a)   FEMALES IN THE RESIDENT LABOUR FORCE

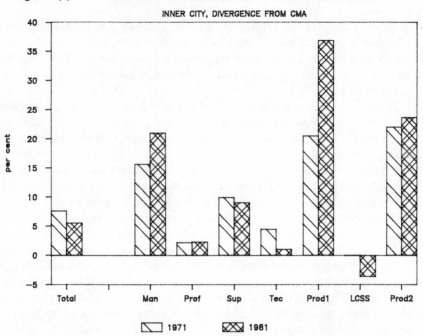

5(b)   FEMALES IN THE RESIDENT LABOUR FORCE

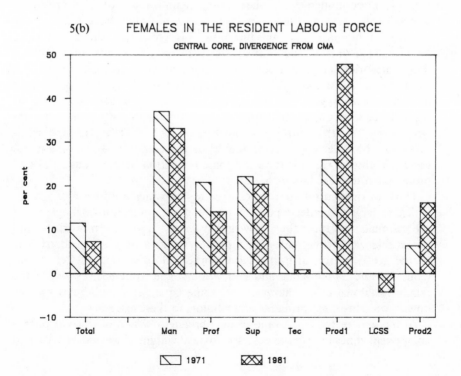

finding presumably reflects the vast growth in female jobs in retailing in the
suburban areas since our cross-tabulations show that, comparing the inner
city to the CMA as a whole, the female work force in the inner city was less
likely to be in retail trade and was more concentrated in personal, food, and
recreational services.

The labour force in the inner city and its core is more female than that of
the CMA, although the gap has decreased since 1971, notably for
upper-level white-collar workers. Yet both the managerial and the semi- and
unskilled blue-collar work force in the inner city have become more female
at a faster rate than in the CMA. In view of the lower earnings of women,
two of these gender-linked trends exacerbate the degree of bipolarization, an
important nuance not revealed by our simple index. First of all, the high
proportion of the semi- and unskilled blue-collar work force in the inner city
heightens the import of the increase in bipolarization created by the growth
of the lower end of the job spectrum. Secondly, the decline in upper-level
white-collar and technical women workers (a decline occurring, according to
our cross-tabulations, mainly in the heavily unionized and thus reasonably
paid education, health, and social services sectors) contributes to the decline
in the middle stratum of women workers. On the other hand, the fact that
women comprise a large share of the new managerial work force living in the
inner city, combined with the strong feminization of the group of
professionals resident there, could possibly mitigate the effects of the
increase in bipolarization produced by this growth at the upper pole,
because the incomes of such women are much lower than those of men in the
same categories. (This is not to deny the combined earning power of a
two-earner professional household, but in fact a relatively small proportion
of professionals in gentrifying areas are in two-earner households, since, as
we shall see later on, the majority of professionals in gentrifying areas are
not married.)[9] In the central core, however, no such mitigation of bipolarization could be expected, since although the percentage of women managers
there is high, the trend is toward a masculinization of the managerial and
professional resident labour forces.

Thus, in the central core we can see a sharp increase in bipolarization
which is largely gender-typed: at one end we find male managers and
professionals; at the other, low-skilled female production workers and
non-specialized office, sales, and service workers of both genders. The
partial gentrification of parts of the working-class districts of Centre-Sud
(zone 44) and Sainte-Anne and Petite-Bourgogne (zone 83), as well as the
relatively 'downscale' character of some apartment buildings on the
downtown fringe, are probable contributors to these extremes.

At the level of the CMA (and using a broader division of thirty-two large
component zones in order to ensure statistical viability), we have also carried

out an analysis of bipolarization within the female work force alone, differentiated by economic sector (see Villeneuve and Rose, 1985). According to our technique for measuring polarization, it is the business services sector—a major growth area for female employment (Rose and Villeneuve, 1985) and one where most of the jobs are in the downtown area (Polèse et al., 1984)—that has shown the greatest tendency for increased bipolarization among women. This is particularly evident in the resident labour force downtown and in adjacent "gentrifying" neighbourhoods. (Office cleaners, as well as architects, fall within the category of business services.) Within the education, medical, and social services sectors, bipolarization among women increased in the downtown area and the heavily professional and managerial communities of Westmount and Outremont (the latter's old neighbourhoods were almost completely gentrified in the 1970's). This change was attributable in the main to an absolute decline in the numbers of upper-level white-collar and technical workers living in those zones.

This brief discussion of the trends of feminization and bipolarization of the labour market structure in the inner city forms the backdrop for the next section. We now turn to the growth of the professional labour force in the inner city and its degree of feminization. Examining the household characteristics of women professionals, we explore the possible impacts of these trends on the form taken by gentrification of the inner city in light of the bipolarization processes outlined above. We look at the group of low-paid female workers rather than at managerial workers because at the fine level of spatial disaggregation which is required for the latter, the numbers are too small (especially for women) to guarantee significance. In the final section of the paper, we present some speculations about the implications of a strong presence of professional women among gentrifiers for community structure and service provision, and for the ongoing presence of semi- and unskilled women workers in the same or adjoining neighbourhoods.

FEMALE PROFESSIONALS AND GENTRIFICATION

In inner zones with a high overall concentration of professionals in 1981, the feminization of the professional labour force is higher than the CMA figure in only two: Outremont and Notre-Dame-de-Grâce (NDG) East—both of which are, incidentally, zones with a high proportion of professional couples. These excepted, the zones where a high percentage of professionals are female are zones where the overall proportions of professionals in the work force are *low*: the eastern part of the Plateau, excluding zone 73;

Saint-Louis/Mile End; Verdun east, and Pointe-St-Charles. One is immediately led to speculate that these zones attracted female professionals because
of relatively modest housing prices and accessibility to inner-city work
places. If we examine the *mean employment income* data for women
professionals, we find that in almost every one of the non-professional zones
where women represented a disproportionate number of all professionals,
their mean incomes in 1981 are below the CMA mean income for women
professionals and, in some cases, significantly below (for example, 82.3 per
cent in zone 72 and 68.8 per cent in zone 70). There seems to be a direct
relationship between the overall employment income level of these zones and
the income of their female professionals.

Women professionals living in the inner city are, like those in the CMA as
a whole, heavily concentrated in one sector: education, medical, and social
services (Rose and Villeneuve, 1985). Between 1971 and 1981 however, their
placement became more diverse, with an increasing involvement in the
business services sector and in the group including communications,
cultural, recreational, and personal services. Most professionals in this
group of sectors are actually in communications and recreation, particularly
in television, radio, and the literary and performing arts (Dansereau and
Beaudry, 1985). Indeed, compared to women professionals in the CMA,
although all the trends are in the same direction, there is a much higher
concentration in the communications-cultural-recreation sector in the inner
city. In the Plateau Mont-Royal, the proportion of female professionals
employed in this sector doubled, from 10 per cent to 20 per cent. A high
proportion of these women evidently work downtown, and we could suggest
that in this sector the prevalence of work at unusual hours and the nature of
contract work (which requires personal contacts) are factors encouraging a
central location.

So far we have remarked on the increased concentration of both male and
female professionals in the inner city. We have implied that, especially for
women, this, combined with a declining proportion of middle-level
white-collar workers and technicians, is increasing the bifurcation of the
work force. However, once we begin to disaggregate professionals by income
level as well as gender, this inference may need modification. We shall now
examine trends in the incomes of male and female professionals in different
parts of the inner city.

To place the discussion in context, we must understand the mean
employment income of the total employed labour force in the inner-city
zones, without regard to occupation or gender. The mean incomes are
consistently lower than in the metropolitan area as a whole, and in some
cases (Villeray and Côte-des-Neiges, for example) they have not kept pace
with the general increase in the CMA (10.3 per cent in constant dollars). The

largest increases have occurred in Downtown west (zone 77: 23.3 per cent), the zone of the Plateau closest to the CBD (zone 73: 32.3 per cent) and Downtown-east/Centre-Sud (zone 44: 20.5 per cent). (The latter is still a poor area but since the construction of CBC/Radio-Canada's Quebec headquarters there, it has seen considerable gentrification, notably through an increase in male managers and professionals.)

In a number of cases, the influx of male professionals has been accompanied by a larger increase in mean male professional employment income than the CMA average increase, notably in zones 70 and 73. All the same, the incomes remain below the CMA average for male professionals ($26,961 in 1981.) Relative to the CMA, 1981 mean incomes were marginal in inner-city areas other than downtown, Outremont, Westmount, and NDG.

In 1981, the mean employment income of female professionals in the Montreal CMA was only $16,960, or 62.9 per cent of that of their male counterparts. In inner-city zones the discrepancy was slightly lower, there being less spatial variation in the earnings of female professionals than those of males. The spatial patterning of female professionals' mean employment incomes follows, in general, that of the total labour force. A number of points are striking, however. In most inner-city zones, the increase since 1971 has been close to or a little higher than that for the CMA as a whole, although many zones still remain below the CMA average. The most noticeable increase is in Lower Outremont (zone 69), where female professionals' incomes were 100.8 per cent of the CMA average in 1971 but 121.3 per cent in 1981. In two zones that experienced an influx of women professionals (zones 70 and 71), the mean incomes of female professionals actually decreased in constant dollar terms, which suggests that many of those who moved in were economically marginal.

Rose (1984) has proposed that not all gentrifiers corresponded to the Young Urban Professional ("yuppie") image, with its connotations of upward mobility and conspicuous consumption by households with two professional or managerial jobs (see, for example, Beauregard, 1986). It was argued that, at least in some cities, with a large stock of modestly priced housing in the inner city, there were also "marginal gentrifiers": young people in occupations that were certainly professional but irregular and not well paying; not-so-young people whose career trajectories were blocked by recession or retrenchment in the public sector; and other groups for whom suburban environments did not offer the appropriate combination of affordable housing, fast access to work and services (such as day care), and social networks. Female single parents with professional jobs are a typical example of this latter group (Rose and Le Bourdais, 1986; Saegert et al., 1985); another example is groups with so-called alternative lifestyles which can be lived more easily in the inner city, such as gay men in the arts and media. This label of marginal gentrifiers is not fully satisfactory; over time, some people in this group doubtless become more upwardly mobile and obtain more stable work. However, the uncertainty brought about by the present phase of economic restructuring makes this dubious for many (Ehrenreich, 1986; Wessel, 1986).

To what extent can marginal professionals, a high proportion of whom are female, be said to be active in the gentrification process? What are the social implications of this activity? If homeownership in the inner city is one indication of gentrification, there is a fair amount of anecdotal evidence from Montreal to show that women professionals are over-represented among owners of undivided condominium duplex and triplex units. This form of tenure, which has grown rapidly since the early 1980's, has offered an inexpensive form of homeownership as well as the advantages of knowing one's neighbours and perhaps exchanging services. All the same, home-ownership was still a rarity in the inner city in 1981, even among households headed by a professional. The relative concentration[10] of homeownership among professionals is increasing in the downtown area, Outremont, Westmount, Saint-Louis/Mile End, and the Plateau. However, in the Plateau, professionals are still *under-represented* among homeowners. This can be looked at in two ways: either you do not have to be a homeowner to be a gentrifier; or you may be part of the influx of professionals but you cannot afford homeownership because your income is too low or insecure. It is probable that both of these contain elements of truth, especially in view of the general context of homeownership rates in the city, which never exceeded 20 per cent in 1981 among all households.

In order to cast further light on the possible neighbourhood-level impacts of the growth in numbers of female professionals, we also examined their marital status and the presence of children at home. For these purposes we have focused on three gentrifying neighbourhoods: Carré Saint-Louis/ Milton-Parc east (zone 73, and most gentrified as of 1981), Saint-Louis/ Mile End west (zone 70) and the central core of the Plateau Mont-Royal (zone 72).

The relative importance of female professionals in these zones can be inferred by looking at more general trends. Overall, the total labour force in the three zones (excluding those whose occupation was not declared) increased only slightly in number from 1971 to 1981 (from 34,005 to 34,590). The female labour force, however, increased by 11.4 per cent (from 13,005 to 14,490), to comprise 41.9 per cent of the work force (slightly higher than the CMA figure of 41.4 per cent). Without this increase the resident labour force would have declined in numbers; we can thus see one concrete indication of the social importance of women's increased labour force participation. Among the resident female labour force of these three zones in 1981, 15.2 per cent were professionals, compared to 12.2 per cent in the CMA as a whole. By way of comparison, women occupied 31.3 per cent of the lower-level clerical, sales, and service jobs, similar to the CMA average. Women professionals made up about one in sixteen of the total labour force (both sexes), compared to about one in twenty in the CMA as a whole. Although women professionals are still not as important numerically in the gentrifying zones as their male counterparts (about one in twelve members of the total work force), a higher proportion of the professional labour force is female (42.8 per cent) than in the CMA (40.0 per cent); the numerical increase of women professionals from 1971 to 1981 was greater in zones 70 and 72 than that of males, bringing the female shares up to 46.8 per cent and 46.3 per cent respectively. Thus there seem to be strong grounds for exploring the structure and possible impacts of the resident female professional work force in these zones.

Combining these three zones and both genders, we found that the percentages of both single and separated or divorced professionals were nearly twice as large as in the CMA as a whole, consistent with the broader trend for the inner city to become less family-oriented (see, for example, Mathews, 1986, pp. 107-11). However, the degree of over-representation (measured by means of the location quotient)[11] declined from 1971 to 1981, as the percentage of non-married professionals increased throughout the CMA. (In the census, "married" includes couples living together outside marriage.) Interestingly, the degree of over-representation in 1981 was much lower among women professionals than among their male counterparts, while there was considerable variation between zones: in zone 70, 40.6 per cent of female professionals were married (still much lower than the CMA average of 56.7 per cent); in zone 72, 35.9 per cent; and in zone 73, only 32.8 per cent.

By way of comparison, the trends in marital status among women in lower-level clerical, sales, and service occupations were not entirely similar, although the overall tendency for an increased percentage to be married rather than never-married was the same (a simple reflection of the general growth in married women's labour force participation). While in the CMA as a whole there was a slight increase in the proportions separated or divorced (from 7.4 per cent to 7.7 per cent), in the three neighbourhoods experiencing some gentrification, the trend was in the opposite direction, especially in zone 72 where the proportion dropped from 12.1 per cent to 6.2 per cent. The size of the never-married group has fallen in absolute as well as in relative terms in zones 72 and 73, while it has increased in zone 70. Although the reasons for these trends are not fully clear, one wonders whether by 1981 gentrification was already having an impact on the abilities of non-married women in this low-wage occupational category to pay for housing in these neighbourhoods. (In zone 70, there was an increase in the stock of moderately priced high-rise units, which probably accounts for the increase in numbers of never-married, low-level white-collar and service workers in this area.)

The high proportions of non-married women among female professionals, combined with the fact that women professionals' incomes tend to be modest in these zones, leads one to suggest that the housing demands of this fraction may not have a drastic inflationary impact on the housing market. Indeed, on the basis of anecdotal evidence, it would seem that women professionals living independently and with limited or unreliable incomes are attracted to non-profit housing cooperatives in Mile End and the Plateau Mont-Royal. At the same time, in the privately rented market, even the more marginal women professionals can still outbid the much lower paid sales and service workers who also want or need to live in these neighbourhoods. Among the latter a good number are probably single parents; and over a quarter of them live by themselves.

Comparing actual and potential gentrifiers in Montreal to other Canadian cities (see Ley, 1985), the relatively small proportion of dual-income couples among professionals in 1981 is probably closely related to the nature of the housing stock in Montreal's inner city. The prevalence of large three-flat row dwellings (triplexes) has historically helped to keep rents affordable (Choko, 1986). As gentrification was experienced in combination with a scarcity of single-family housing,[12] middle-class couples and singles with quite modest incomes were encouraged and enabled to purchase flats in undivided co-ownership tenure. Those with a little more money converted two-flat dwellings (duplexes) into single-family units or bought such units already renovated. As a result of these trends, rents drastically increased. The trends have accelerated since the 1981 census so one would suspect that one-income households are finding it increasingly difficult to afford their accommodation. The recent formation of a group bringing together women wishing to share accommodation in the Plateau Mont-Royal district is one indication of this problem.

Women professionals, regardless of their marital or household status and given their higher household incomes, inevitably contribute to the problem caused by gentrification. Yet one could venture to say that the relatively higher proportions of married people (as well as single parents) among women professionals could lend a more familial character to the gentrification process. This is less likely to be the case where male professionals dominate the process. The almost total absence of families is generally seen as one of the most negative features of gentrification. The negativity is not so much because of a pro-nuclear family bias in the literature but because

TABLE 2(a)

Presence of children at home, in all households whose "head" had a professional occupation, selected gentrifying neighbourhoods, Montreal, 1971 and 1981*

		1971				1981		1971-81
	ZONE		With	Location		With	Location	Relative change
		Total	children	quotient	Total	children	quotient	quotient
#	Name			(children)			(children)	(children)
70	Saint-Louis/ Mile End (west)	315	95	0.507	1030	195	0.378	0.745
72	Plateau Mont-Royal (Centre)	585	185	0.532	1345	310	0.460	0.865
73	Carré Saint-Louis/ Milton-Parc (east)	800	90	0.189	1525	165	0.216	1.142
	Subtotal: 3 gentrifying neighbour- hoods	1700	370	0.366	3900	670	0.343	0.937
	CMA	82450	49045	1.000	11055	55185	1.000	1.000

* See note 11.

gentrification tends to produce "consumption landscapes": areas providing specialized services and amenities antithetical to the needs of low-income families trying to survive in the same neighbourhoods. This stress on the non-family orientation of gentrifiers is largely owing to the American bias of most gentrification literature. As Goldberg and Mercer (1986, pp. 154-66) point out, Canadian inner cities, especially in central and eastern Canada, contain a higher proportion of families with children at home than do American cities, and these families are far less likely to be of low income.

With respect to gentrifying neighbourhoods in Montreal, although our data do not enable us to quantify the trend, a certain number of non-married female professionals head single-parent families with dependent children. This group is notably evident among condominium purchasers

TABLE 2(b)

Presence of children at home, in all family households whose "head" had a
professional occupation, selected gentrifying neighbourhoods, Montreal, 1971 and
1981*

#	ZONE Name	Total	1971 % of all prof. households	Location quotient (children)	Total	1981 % of all prof. households	Location quotient (children)	1971-81 Relative change quotient (children)
70	Saint-Louis/ Mile End (west)	165	52.4	0.782	405	39.3	0.688	0.880
72	Plateau Mont-Royal (Centre)	335	57.3	0.750	590	43.9	0.751	1.002
73	Carré Saint-Louis/ Milton-Parc (east)	240	30.0	0.509	870	24.3	0.638	1.252
	Subtotal: 3 gentrifying neighbour- hoods	740	43.5	0.679	1365	35.0	0.702	1.034
	CMA	66615	80.8	1.000	78905	71.6	1.000	1.000

* See note 11.

for instance (Choko and Dansereau, 1986). We cannot, unfortunately,
identify presence of children at home in all households where a female
professional is present, since our data are tabulated with reference to the
occupation and sex of the 'household head' (1971) and 'person one'(1981).[13]
Moreover, since these two categories are not comparable we are unable even
to do a longitudinal analysis of presence of children in households where the
head or person one is a female professional. Instead, for the three zones used

earlier, and in comparison to trends across the CMA as a whole, we have simply looked at presence of children at home, among households headed by a professional, regardless of sex. Tables 2(a) and 2(b) present our findings.

The location quotients relative to *all* households show clearly the low representation of families with children among professionals in these neighbourhoods. (It should be remembered that, in the census, a family consists of a female-male couple, with or without children, or a single parent with a never-married child living at home). Interestingly, however, in zone 73 (one of the first to be gentrified) the number of children increased slightly between 1971 and 1981. If we now examine only family households headed by a *professional,* the relative change quotient[14] of zone 73 is greater; in zone 72 there is no relative change; and in zone 70 the decline is less drastic. Since these data are five years old at the time of writing, and since we may speculate that a mini-baby boom among professional women over thirty seems to be occurring, it is possible that before the end of the 1980's the presence of women professionals in inner-city neighbourhoods may have gone some way toward reversing the trend toward low numbers of children in inner cities. Already, we have seen signs of gentrifiers participating in fights against elementary school closings (Schulze, 1986) as well as being active in parent-run day-care centres.

CONCLUSION

In this paper we have shown that the labour force residing in the Montreal CMA became increasingly bifurcated from 1971 to 1981, between professional and managerial occupations at one end and unskilled blue-collar and non-specialized white-collar and service occupations at the other. We have suggested that this is a result of the form taken by economic restructuring in Montreal between 1971 and 1981. The development of a 'regional city' with important control and knowledge functions for the new international economic order necessitates an increase in the numbers of managers and professionals, at the same time as building a large corps of low-level white-collar and service workers to service both the downtown infrastructure and the new labour fractions. In Montreal's inner city, the move toward advanced services has taken place in a context where increasingly marginalized, labour-intensive manufacturing also persists. Further, we have pointed out the gender-typing of this bipolarization such that the bulk of those at the bottom are female.

The particularly strong reflection of the bifurcation trend among the work force *resident* in the inner city is the result of a number of factors. Here we have touched on but one aspect—gentrification in or near zones where there has traditionally been a pool of low-cost housing. In some areas the social effects of gentrification have been negative from the point of view of existing communities, particularly in terms of housing and neighbourhood services. This has been evident in the strong working-class opposition to gentrification and the mobilization of housing cooperatives in Centre-Sud, for example.

At the same time, we have suggested that in some zones the gentrifiers may not all be "yuppies," especially in terms of their income prospects. Furthermore, by using data on gender, marital status, and household we were able to shed some light on modes of reproduction of these new fractions of labour. That is, we have been able to show that women professionals with fairly modest incomes—of whom a good number are in family households— are an important part of the total picture. Theoretically, there is a reciprocal and dialectical relationship between modes of reproduction and the consumption patterns of the new fractions of labour produced by the current round of economic restructuring.

This leads us to some more speculative comments, particularly concerning gentrifiers with young children. These appear to be on the increase. Conceivably, when gentrifiers have young children there may be less of a clash with the existing community and its needs. Nonetheless, without intervention to ensure affordable and secure housing these gentrifiers put severe pressure on the low rental housing stock. An option would be to expand the stock of cooperative housing.

We would suggest in particular that whether or not gentrifiers have children is central. Indeed, it could be as important a factor as their income levels and the trajectory of their job prospects over time in differentiating the social implications of gentrification and assessing what political strategies can be adopted. One- and two- parent families with children and paid jobs must continually juggle their responsibilities for both child care and breadwinning, especially when children are very young. Certain types of neighbourhoods, well-provided with support services of a formal and informal nature, can be supportive of families with these multiple responsibilities. Such pressures are faced by the professional and the immigrant clothing industry home-worker alike, but of course the former has more resources at her disposal to deal with them. To the extent that gentrifiers mobilize for improved provision of publicly supported child care services in a neighbourhood, this could also benefit the immigrant mother living not too far away, who has "chosen" to do piece work at home in order to be able to mind her child.[15] The active role of women in urban community struggles has been widely noted (see, for example, Andrew, 1984), but analyses of gentrifiers as urban activists or supporters of urban reform movements have never specifically looked at women.[16] Of course, gentrification with a strong family component can bring with it a new kind of unintended elitism, as Ley (1985) has put it. This has occurred in Canadian inner cities where the progressive middle class has successfully fought to prevent subdividing single-family dwellings, thus excluding low-to-modest income non-couple households (ibid.). Toronto is an excellent example. Clearly, any potentially positive spill-over effects of gentrifiers' pressure for improved community services can only be actualized to the extent that strong measures are taken to maintain the social and demographic heterogeneity of such neighbourhoods.

These observations, together with the fact that the housing stock of gentrifying neighbourhoods across Canada varies greatly, suggest that we need case studies which examine the different kinds of local social movements generated in gentrifying neighbourhoods with different social and income mixes, household structures, and housing stocks. It seems important to make use of the political leverage as well as the time, experience, and resources of the more community-oriented gentrifiers to help fight for neighbourhoods supportive of families of a range of different income levels, slotted into different fractions of the labour force. If we do not want to accelerate the apparent tendency for newly marginalized strata and their children to be forced into poor quality suburban apartment buildings without good access to services (Rose and Le Bourdais, 1986), we shall have to find imaginative ways of developing inclusionary instead of exclusionary urban revitalization in all the existing city neighbourhoods where it is not already too late.

NOTES

1. This chapter is a substantially revised and enlarged version of a paper presented at the Canadian Urban Studies conference, Winnipeg, August 1985. We wish to thank the editors, Francine Dansereau, Anne Gilbert, Alex Kowaluk, Janet McClain, and three anonymous referees for their helpful suggestions. Julie Archambault prepared the map. The research project on which this article is based was funded by the Social Sciences and Humanities Research Council of Canada, whose assistance we gratefully acknowledge.
2. We use the neologism "bipolarization" instead of the term "polarization," used in everyday English, in deference to our colleagues in the regional science milieu for whom the latter term has completely different theoretical connotations.
3. Unless otherwise indicated, all statistical information cited in the remainder of this article is based on calculations using special tabulations of the 1971 and

1981 censuses obtained for the larger research project.

4. Our occupational categories are based on various recent attempts to derive class, rather than status, indicators from census data (see e.g. Hunter and Manley, 1986; Légaré, 1977; Pelletier, 1982). (For instance, a nurse is seen as a technician, not a professional.) The classification is centred on the notion of *social relations of power*, power being considered as a relation exercised through the control of information in the broadest sense, and, where necessary, with recourse to coercion. Our categories are thus related to each other through asymmetrical relations of power based on differential control of information. We also distinguish power over others (managers or supervisors, for example) from power over specialized or technical knowledge (professionals or technicians), although in reality one form of power is likely to entail the other. Finally, the distinction between white- and blue-collar workers reflects on conceptions of "fractions" of capital, although it is clear that in manufacturing, white-collar workers have been increasing in proportion over the years.

Inevitably, the assignment of four-digit census occupational categories to one of our seven groups can be arbitrary at times. This has been minimized by referring to the detailed definitions of occupations found in *Occupational Classification Manual: Census of Canada*, 1971. Cat. 12-536. (We used the 1971 rather than the 1980 classification because the former can be used for both 1971 and 1980.)

5. This observation is drawn from a preliminary analysis of place-of-work by place-of-residence data obtained from Statistics Canada as part of the larger research project.

6. The area thus delimited bears a close resemblance to that used by Mathews (1986, pp. 45-47). The larger research project uses a division of the CMA into 94 zones, initially drawn up for a concurrent study (based at INRS-Urbanisation) on single-parent families in Montreal. As far as possible, the zones represent recognizable neighbourhoods.

7. We have retained three decimal places in these indices because a small change (about 0.02) in the values of either statistic is of statistical significance. For a discussion see Villeneuve and Rose (1985).

8. All the same, our preliminary analysis shows that, as of 1981 there was little decentralization of white-collar employment from the inner city of Montreal to the suburbs. Employment in the finance, insurance, and real estate sectors, as well as in business services—sectors closely associated with the "corporate city"—was concentrated in the central core (see also Polèse *et al.*, 1984). Moreover, there was little "reverse commuting" among the labour force resident close to downtown.

9. Furthermore, although the great majority of married women professionals have spouses who are employed, the proportions are a little lower in some gentrifying neighbourhoods; this suggests that some may be supporting their husbands financially.

10. By relative concentration we refer to the ratio of the proportion of homeowners in a zone that are professionals to the proportion of all households in a zone that are professionals.

11. The location quotient is the ratio of the proportion of professional households in a certain zone with children at home to the proportion of professional households in the whole of the CMA with children at home. The index can vary between 0 and infinity. A value of 0.5 indicates that the concentration in a zone is only half that found in the CMA; a value of 2 indicates a concentration twice that in the CMA. It should be noted that when the values of numerator or denominator are very small, the index is much less reliable.

12. Exceptions were Outremont and Notre-Dame-de-Grâce, which rapidly became very expensive from the late 1970's on.

13. In the 1981 Census Statistics, Canada replaced its previous concept of "household head" with that of "person one," defined as the person in a household responsible for payment of rent, mortgage, taxes, or electricity. Although this was supposed to get rid of sexist bias, in reality numerous problems remain in this respect (see Armstrong and Armstrong, 1983 for discussion). Moreover, the new definition is still unable to take account of households where two adults share equally in financial responsibilities.

14. The relative change quotient is the 1981 location quotient divided by that of 1971.

15. As Meintel, Labelle and Turcotte (1985) have suggested, immigrant women may also be short of support either because selective immigration has fractured kinship networks or because their kin and friends also have to work long hours.

16. For an illustration of this point, see Ley and Mills's (1986) study of gentrification and political activism in Montreal in 1982.

REFERENCES

Andrew, Caroline (1984). "Women and the Welfare State." *Canadian Journal of Political Science, 17*(4), pp. 667-83.

Armstrong, Pat (1984). *Labour Pains: Women's Work in Crisis.* Toronto: The Women's Press.

Armstrong, Pat and Armstrong, Hugh (1983). "Beyond Numbers: Problems with Quantitative Data." *Alternate Routes: A Critical Review, 6*, pp. 1-40.

Aydalot, Philippe (1981). "Politiques de localisation des entreprises et marchés du travail." *Revue d'économie régionale et urbaine, 1*, pp. 107-28.

Beauregard, Robert (1986). "The Chaos and Complexity of Gentrification." In Neil Smith and Peter Williams (Eds.), *Gentrification of the City* (pp. 35-55). Boston: Allen and Unwin.

Bernèche, Francine (1983). "Immigration et espace urbain: Les regroupements de population haïtienne dans la région métropolitaine de Montréal." *Cahiers québécois de démographie, 12*(2), pp. 295-324.

Bradbury, John (1985). "Regional and Industrial Restructuring Processes in the New International Division of Labour." *Progress in Human Geography, 9*(1), pp. 38-63.

Choko, Marc (1986). "Evolution of Rental Housing Market Problems." Resource Paper submitted to CMHC for the project "Housing Progress in Canada since 1945"; INRS-Urbanisation, Montreal and Centre for Urban and Community Studies, University of Toronto.

Choko, Marc and Dansereau, Francine (1986). "Restauration résidentielle et copropriété au centre-ville de Montréal." Research report submitted to CMHC; INRS-Urbanisation, Montreal.

Cohen, R. B. (1981). "The New International Division of Labor, Multinational Corporations and Urban Hierarchy." In Michael Dear and Allen J. Scott (Eds.), *Urbanization and Urban Planning in Capitalist Society* (pp. 287-315). London and New York: Methuen.

Dansereau, Francine and Beaudry, Michel (1985), "Les mutations de l'espace habité montréalais: 1971-1981." Paper presented at the ACSALF symposium, "La morphologie sociale en mutation au Québec," Chicoutimi (May); INRS-Urbanisation, Montreal.

Ehrenreich, Barbara (1986), "Is the Middle-class Doomed?" *New York Times Magazine,* Section 6, 7 September, pp. 44, 50, 54, 62, 64.

Goldberg, Michael and Mercer, John (1986). *The Myth of the North American City: Continentalism Challenged.* Vancouver: University of British Columbia Press.

Greater London Council, Industry and Employment Branch (1985). *The London Industrial Strategy.* London: Greater London Council.

Harrison, Bennett (1982). "Rationalization, Restructuring and Corporate Reorganization: The Economic Restructuring of New England since World War II." *MIT-Harvard Joint Center for Urban Studies. Working Papers*, No. 72.

Holcomb, Briavel (1984). 'Women in the Rebuilt Urban Environment: The United States Experience." *Built Environment, 10*(1), pp. 18-24.

Hunter, Alfred and Manley, Michael C. (1986). "On the Task Content of Work." *Canadian Review of Sociology and Anthropology, 23*(1), pp. 47-71.

Labelle, Micheline, Meintel, Deirdre, Turcotte, Geneviève, and Kempeneers, Marianne (1984). "Immigrées et ouvrières: un univers de travail à recomposer." *Cahiers de recherche sociologique, 2*(2), pp. 9-48.

Labour Canada Women's Bureau (1983). *Women in the Labour Force. Part 1: Participation.* Ottawa: Labour Canada.

Lamonde, Pierre and Polèse, Mario (1984). "L'évolution de la structure économique de Montréal, 1971-1981: désindustrialisation ou reconversion?" *L'Actualité économique. Revue d'analyse économique 60*(4), pp. 471-94.

Légaré, Anne (1977). *Les classes sociales au Québec.* Montreal: Les Presses de l'Université du Québec.

Ley, David (1985). "Gentrification in Canadian cities: Patterns, Analysis, Impacts and Policy." Research report submitted to CMHC; Department of Geography, University of British Columbia.

Ley, David and Mills, Caroline (1986). "Gentrification and Reform Politics in Montréal, 1982." *Cahiers de géographie du Québec, 30*(81), pp. 419-427.

Lipietz, Alain (1986). "New Tendencies in the International Division of Labor: Regimes of Accumulation and Modes of Regulation." In Allen J. Scott and

Michael Storper (Eds.), *Production, Work, Territory: The Geographical Anatomy of Industrial Capitalism* (pp. 16-40). Boston: Allen and Unwin.

Mackenzie, Suzanne (1983). "Gender and Environment: Reproduction in Post-War Brighton." D.Phil. Thesis, University of Sussex, Brighton, England.

Maroney, Heather (1983). "Feminism at Work." *New Left Review,* 141, pp. 51-71.

Massey, Doreen (1984). *Spatial Divisions of Labor.* London: Macmillan.

Mathews, Georges (1986). "L'évolution de l'occupation du parc résidentiel plus ancien de Montréal de 1951 à 1979." *Etudes et Documents, 46.* Montreal: INRS-Urbanisation.

Meintel, Deirdre, Labelle, Micheline, and Turcotte, Geneviève (1985). "La nouvelle double journée du travail des femmes immigrantes au Québec." *Revue internationale d'action communautaire 14*(54), pp. 33-44.

Menzies, Heather (1982a). *Computers on the Job.* Toronto: James Lorimer.

Menzies, Heather (1982b). *Women and the Chip.* Montreal: Institute for Research on Public Policy.

Menzies, Heather (1985a). "Une approche féministe des nouvelles technologies." In *Apprivoiser le changement: Actes du colloque CEQ sur les nouvelles technologies. La division du travail, la formation et l'emploi* (pp. 37-43). Montreal: Centrale de l'enseignement du Québec.

Menzies, Heather (1985b). "Un avenir peu prometteur pour les femmes." In *Apprivoiser le changement: Actes du colloque CEQ sur les nouvelles technologies, la division du travail, la formation et l'emploi* (pp. 227-31). Montreal: Centrale de l'enseignement du Québec.

Messier, Suzanne (1984). *Les femmes, ça compte: profils socio-économique des Québécoises.* Gouvernement du Québec. Conseil du statut de la femme.

Morin, Richard (1984). "Désindustrialisation et mutations des quartiers anciens." *Actualité immobilière, 8*(3), pp. 8-13.

Payeur, Christian (1985). *Nouvelles technologies et conditions de travail: matériaux pour une stratégie syndicale.* Quebec: Centrale de l'enseignement du Québec.

Pelletier, Lyse (1982). "Pouvoir politique et classes sociales: l'exemple de la ville de Québec." Master's Thesis, Département de géographie, Université Laval.

Polèse, Mario, Johnson, Lynda, and Tessier, François (1984). "L'activité tertiaire." Pierre Lamonde, Jacques Ledent, and Mario Polèse (eds.), "Perspectives d'emplois et de population pour la région métropolitaine de Montréal, par zone d'analyse-Horizon 1996." Study conducted for the Service de la planification du territoire de la Communauté urbaine de Montréal; Centre de documentation, INRS-Urbanisation, Montreal.

Pred, Allan (1978). *City-Systems in Advanced Economies.* London: Hutchinson.

Rose, Damaris (1984). "Rethinking Gentrification: Beyond the Uneven Development of Marxist Urban Theory." *Environment and Planning D: Society and Space,* 2(1), pp. 47-74.

Rose, Damaris and LeBourdais, Céline (1986). "The Changing Conditions of Female Single Parenthood in Montreal's Inner City and Suburban Neighborhoods." *Urban Resources,* 3(2), pp. 45-52.

Rose, Damaris and Villeneuve, Paul (1985). "Women and the Changing Spatial

Division of Labour in Montreal.'' Paper presented at the Annual Meeting of the Association of American Geographers, Detroit (April); INRS-Urbanisation, Montreal.

Rose, Ruth and Grant, Michel (1983). *Le travail à domicile dans l'industrie du vêtement au Québec*. Montreal: Fédération des Travailleurs du Québec (Protocole UQAM-CSN-FTQ).

Ross, Robert and Trachte, Kent (1983). ''Global Cities and Global Classes: The Peripheralization of Labour in New York City.'' *Review: A Journal of the Fernand Braudel Center,* 6(3), pp. 393-431.

Saegert, Susan, Liebman, Theodore, and Melting, Alan (1985). ''Working Women: The Denver Experience.'' In Eugenie Ladner Birch (Ed.), *The Unsheltered Woman: Women and Housing in the 80s* (pp. 83-100). New Brunswick, New Jersey: Rutgers University, Center for Urban Policy Research.

Sassen-Koob, Saskia (1984). ''The New Labor Demand in Global Cities.'' In Michael P. Smith (Ed.), *Cities in Transformation: Class, Capital and the State* (pp. 139-71). Urban Affairs Annual Reviews, vol. 26. Beverley Hills: Sage.

Schulze, David (1986). ''Des parents anglophones sauvent l'école Bancroft.'' *Liaison St-Louis* (5 February), p. 1.

Semple, Keith and Green, Milford (1983). ''Interurban Corporate Headquarters Relocation in Canada.'' *Cahiers de géographie du Québec*, 27(72), pp. 389-406.

Smith, Joan (1984). ''The Paradox of Women's Poverty: Wage-earning Women and Economic Transformation.'' *Signs: Journal of Women in Culture and Society*, pp. 291-310.

Smith, Neil (1986). ''Gentrification, the Frontier and the Restructuring of Urban Space.'' In Neil Smith and Peter Williams (Eds.), *Gentrification of the City* (pp. 15-34). Boston: Allen and Unwin.

Villeneuve, Paul and Rose, Damaris (1985). ''Technological Change and the Spatial Division of Labour by Gender in the Montreal Metropolitan Area.'' Paper presented at a Meeting of the Commission on Industrial Change, International Geographical Union, Nijmegen, The Netherlands (August); Département de géographie, Université Laval, Québec.

Weiss, M. A. (1985). ''High-technology Industries and the Future of Employment.'' In Peter Hall and Ann Markusen (Eds), *Silicon Landscapes* (pp. 80-93). Boston: Allen and Unwin.

Wessel, David (1986). ''Growing Gap: U.S. Rich and Poor Increase in Numbers; Middle Loses Ground.'' *Wall Street Journal*, 22 September, pp. 1, 19.

Williams, Peter (1986). ''Class Constitution through Spatial Reconstruction?: A Re-evalution of Gentrification in Australia, Britain and the United States.'' In Neil Smith and Peter Williams (Eds.), *Gentrification of the City* (pp. 56-77). Boston: Allen and Unwin.

3

Practical Idealism: Women in Urban Reform, Julia Drummond and the Montreal Parks and Playgrounds Association

JEANNE M. WOLFE and GRACE STRACHAN

INTRODUCTION

The urban reform movements in Canada between 1880 and 1920 have been well documented (Rutherford, 1974; Stelter and Artibise, 1977; Weaver, 1977; Germain, 1984) as have the conditions of our cities and towns during the middle and late nineteenth century that triggered the reforms (Ames, 1897; Woodsworth, 1911; Hart, 1919; Copp, 1974; Linteau, 1979). However, there has been scant attention paid to the contribution of women in these movements. Women were the prime actors in welfare organizations, often wielding power through their husbands. In Montreal during this period, women were responsible for the foundation of the Charity Organization Society (later to become the Family Welfare Association), they were prominent in the University Settlement Movement, founders of the Parks and Playgrounds Association, and central to the establishment of the Victorian Order of Nurses through the National Council of Women. Women also coordinated traditional charities such as foundling hospitals, Ladies Benevolent Societies, and associations for the protection of women and children.

This paper examines some aspects of the role of women active in urban reform in Montreal at the turn of the century. It is clear that women's concerns focused on the domestic, family, and environmental aspects of urban life rather than on the political, administrative, and economic. There are two reasons for this: first, caring and children are traditionally the concern of women; second, women were simply not enfranchised in most areas of public life.

This preliminary examination of the role of women focuses mainly on the foundation and evolution of the Montreal Parks and Playgrounds Association (MPPA) and on the life of Lady Julia Drummond. The Montreal Parks and Playgrounds Association began as a women's protest movement, and the breadth of its activities and its longevity are noteworthy. It is one women's organization among many that has had an enduring effect on urban life. Similarly, the work of Julia Drummond illustrates the scope of reform activities among and for women, children, and working-class families. Many other women of this period did similar work for a similar range of organizations; activists such as Lady Hingston, Mrs. John Cox, and Josephine Gérin-Lajoie were, like Drummond, amateurs and philanthropists. Other later ones, such as Professor Carrie Derick, a botanist, Maud Abbott, a lawyer, and Dr. Grace Ritchie England and Helen Y. Reid, social workers, were pioneer professionals with wide-ranging interests. However, both groups shared common interests and common approaches to the problems of the times.

We make no apologies for starting our enquiry through examination of the work of a member of the elite; sources about working-class women of this period are scarce, possibly non-existent, although more is becoming known about their working lives. (See Cross 1977; Dumont et al., 1982; Lavigne, Pinard and Stoddart, 1977; and Lavigne and Stoddart, 1983.)

URBAN REFORM

The urban reform movement in Montreal, as elsewhere, arose at the beginning of the twentieth century in response to the conditions created by large-scale industrialization and immigration. From a population of 78,000 in 1851, just before the building of the Grand Trunk Railway, greater Montreal grew to a third of a million by the turn of the century and had passed the one million mark by 1931. As migrants streamed into the city to fill unskilled jobs, so health, crowding, and sanitation problems compounded. Concern for the city's poor, voiced only by a scattered few in the late 1800's, foreshadowed the rise of urban reform movements, which led to town planning in the 1910's and 1920's.

Urban reform in the nineteenth century focused on: (1) public health and housing concerns, (2) the city beautiful movement, (3) the parks and playgrounds drive, (4) civic administrative reform, and (5) the conservation movement (Lubove, 1967; Spragge, 1975). In many respects reformers pursued similar ends but approached the problems from different perspectives.

THE PARKS AND PLAYGROUNDS MOVEMENT

The Parks and Playgrounds Movement in North America dates from the mid-nineteenth century. Its beginnings are marked by the passage of the First

Park Act by the New York State legislature in 1851. Previous to this, there is no recorded example in North America of outdoor recreational space on land acquired and owned by a public authority, developed with public funds, and open indiscriminately to all, although various civic and ornamental squares existed (Newton, 1971, p. 267). The first steps in the acquisition of Central Park in New York City date from this time; other cities rapidly followed suit, including Boston, Chicago, Buffalo, San Francisco, and San Diego, and, almost twenty years later, Montreal. The act authorising the purchase of Mount Royal was passed in 1869 and some 485 acres had been acquired by 1875, despite various disputes (Jenkins, 1966, p. 413). In 1873, Frederick Law Olmstead was retained as designer for the park (Marsan, 1983, pp. 301-4).

The parks movement pre-dates the playground drive by a few years: the first focused on large-scale natural open space; the second concentrated on organized play areas as an alternative to cluttered streets. The parks movement, urged on by the developing profession of landscape architecture, can be considered as the urban counterpart of the conservation movement. Conservation experts in the United States such as Gifford Pinshott, John Wesley Powell, Elwood Mead, and Benton Mackaye first introduced the concept of scientific resource management, but they soon moved beyond natural resource policy into the realm of social and community theory (Lubove, 1967, p. 2). Thus the idea of large urban parks with naturalistic landscaping evolved in response not only to rapid urbanization and the distancing of the countryside from city dwellers but also to an emerging idea of a rural-urban continuum satisfying aesthetic and emotional needs (Fein, 1972). The impetus for acquiring and developing parkland came then, as now, from the upper middle classes (Harry, Gale and Hendee, 1969).

The playgrounds movement followed rapidly, prompted by concerns about urban crowding, sanitation and hygiene, and juvenile delinquency. Sand "gardens," a new idea introduced from Germany, were prescribed for the very young as a creative form of play and learning. Organized games emphasizing discipline and good sportsmanship were recommended for older children, along with useful lessons such as woodwork and metalwork for boys and cooking and sewing for girls. These playgrounds would (1) keep children from slum areas off the streets where they might be injured or subjected to all sorts of temptations, (2) get them out into the sunshine to improve their health, and (3) train them to be better citizens (MPPA, 1901, 1904).

The Parks Protective Association, forerunner of the Montreal Parks and Playgrounds Association (MPPA), was founded in the winter of 1895-96. Its purpose was to save Mount Royal from the threat of disfiguring development, prompted by the Montreal Street Railway Company's attempt to build a railway through the park to provide improved access. (After the opening of

Mount Royal park in 1876, a privately operated incline railway had been built to provide access to the summit, but it was unreliable, costly, and underused. However, Fletcher's Field, on the eastern foot of the mountain, was always crowded [Ewing, 1922], prompting the railway company to seek a franchise there.) Reaction was immediate: a Park Protective Association was formed by a group of well-connected women under the leadership of Lady Hingston. Popular sentiments were divided, however. Some feared that, without rail access, the top of the mountain "would only be for the rich who could reach it in their carriages" (letter to the *Montreal Star*, 25 July 1891).

Lady Hingston, wife of Dr. William Hingston who had officiated as mayor at the opening of the park twenty years earlier, agreed with Frederick Law Olmstead's passionate belief in the dangers of encroachment on naturalistic landscape. Olmstead was a leading American promoter of the view that the market system did not create environments conducive to the socialization of urban dwellers. Lady Hingston rapidly organized a petition of twenty thousand signatures to persuade the legislature to refuse the franchise. On the very day it was presented, the company, sensing defeat, withdrew its request (MPPA, archives MG.2079.c13. File 313). The committee of ladies then met with the city council and persuaded it to amend the city charter so that the mountain would forever be preserved in its natural beauty (MPPA, *Annual Report*, 1901).

In spite of the women's success, the mountain continued to be threatened by development schemes. In early 1900, for instance, a member of the Quebec legislature moved to amend the city charter with a view to alienating the southwest corner of Fletcher's Field. Although protested vigorously, the amendment went through, though in modified form. The women of the Parks Protective Association sensed that their informal watchdog group was not strong enough to withstand development pressures, and they moved to incorporate a more forceful and durable society (MPPA, archives MG.2079.c8. Scrapbooks).

Meanwhile it was becoming clear that the mountain was not the only open space issue. Working-class areas suffered an appalling lack of parks and playgrounds. The 38,000 residents of the western section of the lower city only had two public squares, Richmond and St. Patrick's. Similarly, the 26,000 residents of St. Louis ward had access only to Viger Square. For the people of St. Laurent ward there was only Dufferin Square which, like Dominion Square, had been a cemetery (Robert, 1928). Lafontaine Park, (Logan's Farm), a military training ground from 1845 to 1888, did not become a park until towards the end of the century, and St. Helen's Island, also a military base from 1818 to the late 1870's, was accessible only by ferry. Its southern tip became a park in 1874, but the city did not purchase the whole island until 1907 (Atherton, 1914, Vol. 2, p. 644; Marsan, 1981, p. 306).

Most of the women of the Parks Protective Association were affiliated with other groups, notably through the Montreal Local Council of Women (MLCW), and a vigorous chapter of the National Council of Women of Canada (NCWC) founded by Lady Aberdeen in 1893 (Strong-Boag, 1976) which brought together members of women's philanthropic, charitable, and cultural associations for mutual benefit. The ladies of the Parks Protective Association, through their work in other organizations, were only too well aware of the deficiencies of slum neighbourhoods. They recognized the need for a dual-purpose open space organization, first to protect existing open spaces, and second to foster the development of playgrounds and the ideals of the growing playground movement.

The so-called play movement came to Canada through the United States from Germany. Before its inception, sports such as football, cricket, and athletics were practised on open space such as the town commons of New England, and on vacant land in the outskirts of town such as Fletcher's Field in Montreal. These manly sports were replaced by curling, hockey, and snowshoeing in winter, usually organized through private clubs and catered primarily, though not exclusively, to middle- and upper-class men (Metcalfe, 1978). Play space for children was simply not considered.

The idea of sand gardens was brought to Boston from Germany by Dr. Marie Zakrewski in the late 1880's and was popularized by Miss Ellen Tower of the Massachusetts Emergency and Hygiene Association. There was great excitement over sand play, and Miss Tower was invited to Montreal to lecture on the subject in 1902 (MPPA, *Annual Report*, 1903). Her ideas were gladly incorporated into the fledgling parks movement (Wilson, 1953).

The Parks and Playgrounds Association was formally launched in 1902, with Mrs. William Peterson, wife of the principal of McGill University, as president. In the first year two Protestant School Board yards, at Berthelet and Royal Arthur schools, were rented for the summer and set up as play centres; members of the association worked as volunteer leaders. A total of 12,912 children attended over a nine-week summer period, with total expenditures of $386.43 (MPPA, *Annual Report*, 1902).

Meanwhile the association set in motion an Act of Incorporation. The petition was signed by most of the leading figures of the day, including George A. Drummond, William Hingston, Raoul Dandurand, Frederick L. Beique, Mayor Hormidas Laporte, Dr. William Peterson, Sir Alexandre Lacoste, and many others, along with a great list of their wives, including Julia Drummond. In 1904, the association received its Quebec Charter, and at the annual meeting a group of distinguished gentlemen were elected to the board, with the Hon. George A. Drummond as president (MPPA, *Annual Report,* 1904).

The presence of men on the governing board of an organization started by women can be explained by a speech made by Julia Drummond some years later. She enumerated three conditions necessary for the success of an organization: "It must have women in it"; "its governing board must be composed largely of business men. . . . that business men should think it worth their while as citizens to put into charity those same principles of order, economy and adaptation of means to ends which characterize all business"; and "everyone should make use of it" (Drummond, 1907, pp. 136-37). The annual reports of the MPPA for the first years consistently show a male board of directors, while the two committees, one for parks and the other for playgrounds, were composed entirely of women, whom, Julia Drummond said, have more "sense and sensibility" (1907, p. 136).

GRACE JULIA DRUMMOND

Grace Julia Drummond was born in Montreal in 1859, the third daughter of Alex Davison Parker, an insurance broker, and Grace Parker, a former lady-in-waiting to Lady Elgin, wife of the Governor General. Julia was raised and educated in Montreal; she was fluent in French and an advocate of bilingualism (Osborn, 1919). At the age of twenty, she married an Anglican clergyman, George Hamilton, who died the following year. In 1884, she married George A. Drummond, a prosperous, Scottish-born sugar merchant, financier, company director, patron of the arts, and well-known philanthropist. He was fifty-five and she was twenty-five. George Drummond was later to be made a senator and knighted. They had two sons, Julian, born in 1885, who died in infancy, and Guy, born in 1887, who was killed at the second battle of Ypres on 22 April 1915.

The first record of Julia Drummond's involvement with activities outside the domestic sphere is as a member of the Women's Historical Society and the Women's Art Association, both "normal" pursuits for a Victorian woman of her class. The Women's Art Association was particularly suitable for Julia since her husband was a collector of paintings and served as president of the association from 1896 to 1899. Her first independent step into public life was in 1893, when she became the first president of the Montreal Local Council of Women (MLCW).

Lady Aberdeen had come to Canada as wife of the Governor General and was already an activist in the rapidly evolving women's club movement (Strong-Boag, 1977); she was elected president of the International Council of Women at their founding convention in Chicago in 1893. Arriving in Canada later that year, she immediately set about founding a national organization with chapters in each major city. Not unsurprisingly, she became president of the Canadian Council. A note in the Aberdeen diaries gives a clue to why Julia Drummond was elected president of the Montreal group. Dated Thursday, 30 November 1893, and written at the Windsor Hotel in Montreal, the entry reads: "Dr. Barclay has happily suggested the name of Mrs. Drummond as Pres. of Local Council. She is the wife of Senator Drummond and a very distinguished charming looking women . . . . Mrs. Cummings [née Emily Ann Short, a Toronto activist] went around to explain things to her this morning & she readily accepted and spoke a few words saying Yes in a v. dignified and pleasant way" (Saywell, 1960, p. 36).

Dr. James Barclay, a presbyterian minister who had emigrated to Canada in 1844, was a highly influential person. He had a great reputation as a preacher, lecturer, sportsman, and philanthropist, and his fame was such that he was often summoned to Balmoral to preach to Queen Victoria (ibid., p. 485). He was a great friend and confidant of the Aberdeens. Thus, it appears that Julia Drummond was really chosen rather than elected first president of the MLCW.

Julia Drummond served as president of the MLCW for the first five years of its life. The Montreal council was a voluntary federation of both women's groups and individual members. The main aim of the council was to promote unity among women; its secondary objectives were aid to women and children and social reform. Respecting but not necessarily supporting the views of its member groups, the MLCW remained non-sectarian and non-political, although it started in an essentially Anglo-Protestant milieu. The council was soon joined by groups such as the Girls Friendly Society, the YMCA, the Child Welfare Association, the Day Nursery, the Foundling and Baby Hospital, the Ladies Benevolent Society, the Women's National Immigration Society, the Child Welfare Association, the Montreal Women's Club, the Women's Art Association, and the Alumnae Society of McGill University (Strong-Boag, 1976). A number of prominent French-Canadian women also joined, despite the opposition of their church, including: Mme Rosaire Thibaudeau (Marie Loulou Lamothe), founder of the Notre Dame hospital; Josephine Marchand Dandurand; Marie Gérin-Lajoie, daughter of Lady Lacoste; and Caroline Beïque. All were to gain valuable organizational experience and to hold office in the council (Pinard, 1977). In 1907, they formed a French-Canadian parallel to the MLCW, the Fondation des Dames Patronnes de l'Association St-Jean Baptiste, and although their work with the Local Council provided them with a durable model, they soon drifted away from the MLCW (Lavigne et al., 1977; Johnson, 1968).

Julia Drummond's work with the MLCW also prompted her to take a decisive role in the newly emerging Charity Organization movement which, like the Parks and Playgrounds movement, was a direct import from the

United States. The idea at first was to coordinate all charitable activity in the city and have all paupers registered so that they could not exploit several different agencies. The available funds would thus go further, and the truly needy would have more chance of getting relief. As Drummond said, "We hear from another city of a woman who has buried her husband seventeen times. He is still going about and able to enjoy his dinner" (1907, p. 138).

An earlier attempt to found a Charity Organization Society under the leadership of the Reverend Dr. Barnes had failed, so the women decided to put all their support behind this movement. Local councils set up study groups, and they surveyed the various methods used in dealing with unemployment and want in "civilized countries." Mrs. John Cox (wife of a McGill University professor) became convenor, and Julia Drummond was a moving force on the executive committee. A public meeting was held to air the issues in October 1899; presided over by the mayor, it was attended by all the notables of the city and Lady Minto, wife of the Governor General. Dr. Gordon Taylor and Lady Drummond gave addresses (Derick, n.d.); Julia's was the first public speech by a woman in Montreal (Collard, 1982), and it was much praised for its lucidity and elegance. Sir George Drummond was elected president, a position he was to hold until his death in 1910. Lady Julia then took over this task, a sign of both the changing times and the changing attitudes of Lady Julia herself.

The Victorian Order of Nurses (VON) was founded in a similar way. The NCWC was looking for a suitable way to commemorate the Queen's jubilee, and it was also concerned about the lack of medical care for rural women and children. Encouraged by the activities of Florence Nightingale and the establishment of nursing services in rural England and Ireland, the VON was created. Sir George Drummond agreed to serve as a trustee (Gibbon, 1947), and Lady Julia sat on the organizing committee, later becoming a vice-president.

Julia Drummond's public speaking abilities became famous. She addressed not only the women's and charitable organizations but also such groups as graduating nurses at McGill, women's church groups on "How to Be Happy," and the working men of the Sunday Afternoon Society of Point St. Charles, in addition to addresses to the British nobility (Drummond, 1907). She was familiar with the classical philosophers, knew the work of Charles Booth and John Ruskin, was aware of "a fierce form of socialism" (1907, p. 116), and was horrified by one contemporary commentator's notion that women were incapable of further intellectual development after the age of twenty-five.

These sentiments inevitably led Julia Drummond into the suffrage movement. The International Council of Women had debated suffrage in 1904 and 1909, but it was not until 1910 that the Canadian Council overtly expressed sympathy with the movement. This caution seems to have been more because of the council's avowed non-political stand than because of disinterest. Many members firmly believed, like the women of the Women's Christian Temperance Union, that the only way to ensure legal rights for women was through the franchise (Cleverdon, 1950; Bacchi, 1977, 1978).

The local council of women had long been struggling for women's rights on issues such as property, injurious assault, child support, stools for shop assistants to rest on, and higher education for women. It was not until 1888 that McGill timidly admitted the first women; even then, they were not permitted in professional faculties (Gillett, 1981). By 1913 the MLCW decided it must take a real stand. Under the leaderhip of Professor Carrie Derick, a botanist and the first female professor at McGill, the Montreal Suffrage Association was formed. It was quick to explain that it was not militant in the way of some American feminists, but that it sought equal rights for all.

A special issue of the *Montreal Herald* was produced on 26 November 1913 to launch the suffrage campaign. In it Julia Drummond wrote an article titled "A Great Movement: Its Trend and Significance." She reviewed the achievements of the Montreal Council, including work on sanitary conditions and public health, propaganda lectures on diet, child care, and disease prevention, work in the Pure Milk League, the anti-tuberculosis campaign, the establishment of the Royal Edward Institute for pulmonary diseases, agitation for medical inspection of schools, certificates of training for teachers, and pressure to allow women to study medicine. On the civic scene they included the parks and playgrounds drive, housing standards, and the construction of public baths.

Meanwhile the Parks and Playgrounds Association continued its activities. Public subscriptions and city contributions enabled it to employ professionally trained graduates from McGill to work with children in the parks and school yards each summer. Their ranks were swelled by workers from the Montreal University Settlement, which was founded by the McGill Alumnae Society following the model of Toynbee Hall in London as popularized by Octavia Hill and by Jane Addams in Chicago (Morton, 1953). The concept was that young university people should live in low-income areas in order both to help the residents with educational and recreational programmes and to learn the true nature of social problems. The University Settlement and the MPPA worked closely together for many years to provide activities for children. By 1919, the MPPA had five playgrounds in operation in the summer; slides, sandboxes, and swings in many localities; and recreational programmes for all age groups.

The MPPA also became a member of the Montreal City Improvement League, a federation which included the Province of Quebec Association of

Architects and the Greater Montreal Housing Association, whose prime aim
was to campaign for town planning as a remedy for all urban evils. The
MPPA also became a member of the Charity Organization Society and was
from its beginning a member of the MLCW. All these groups lobbied the
city to set up a real Parks and Playgrounds Department. By 1913 the city was
giving $10,000 per year for playgrounds, but publicly organized recreation
did not become a fact until after the Second World War. Until that time the
MPPA ran the children's programmes in the city parks (*Canadian Municipal
Journal*, 1913; McFarland, 1970).

CONCLUSION

Various conclusions can be drawn from this account of the operation of a
women's organization at the turn of the century and its role in urban reform.
The first, and most striking, is that with the exception of the Parks
Protective Association, the ideas of women were not native to the local
scene, nor even to Canada. The parks and playgrounds movement, the
National Council of Women, the Charity Organization Society, the
Victorian Order of Nurses, and the Montreal University Settlement all had
their antecedents in the United States and England. Canada was very much
the colonial society, obeying the wishes of the Governor General and his
wife and absorbing social movements from south of the border.

Networking, a concept that receives much contemporary scholarly
attention, was highly developed among the women of late nineteenth-
century Canada. It was in fact formalized through the various overlapping
federations of volunteer associations and societies. The Montreal Local
Council of Women, the National Council of Women of Canada, the
Charity Organization Society, and the City Improvement League were all
umbrella groups bringing together diverse single-purpose agencies; they
could all rapidly muster support for causes.

At the beginning of the reform period, power was exercised through
husbands. This is well illustrated by Lady Hingston's mustering of 20,000
signatures: she simply had the association write to each of her husband's
friends and associates, encouraging them to ask their employees to sign the
petition! Later, as associations gained credibility and women gained
confidence, and took advantage of increased educational opportunities,
women started to organize independently.

Feminist perspectives also prompted a change in conventional wisdom
about the nature of urban ills. The urban environment was full of
temptations and evil influences: drink, prostitution, thievery and vagrancy.
Early reformers believed that human nature was weak and impressionable,

and that children were especially vulnerable to destructive forces (Hart, 1919). By the early twentieth century, the notion that the poor were somehow responsible for their own miseries was being diluted. Julia Drummond gives us a fine illustration of this; writing in 1913, she says "take only Montreal with its noble site and splendid possibilities—and its slums and bad housing and lack of open spaces, with all that these bring of physical and moral degradation—are not these miserable actualities of today the direct result of the lack of public conscience, of the seeking only for immediate and personal profit in Montreal of the past?" (*Montreal Herald*, 26 November 1913).

Lubove (1967) has interpreted the parks and playgrounds movement as the introduction of a form of social control, similar to other reform initiatives. We prefer to think that it stemmed from heartfelt and sincere concern. Victorian volunteers had to tread daintily between images of "Lady Bountiful" and charges of "slumming it" for their own gratification. However, it is clear that many of them went far beyond what was perceived as the path of duty for women of their class, and one can only speculate on the ire these activities must have raised in their own families.

EPILOGUE

Julia Drummond went on to become more and more famous. During the First World War she went to England to work for the Canadian Red Cross and became head of its information services. She founded the Maple Leaf Clubs for Canadian servicemen overseas, meanwhile maintaining her interest in the Charity Organization Society. She received many honours; among others, she was made a Lady in her own right by the Order of St. John of Jerusalem in 1919, and she was awarded an honorary LL.D. from McGill in 1921. After the war she resumed her Canadian volunteer activities, remaining active until her death in 1942 at the age of eighty-three. The biography of this remarkable woman has yet to be written; perhaps a "trained intellect," her own expression for a university-educated woman, could take up the challenge?

BIOGRAPHY OF GRACE JULIA DRUMMOND, 1859-1942

Born: 17 December 1859, Montreal.
Baptised: Presbyterian Crescent Church, 3 May 1860.

Parents: Alex Davison Parker, who came from Edinburgh in 1846 to open the first office of Standard Life Insurance Co.

Grace Parker, formerly Grace Gibson, lady-in-waiting to Lady Elgin, wife of the Governor General.

First husband: Rev. George Hamilton, Anglican clergyman, son of Robert Hamilton, a Quebec merchant. Married 1879; died 1880.

Second husband: George A. Drummond, 1829-1910

    1854: came to Canada from Scotland, aged 25.

        entered sugar business (Redpath).

    1857: married Helen Redpath (sons: Huntley R. and Arthur L.; three others, Maurice, Edgar and George, died young).

    1872: ran unsuccessfully for Parliament (Conservative).

    1874-78: in Europe.

    1878: founded Canada Sugar Refining Company.

    1882: became a director of the Bank of Montreal.

    1884: married JULIA.

    1888: made a Senator.

    1894: founded Home for Incurables (Sisters of St. Margaret).

    1896-99: President of the Art Association.

    1897: trustee for Victorian Order of Nurses.

    1900-10: President, Charity Organization Society.

    1904: Charter member, Montreal Parks and Playgrounds Association.

    1904: Knighted.

    1904-5: President, Montreal Parks and Playgrounds Association; President, Royal Edward Institution.

    1905: President, Bank of Montreal.

    1910: died, aged 81.

Children: Julian 1885-86.

    Guy 1887-1915. Killed at age 28 at the second battle of Ypres, 22 April 1915. Married 18 April 1914 to Mary Hendrie Braithwaite; one son, Guy Melfort Drummond, lawyer.

Work:

Women's Historical Society, 1893.

Art Association.

National Council of Women of Canada:

    First President, Montreal Local Council of Women, 1893-97.

    Victorian Order of Nurses, Organizing Committee, 1897.

    Convenor, NCWC presentation for the Paris International Exhibition, 1900.

    Convenor, Reformatory Committee, 1908-10.

    Quebec Tercentennial Celebrations Committee, 1908.

    Montreal Suffrage Association, Organizing Committee, 1913.

    Political Speech for reform candidate, 1 April 1913.

    Life patron, NCWC, 1915.

Parks and Playgrounds Association:

    Parks Protective Association, 1895-1904.

    Charter member, 1904.

    Board member, 1904-8.

Charity Organization Society (later the Family Welfare Association and the Council of Social Agencies):
Organizer, 1899.
(Husband president, 1900-10).
Executive Committee, 1900-10.
President, 1910-20.
Mothers' Aid Branch of the Family Welfare Association, 1922.
Montreal Women's Canadian Club: First President, 1907-8.
War Work
Canadian Red Cross Society:
Head of Information Bureau in England, 1914-18.
Founder and President of King George V and Queen Mary Maple Leaf Clubs for soldiers on leave, 1914-18.
Post-war
Family Welfare Association:
Honorary President, 1920-32.
Board of Directors, 1920-22.
Mothers' Aid Branch, Executive, 1920-22.
Womens Directory of Montreal (organized in 1914 to help unmarried mothers) Honorary President.
Montreal Parks and Playgrounds Association: Board member, 1931.
Montreal Industrial Institute for Epileptics (providing training for the mentally and neurologically handicapped; 17 pupils): Committee member.
Montreal University Settlement: Life Governor, 1922
Murray Bay Convalescence Home (196 patients): Director.
Victorian Order of Nurses:
Honorary Vice President.
Local Board of Management, 1922.
Honours
Royal Montreal Ladies Golf Club Cup, 1905.
Médaille de Reconnaissance, France.
British Red Cross Medal.
Serbian Red Cross Medal.
Lady of Grace, Order of St. John of Jerusalem, 1916.
Lady of Justice, Order of St. John of Jerusalem, 1919.
Honorary LL.D., McGill University, 1921.

NOTE

1.   Julia Drummond's grandson, Guy Melfort Drummond, a Montreal lawyer, has kindly helped with information for this paper. We are greatly indebted to Miss Barbara Whitley, Past President of the Women's Canadian Club of Montreal, for her generous help in providing materials concerning Lady Drummond.

REFERENCES

Aberdeen, Lady (Ishabel Maria Marjoribanks) (1925). *"We Two": Reminiscences of Lord and Lady Aberdeen* (2 vols.). London: Collins.

Ames, Herbert B. (1897). *The City Below the Hill*. Toronto: University of Toronto Press, reprint 1972.

Atherton, William H. (1914). *Montreal 1535-1914* (3 vols.) Montreal: S. J. Clarke.

Bacchi, Carol (1977). "Liberation Deferred: The Ideas of the English Canadian Suffragists 1877-1918." *Histoire sociale/Social History*, *10*(20), pp. 433-34.

Bacchi, Carol (1978). "Race Regeneration and Social Purity: A Study of the Social Attitudes of Canada's English-speaking Suffragists." *Histoire sociale/Social History, 11*(22), pp. 460-74.

Canadian Municipal Journal (1913), *9*(6), p. 212.

Cleverdon, Catharine L. (1950). *The Woman Suffrage Movement in Canada: The Start of Liberation 1900-20*. Toronto: University of Toronto Press, reprint 1974.

Collard, Edgar A. (1982). "Montreal's Lady Drummond." *Gazette*, 22 May.

Copp, Terry (1974). *The Anatomy of Poverty: The Condition of the Working Class in Montreal, 1827-1929*. Toronto: McClelland & Stewart.

Cross, D. Suzanne (1977). "The Neglected Majority: The Changing Role of Women in 19th Century Montreal." In Susan Mann Trofimenkoff and Alison Prentice (Eds.), *The Neglected Majority: Essays in Canadian Women's History* (pp. 66-86). Toronto: McClelland and Stewart.

Derick, Carrie M. (n. d.). *The Origin of the Charity Organization Society of Montreal*.

Drummond, Julia (1894a). "The Aims and Work of the National Local Councils." *NCWC Report*, pp. 216-22.

Drummond, Julia (1894b). "Cooperation as Shown in Associated Charities." Paper presented to the annual conference of NCWC.

Drummond, Julia (Ed.) (1900). *Women of Canada: Their Life and Work*. Paris International Exhibition 1900, Canadian Commission. Ottawa: Department of Agriculture.

Drummond, Julia (1907). *Some Addresses*. Montreal: Gazette Printing.

Drummond, Julia (1912). "Foreword." The 12th Annual Report of the Charity Organization Society. Montreal: Charity Organization Society.

Drummond Julia (1915). "Practical Idealism." *MLCW 21st Anniversary 1893-1915*. Montreal: MLCW. Originally delivered at the 18th Annual Meeting, MLCW, 7 May 1912.

Drummond, Julia (1913). "A Great Movement: Its Trend and Significance." *Montreal Herald*, Women's Edition, 26 November 1913.

Drummond, Julia (1915). "Foreword." *Annual Report 1914-15*. Montreal: Charity Organization Society.

Dumont, Micheline, Jean, Michèle, Lavigne, Marie, and Stoddart, Jennifer (1982). *L'Histoire des femmes au Québec depuis quatre siècles*. Montreal: Les Quinze.

Ewing, James (1922). "Suggested Mountain Roadway for Mount Royal Park." *Journal of the Town Planning Institute of Canada, 1*(7), p. 6.

Fein, Albert (1972). *Frederick Law Olmstead and the American Environmental Tradition*. New York: Brazillier.

Germain, Annick (1984). *Les mouvements de réforme urbaine à Montréal au tournant du siècle*. Montreal: Les Cahiers de CIDAR, Département de Sociologie, Université de Montréal.

Gibbon, John Murray (1947). *The Victorian Order of Nurses for Canada: 50th Anniversary 1897-1947*. Montreal: Southam.

Gillett, Margaret (1981). *We Walked Very Warily: A History of Women at McGill*. Montreal: Eden Press.

Harry, J., Gale, R., and Hendee, J. (1969). "Conservation: An Upper-Middle Class Social Movement." *Journal of Leisure Research, 1,* pp. 246-64.

Hart, E.I. (1919). *Wake Up Montreal!: Commercialized Vice and its Contributaries*. Montreal: Witness Press.

Hayden, Dolores (1982). *The Grand Domestic Revolution*. Cambridge, Mass.: MIT.

Jenkins, Kathleen (1966). *Montreal: Island City of the St. Lawrence*. New York: Doubleday.

Johnson, Micheline D. (1971). "History of the Status of Women in the Province of Quebec." In *Cultural Tradition and Political History of Women in Canada*. Studies of the Royal Commission on the Status of Women in Canada, vol. 8, Ottawa.

Kaminer, Wendy (1984). *Women Volunteering: The Pleasure, Pain & Politics of Unpaid Work from 1830 to the Present*. New York: Doubleday.

Lavigne, Marie, Pinard, Yolande, and Stoddart, Jennifer (1977). "La Fédération nationale St-Jean-Baptiste et les revendications féministes au début du 20e siècle." In Marie Lavigne and Yolande Pinard (Eds.), *Les femmes dans la société québécoise: aspects historiques* (pp. 89-108). Montreal: Boréal Express.

Lavigne, Marie and Stoddart, Jennifer (1977). "Women's Work in Montreal at the Beginning of the Century." In Marylee Stephenson (Ed.), *Women in Canada* (pp. 129-47). Don Mills: General Publishing.

Lavigne, Marie and Stoddart, Jennifer (1983). "Ouvrières et travailleuses montréalaises, 1910-1940." In Marie Lavigne and Yolande Pinard (Eds.), *Travailleuses et féministes: Les femmes dans la société québécoise* (pp. 99-103). Montreal: Boréal Express.

Linteau, Paul André, Durocher, René, and Robert, Jean-Claude (1979). *Histoire du Québec contemporaine: De la confédération à la crise*. Montreal: Boréal Express.

Lubove, Roy (1967). *The Urban Community: Housing and Planning in the Progressive Era*. Englewood Cliffs, New Jersey: Prentice Hall.

Marsan, Jean-Claude (1981). *Montreal in Evolution*. Montreal: McGill-Queen's University Press.

McFarland, E. M. (1970). *The Development of Recreation in Canada*. Ottawa: Parks and Recreation Association.

Metcalfe, Alan (1978). "The Evolution of Organised Physical Recreation in Montreal, 1840-1895." *Histoire Sociale/Social History, II*(21), pp. 144-66.

Montreal Parks and Playgrounds Association (MPPA) (1955). *A Half Century of Community Service, 1902-1952*. Montreal: MPPA.

Montreal Parks and Playgrounds Association. *Annual Reports,* 1902 onwards.

Montreal Parks and Playgrounds Association, Archives. McGill University Archives. MG.2079.

Morton, Irving (1953). "Program Development at the University Settlement of

Montreal." Master's of Social Work thesis, McGill University.

Newton, Norman T. (1971). *Design on the Land: The Development of Landscape Architecture.* Cambridge, Mass.: Harvard.

Osborn, E. B. (1919). *The New Elizabethans.* London: John Lane.

Pinard, Yolande (1977). "Les débuts du mouvement des femmes." In Marie Lavigne and Yolande Pinard (Eds.), *Les femmes dans la société québécoise: aspects historiques* (pp. 61-87). Montreal: Boréal Express.

Plumptre, H. P. (1914). "The National Council of Women and Conservation." In Commission of Conservation, *Report of the Fifth Annual Meeting.* Ottawa, 1914, pp. 25-30.

Robert, Percy A. (1928). "Dufferin District." Thesis, McGill University.

Rutherford, Paul (Ed.) (1974). *Saving the Canadian City.* Toronto: University of Toronto Press.

Saywell, John T. (Ed.) (1960). *The Canadian Journal of Lady Aberdeen, 1893-1898.* Toronto: Champlain Society.

Shepherd, William F. (1957). *Genesis of the Montreal Council of Social Agencies.* Master's of Social Work thesis, McGill University.

Spragge, Godfrey (1975). "Canadian Planners' Goals: Deep Roots and Fuzzy Thinking." *Canadian Public Administration, 18*(2), pp. 216-34.

Stelter, Gilbert A. and Artibise, Alan F. J. (Eds.) (1977). *The Canadian City: Essays in Urban History.* Toronto: McClelland & Stewart.

Strong-Boag, Veronica (1976). *The Parliament of Women: The National Council of Women of Canada 1893-1929.* Ottawa: National Museums of Man.

Strong-Boag, Veronica (1977). "Setting the Stage: National Organization and the Women's Movement in the Late 19th Century." In Susan Mann Trofimenkoff and Alison Prentice (Eds.), *The Neglected Majority: Essays in Canadian Women's History* (pp. 87-103). Toronto: McClelland & Stewart.

Vicinus, Martha (Ed.) (1977). *A Widening Sphere: Changing Roles of Victorian Women.* Bloomington and London: Indiana University Press.

Vigod, B. L. (1978). "Ideology and Institutions in Quebec: The Public Charities Controversy 1921-1926." *Histoire sociale/Social History, 11*(21), pp. 167-82.

Weaver, John C. (1977). *Shaping the Canadian City: Essays on Urban Politics and Policy, 1890-1920.* Toronto: Institute of Public Administration of Canada.

Wilson, E. Laird (1953). *The Montreal Parks and Playgrounds Association.* Master's of Social Work thesis, McGill University.

Woodsworth, J. S. (1911). *My Neighbour.* Toronto: University of Toronto Press. Reprint 1972.

4

Divergent Convergence:
The Daily Routines of Employed Spouses
as a Public Affairs Agenda

WILLIAM MICHELSON

INTRODUCTION

The increased participation of women in paid employment outside the home is a pronounced trend of our times. Consequently, women's activity patterns seem to resemble what men do, but women's qualitative experience in the daily routine is actually quite different from that of men.

This article explores ways in which the daily experience of employed mothers converges with and diverges from that of their husbands.[1] It also describes how public policies and practices, especially those concerning urban organization, infrastructure, and transportation, compound the difficulties of employed mothers, and it suggests what can be done to increase support for this growing segment of the working population.

WHY PERSONAL DECISIONS ARE OF PUBLIC CONCERN

It is helpful first to give some perspective on reasons for linking public affairs with employment decisions and the daily activities of individuals and families. A laissez-faire approach to maternal employment means that mothers of young children cope individually and independently with the daily activities confronted when they enter the labour force. Some well-meaning how-to books written by women urge other women to devote greater effort to personal organization, but this conveys an impression that a career women who is overburdened has only herself to blame.

Personal lives are in fact played out on a vast stage; forces originating far beyond the self and family influence what people do and how well they can do it. In the case of maternal employment, for example, public policies affect such critical matters as the basic decision to undertake employment and the logistical conditions under which non-household activities are conducted in the daily routine.

Increasing Employment of Women

Neither formal employment nor work as such are new to women. The dramatic new trend in western industrial societies is the extent to which different categories of adult women have joined the labour force. Before the Second World War, women who held jobs were principally those who were poor, single, or childless, or they might be highly educated professionals. The war effort's temporary demands expanded work participation beyond these groups, including women with school-age or older children. The economic expansion after the war, and the absence of traditional sources and levels of immigration, led to even greater increases of "acceptable" female employees, who filled the burgeoning "pink-collar" jobs. This expansion included mothers of young children (Fox and Hess-Biber, 1984; Hayghe, 1982; Mortimer and London, 1984; Oppenheimer, 1982; Ross, Mirowsky, and Huber, 1983).

Employment decisions reflect incentives and disincentives imposed by the public realm and beyond the individual's immediate control. Thus many women were far less likely to enter employment when they were neither needed in work-place roles nor culturally supported in seeking jobs. What women choose to do is not simply the outcome of personal decisions but reflects much larger contexts.

Labour market demands and incentives are one side of the picture, representing forces that pull women to jobs. The other side of the picture is equally important: that is, the influences that push women to jobs. The greater portion of the increase in outside employment among Canadian and American women with children under six—rising from less than 20 per cent in 1955 to about 50 per cent at present—has come since 1970. The 1970-85 period was marked by great increases in the cost of living (particularly housing costs) and in the divorce rate (Michelson, 1985).

There is an undeniable logic behind the movements for women's liberation and equal opportunity. Unquestionably these forces are influential among women with education and career interests. Nevertheless, recent studies consistently show that economic need provides the greatest single incentive for employment among the general population of women. Kamerman, for example, reported that 60 per cent of white married professional women, and as many as 90 per cent of working-class women, worked "for the money" (1980, p. 87).

In short, much more than individual preference is involved when mothers of young children enter the labour force, although each decision is made individually. Labour-force entry reflects major developments in society that most women can scarcely ignore, and such employment trends are inherently matters of public concern.

The 24-Hour Cycle: Time and Space

Some of the everyday needs that occupy part of the 24-hour cycle are attributable to participation in the labour force, such as hours spent at work or commuting. Other activities relate to basic survival: eating, sleeping, eliminating, and so forth. Others are a function of family structure: child care, housekeeping, and chauffeuring. Still others are discretionary, such as the many forms of leisure and social activities. How much an individual is obligated to do clearly relates to the responsibilities he or she has agreed, or is forced, to accept. Since the 24-hour day is inelastic, the multiple obligations people actually discharge during the weekday are complex functions of priority-setting—often dictated by external parties such as employers—and related time trade-offs (Cullen, 1978; Staikov, 1973). The nature of individual activities seldom determines the ease or difficulty of carrying out a given set of daily activities (whether obligatory or discretionary). An everyday routine does not occur in a vacuum, but in a community, which influences the ability to realize sets of activities. In short, the logistics of the typical workday are a legitimate public policy concern.

Some population subgroups—such as infants, prisoners, and hospital patients—may lead their daily lives without thought of changing locations. Most self-sustaining adults, however, have to consider accessibility in time and space in choosing and carrying out activities. Time considerations involve not only the amounts of travel people have to add to the time taken by actual activities within the daily schedule but also such matters as the opening and closing hours of markets and services they may need to patronize.

Space and time considerations are closely inter-related. The greater the travel required for any activity, the more time it will usually demand. The clustering of potential activities, or their distribution over space, will affect the amount of travel and time required to perform them all. Thus, urban land use is pertinent not only to public health and safety (its main statutory justifications) but also to the ease or difficulty with which citizens conduct their daily activities. From the individual's perspective, a major and generally overlooked criterion is how well the individual's pattern of obligations, responsibilities, and desires can be carried out within any particular land-use pattern.

Temporal and spatial dimensions are, however, by no means identical.

The time it takes to travel depends on the availability, nature, routing, scheduling, and speed of transportation facilities. Automobiles may be privately owned and scheduled at will, but the time it takes to get from point A to point B is still a function of the public infrastructure including: the types and patterns of streets, highways, or bridges, and their availability relative to the number of users. Public transportation—whether in the absence of or as an improvement over privately owned means of travel—puts even more emphasis on externally determined influences on everyday behaviour. The location of routes as well as transit spacing, speed, and hours of service per day are all influential.

"Time-Geography" and Constraints on Daily Life

Time-geography (or chronogeography) is a school of analysis founded by Torsten Hägerstrand, a Swedish geographer. His interpretation posited three kinds of constraints placed on daily life and activity by the temporal and spatial conditions of cities (and rural areas [Palm, 1981]):

1. Coupling constraints. These are limits on what is available to obtain or do, given the critical masses of persons within a spatial/temporal proximity necessary to support a given behaviour/good/service. For example, can enough people converge during a weekday to support speciality stores or only a general store?

2. Capability constraints. There are limits to what a person can fit into his or her daily timetable, in the community's spatial/temporal circumstances. For example, do the respective opening and closing hours, locations, and travel characteristics permit visits to a post office or shoemaker during a workday?

3. Authority constraints. These are limits on when activities can or cannot take place, or where they must or must not be located, imposed by decisions by external parties. For example, mandatory closing hours, blue laws, and public service hours are all potential constraints on the individual's behaviour (Hägerstrand, 1969; Pred, 1977).

Hägerstrand does not view his time-geography considerations as determining behaviour. People are cultural beings motivated by a host of group, subgroup, and personal interests. The ease of accomplishing activities, however, is in fact a function of the kinds of constraints Hägerstrand treats (van Paasen, 1981). Practical matters considered under this perspective include: urban transportation, use of medical facilities, factors affecting the inequality or equality of women, regional planning, day care, and societal development (Carlstein, 1982; Hagerstrand, 1970; Lenntorp, 1976; Märtensson, 1977, 1978, 1982; Palm and Pred, 1974). In all cases, daily activity is seen as a complex function of personal and cultural needs and desires, on one hand, and practical circumstances on the other (Chapin, 1965, 1974).[2]

A serious question in the case of maternal employment is how urban conditions (such as transportation) help or hinder accomplishment of the daily obligations, responsibilities, and desires of the woman involved. External societal forces encourage labour-force participation by mothers of young children, but has equivalent recognition been given to the way a community's structure and functioning can facilitate such participation?

LOGISTICS OF MATERNAL EMPLOYMENT: RESEARCH FINDINGS

The following discussion is based on data gathered in metropolitan Toronto in 1980. Members of a research programme called "The Child in the City" concluded that having a mother with outside employment was a new factor in the lives of many urban children. While the provision and financing of sufficient day care places was already an issue in Canadian urban areas, it was less clear what effects maternal employment might have on the lives of various family members. Accordingly, a three-phase study was designed to focus on the logistics and implications of maternal employment for women and their families.[3]

A multiple-stage sampling procedure was used to survey 538 families. (See Appendix: Note on Methodology.) The survey covered school days from March to June 1980, including a variety of weather conditions. A comparative substudy of a random selection of 78 of the same families was conducted during the subsequent summer vacation period, to assess differences in the absence of compulsory schooling on weekdays.

The first phase of the study was an intensive three-day set of interviews and observations, within a much smaller sample of families, assessing in greater depth the relevance of questions and wording to be used in the later survey. This included a validation of self-administered time-budget procedures, through observation of the same time periods (Ziegler and Michelson, 1981). The final phase was a set of group discussions with women who had been part of the survey, conducted after the compilation and analysis of initial results. The purpose was two-fold: to provide feedback to respondents while at the same time benefiting from their assessment of the accuracy and meaning of the conclusions inferred from the data.

We were able to assess the extent to which the daily lives of employed mothers of young children were becoming more like those of their husbands. We also noted the conditions and patterns of activities that might make their situations qualitatively different.

Husband-Wife Convergence

Certain major indicators give the impression that the everyday employment experiences of working women are starting to approximate those of men. Thus, in the amount of time devoted to aspects of the daily routine, full-time working wives resemble their husbands more than part-time or unemployed wives resemble theirs.

By definition, of course, this is true for hours spent at an external place of work. Nonetheless, employed women also resemble their husbands in other ways. Daily travel is an example. Conceivably, employed women might not spend more time in travelling than housewives, since the latter could devote additional time to travel related to family, shopping, recreational, or other noncommuting purposes.In fact, however, employed women actually do travel more than housewives, and they approximate men's traditionally higher daily transit time. For example, women with full-time jobs spent 81 minutes a day travelling, compared to 66 minutes for women with part-time jobs, 44 minutes for housewives, and 87 minutes for husbands.

Women also trade off the time devoted to employment with other activities in the same way as men. The greater the amount of weekday time devoted to a job, the less time both men and women put into housework, child care, shopping, social activity, or both active and passive forms of leisure.

In addition, when women have greater exposure to outside employment, their daily tensions increase, culminating in levels identical to those of men. Tension was calculated over the whole day, weighted by the length of time devoted to contributing activities and with reference to the performance of specific activities. Both men and women view paid employment as relatively high-tension (though men rate it slightly higher), and tension associated with a major daily activity affects employees of either sex in similar ways.

Husband-Wife Divergence

Paid employment is a major responsibility. Of the 24-hour day, a full-time job demands more than half the remaining time left after removing time for sleep and other necessary personal activities, particularly if much commuting is required. Paid employment places great constraints on the extent to which other activities can be undertaken during a workday.

The total pattern of a person's day, however, along with his or her subjective experience of it, is not determined solely by the work responsibility. Activities that occupy the remainder of the day also count. Moreover, this more inclusive conception of everyday life brings out differences between women and their husbands. There is much evidence that the everyday subjective experiences of employed mothers differ markedly from those of their spouses. Although women working outside the home make most of the same daily time trade-offs as their husbands, the absolute amounts of an activity men and women put into the daily routine differ, sometimes greatly. Consequently, the art of fitting activities in and weaving them together will also differ.

Household Work and Child Care

The most prominent differences between employed spouses occur in the use of time related to housework and child care. Women with full-time jobs spend less time than housewives at such tasks, indeed less than half as much. (Women with full-time jobs spend 192 minutes a day versus 436 minutes a day for housewives. Women with part-time jobs are in-between at 356 minutes). Nevertheless *all* women do much more of these activities than do their husbands, who only devote an average of 71.2 minutes to housework and child care. Even women with full-time jobs spend nearly three times as much daily time on housework and child care as their husbands. The latter's contribution to domestic activity also varies little with their wives' employment status.

If one adds employment, housework, and child care responsibilities, and characterizes them as a basic unit of *obligatory daily activity*, it becomes apparent that the daily routines of women with children and outside jobs involve more of such activity than those of men, or indeed, of women with less extensive employment. The mother employed full-time spends nearly 10 hours a day (584 minutes) in obligatory activities (see Figure 1). Moreover, the definition and the data shown in Figure 1 fail to cover related activities such as commuting and shopping, which typically add still another hour per day. The different categories of men typically spend half an hour to an hour less in daily obligatory activities than women with full-time jobs—with the greatest differences reflecting the comparatively low obligatory activity by men whose wives work full-time (in other words, the opposite of expectations that men might compensate for their wives' total loads).

Women and Everyday Travel

These differences between men and women in the nature and juxtaposition of daily activities carry serious implications for everyday travel. The most tension-producing daily activities in women's routines are transitions to and from household responsibilities and outside employment. These tensions are stronger for women than for men, because the women are responsible for what happens both before and after their commuting trips.

**FIGURE 1: Minutes of "Obligatory Time" on a weekday by
Wives and Husbands**

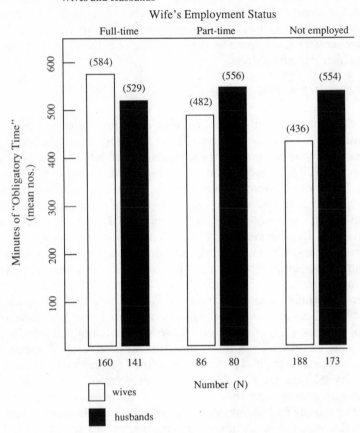

Thus they have to see children off or accompany them to their destinations
yet must still appear at the place of employment on time and ready to work.
In the evenings, they leave work at a fixed hour but upon reaching home
must be available for child care, companionship, dinner preparation, and
other household chores. Since travel can thus exacerbate both of the
demanding portions of women's daily routines, it takes on a different
subjective tone.

Attitudes about travel are intensified because women typically have
relatively marginal travel resources, being described as "transportation
deprived and transit dependent" (Carp, 1974). In families with one
automobile, the husband typically takes the car to work, leaving the wife to
contend with the inflexibilities of public transit systems or to seek a job that

emphasizes proximity to home rather than career enhancement (Koppelman *et al.*, 1978; Levine, 1980). Indeed, women are less likely than men to have acquired driver's licences (Pickup, 1981; Sen, 1978). Yet when taking responsibility for transporting children to their daily locations, women strongly prefer automobile travel because of the relative ease of handling children and their gear (Studenmund *et al.*, 1978). Single mothers who usually have low incomes are especially unlikely to have access to automobiles, despite family travel needs.

Documentation of this and other widely reported information about women's transportation shows that precise travel patterns reflect local and/or national variations in city size and structure, nature of public transportation, socioeconomic status, and the logistics of owning and using a private automobile. Canadian urbanites typically lie between Americans and Europeans in the number of automobiles owned and the use of public transportation. Yet, regardless of the precise nature of the system, differences by gender appear to run in the same direction. Our data support most of these general gender-relevant findings (Michelson, 1983). Our data from Toronto indicate that women are about three times as likely as their husbands to use public transportation, such use being almost exclusively for trips to and from work. Forty-four per cent of their trips are made with chidren, exclusively by foot or automobile. Public transportation is most often used for the relatively long commutes from suburbs to the central city. This reflects both the Toronto public transit system's highly efficient service and the difficulty and expense of centre-city parking. In all, 38 per cent of the women interviewed lacked driver's licences. Among those taking the subway downtown, 50 per cent lacked licences, rising to 73 per cent among those who took the slower and less convenient buses in non-central directions.

Transportation, Time Pressure, and Tension

Being deprived of transportation increases tension. Thus women experience a high degree of tension in travelling, second only to certain other transitional activities such as getting children out of the house in the morning. Travel causes more tension than most routine activities, such as in-house child care and housekeeping. Furthermore, travel by public transportation (which as noted reflects intrafamilial and external conditions more than personal desire) is felt to cause more tension than travel by car, and this is not a function of trip length or duration.

The time pressure that respondents reported experiencing the day preceding the interview was clearly related to both their own and their husbands' mode of transportation to work. Of women taking public transit,

35.1 per cent were in the high time-pressure category (+ 5 to + 10 on a scale from -10 to + 10), compared to only about 19 per cent of those using a car for some or all of the trip to work.

Men typically have more choice than women about their means of travel, and they do not show the same patterns of tension associated with travel as do women. Our more general analyses of tension indicate that the degree of tension associated with an activity is correlated with the extent to which choice is lacking. Thus with respect to public transit, the correlation between tension and lack of choice is + 0.43 for women and + 0.37 for men.

Men's jobs are the only relatively significant source of high tension among their daily activities. But women report employment as only one of half-a-dozen job- and transition-related family responsibilities rated high in tension (see Figure 2). Many of these activities involve travel and, as noted, women often travel with less efficient resources and have fewer choices. Consequently, daily travel requirements should be expected to produce different subjective experiences among employed women than they do among their husbands.

This is illustrated by day care centres and their relation to women's places of employment. Our data show that mothers are about four times more likely than fathers to take a young child to a day care centre. These data further indicate that the divergence of day care locations from optimal locations with respect to the daily commute (that is, near home or work or on a direct line in between) adds a conservatively estimated increment of 28 per cent to the trip. While tension in daily travel was not found to be significantly related to total amount of travel, it is indeed significantly related to how much more the child care drop-off adds to what would otherwise be the mother's commute to work.

Employment Flexibility

An analysis of different kinds of employment flexibility gave other indications of the relationships of tension to transportation and to other aspects of an employed person's day.

Our analysis included comparisons of part-time job-holders with full-time employees, on one hand, and those with no outside employment, on the other (Michelson, 1985). As one would expect, part-time employment moderated the impact of employment responsibilities on non-work activities. Feelings of time pressure and tension among part-time employees fell in-between those reported by housewives and women working full-time. In short, part-time jobs provide needed income but also allow time during the day for shopping and other household tasks, lessening capability constraints on these activities. Respondents appreciated being able to do these things

FIGURE 2: Mean Tension in Selected Daily Activities (women and men)

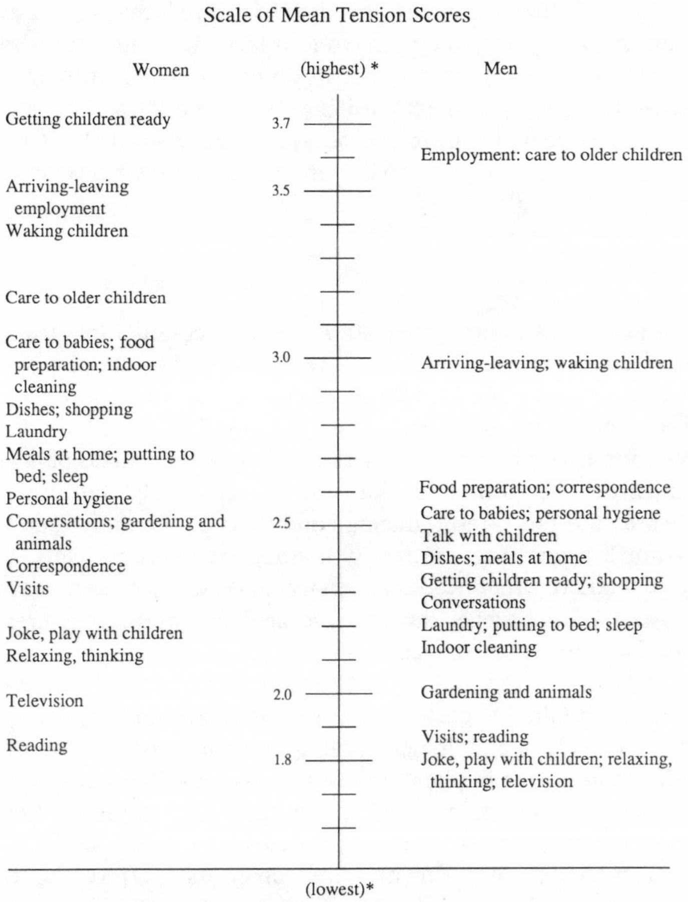

Scale of Mean Tension Scores

Women	(highest) *	Men
Getting children ready	3.7	
		Employment: care to older children
Arriving-leaving employment	3.5	
Waking children		
Care to older children		
Care to babies; food preparation; indoor cleaning	3.0	Arriving-leaving; waking children
Dishes; shopping		
Laundry		
Meals at home; putting to bed; sleep		Food preparation; correspondence
Personal hygiene		Care to babies; personal hygiene
Conversations; gardening and animals	2.5	Talk with children
		Dishes; meals at home
Correspondence		Getting children ready; shopping
Visits		Conversations
		Laundry; putting to bed; sleep
Joke, play with children		Indoor cleaning
Relaxing, thinking		
Television	2.0	Gardening and animals
		Visits; reading
Reading	1.8	Joke, play with children; relaxing, thinking; television

(lowest)*

* Mean tension scores reflect a transformed scale on which raw scores ranged from 1 (ease) to 7 (tension).

themselves during the day, freeing evenings so they can be home and at ease with other family members.

Part-time employment is not, however, a solution to the logistical difficulties of employed mothers. Many need the larger incomes that go with full-time jobs, and many are actively pursuing careers. Furthermore, the terms of part-time employment are often inferior to full-time employment in such matters as wage rates, fringe benefits, and permanence.

We investigated other forms of employment flexibility among employed respondents: how the nature of the work, and/or employer rules, permitted flexibility in hours of employment, and whether women worked a standard

9-to-5 day, 5-day week, or one of the many variations.[4]

Flexibility in either form was associated with reduced daily travel time (15-18 minutes less a day) and with reduced feelings of time pressure. These differences attributable to work-place flexibility held true for both full-time and part-time employees, emphasizing the importance of work place flexibility to people with multiple responsibilities and sources of tension (the circumstances wives confront much more often than their husbands).

Cultural Lag

Our findings thus indicate that women diverge considerably from men in their subjective experience of the average workday, despite superficial appearances of convergence. A better realization of equality at home would clearly ease the logistical challenges that employed mothers face. Transition problems, for example, would be less pressing if immediate obligations at both ends of the commute did not so uniformly fall on women. Nevertheless, the pressure-producing conditions of the daily routine are at least as much external to the family as they are internal. Thus, hours of employment and of other necessary services and facilities, land-use patterns, and transportation systems can increase or decrease the pressures arising from internal domestic arrangements.

If conditions in the public sphere are part of the problem, their amelioration should be part of any solution. Societies typically accept innovations (usually technological) that appear progressive, without considering side-effects, other implications, or the adaptations needed to cope with these influences. This has been called "cultural lag" (Ogburn, 1964), with culture lagging behind technology. In the case under study, acceptance of the virtues of maternal employment have come first, before the full-scale adaptations required as a result of the addition of employment to a host of other traditional women's obligations.

MATERNAL EMPLOYMENT AND PUBLIC POLICY

Some ways public-sector adaptation could help improve the kind of day experienced by employed mothers are now examined. Since transportation is an obvious consideration, its implications are considered first. The data also suggest more fundamental, far-reaching changes, which are subsequently discussed. The accumulation of these arguments suggests the need for a new kind of planning.

Transportation Options

As noted above, employed women travel approximately as much as men, but the conditions of travel and their subjective experiences diverge greatly. Optimizing the number and variety of trips that can safely be taken by public transportation would provide both male and female travellers with more positive choices in travelling. Public measures making public transit "the better way"[5] for a growing number of trips should help reduce travel tension among those taking such transit trips, as well as among those who choose to drive. Fixed-rail transit systems are particularly popular for everyday commuting.

Public transit can have decided advantages for work trips in central or congested areas, such as downtown Toronto. One obvious form of public assistance would be a better distribution of parking lots/garages at non-central subway stations, facilitating safe and inexpensive changes of transportation mode. This would help achieve the most rational choices of travel for the plural activities that must fit into limited time periods.

Can public transit reflect more sensitively the needs of its current or potential users? The use of public transit for more than one purpose—for example, combining trips to the work place, for child care, and shopping— would be facilitated by measures such as economical monthly passes or transfer formulas that permit stopovers. Can the use of public transit be made a more relaxing experience? Many airlines have tried to do this for their passengers, who admittedly spend more money for fewer trips than transit riders. Could better use of light, colour, and sound make public transit more attractive? Could the wide variety of transit employees who meet the public be better trained in interpersonal relations? Some transit systems have pioneered services for the handicapped. Could similar efforts be made to render transit services more appropriate or desirable for use by parents and children?

Non-Transportation Options Affecting Travel and Everyday Logistics

Logistical problems of everyday travel and their outcomes can also be helped by approaches that reach well beyond purely transportation solutions. Policies only indirectly related to transportation can effect travel and daily life. For example, as noted earlier, work-place flexibility can alleviate travel tension and feelings of daily time pressure, giving employees some additional freedom of action (that is, a reduction of capability constraints). Moreover, employment systems that reflect more appropriately the time demands on individual employees need much more attention. Working-hour variations within firms, reflecting individual and family needs, are much more likely to provide positive benefits to individuals than flex-time formulas that merely try to redistribute peak travel loads.

Furthermore, the use of job-sharing by interested employees in regular positions could make the benefits of part-time employment more readily available, without the drawbacks of inferior status and benefits. There is evidence that job-sharing employees maintain unusually high productivity records, presumably indicating how job-sharers feel about and respond to the logistical opportunities offered them (Commission of Inquiry into Part-time Work, 1983; Meier, 1979; Meltz *et al.*, 1981; Nollen *et al.*, 1978).

The evidence on day care location suggests that more suitable sites would help reduce the travel tensions of employed mothers. Land-use regulations should be re-examined and modified where necessary to permit day care centres to operate in the midst of residential clusters, minimizing travel distances from homes and reducing the need for young children to commute. A second alternative is work-place day care, which minimizes travel for the mother, though it maximizes travel for the child. Work-place day care also gives both mother and child opportunities for some daytime access to each other. A third alternative, feasible where public transportation is well developed, is day care facilities located at major transfer points. While commercial facilities are often found in such locations, they rarely include nonprofit or limited-profit enterprises. To sum up, the place of child care in land-use planning merits special concern but is seldom given explicit consideration. Instead, child care is typically one of the last land uses considered when land or buildings are allocated or constructed. Note how many day care centres end up in church basements, because these are the only spaces available.

Clustering and Mixed Uses

Creating more mixed, integrated land uses reduces but does not eliminate the need to travel. People usually cannot find everything they want in one location; moreover, they do not want undesirable or inappropriate land uses (such as factories or warehouses) near their homes. They often prefer to drive even to a nearby store to carry purchases home more easily. Even so, increased clustering is likely to reduce the number of daily trips required. When daily essentials are close to home, the kinds of trips that put pressure on the daily timetable can be more readily absorbed, as can trips in the absence of a car. In any event, our respondents were definitely interested in having a variety of land uses such as stores, banks, and clinics available closer to home, a preference that was pronounced among respondents expressing greater feelings of time pressure.

Extension of Hours

One recent change in community infrastructure is extension of local store hours into the evening and night, as well as Sundays, thereby providing more shopping capability. The private sector has increasingly discovered that many customers find it more convenient to shop and receive deliveries outside traditional store hours. Night-time has been called our last frontier (Melbin, 1978).

Admittedly, some long-term store employees may dislike the new working hours. Others, however, find new schedules fitting better with their other obligations or with the schedules of other family members. Young people, for example, can more easily combine school with employment. Pairs of working parents whose schedules differ can provide home child care without resorting to external sources.

More can be accomplished with greater ease when people are able to fit employment and other obligations in during the day, without constraints caused by a near identity of opening and closing hours. If nonwork opportunities are available when people are not at work, a single family car can be used during the day for more purposes. Longer store and service hours thus take some pressure off transportation systems in several ways. Understandably, most of our respondents favoured such longer hours for many services and facilities.

The public and nonprofit sectors lag behind the private sector in this regard. Many people, for example, continue to find post office hours difficult. The hours of preventive medical services are characteristically inconvenient for children whose parents are both employed. For working parents, arranging the often-vital check-ups and shots is no longer a routine day-time maternal activity. With both parents employed, such visits require a flexible schedule, an agreeable employer who will permit one parent to take time off (and lose wages), the cooperation of a helpful school staff, or a physician who keeps evening hours. Contact with physicians has already begun shifting to evening and weekend hours (Jordan-Marsh, 1981); however, this is principally in crowded emergency wards and hospital clinics, for the treatment of acute illnesses not for preventive medicine.

There have been private sector adaptations with respect to maternal employment, because providing some kinds of service when needed can be profitable. Out-of-hours needs for public- and non-profit-sector services are, however, largely not being met.

CONCLUSION: A NEW KIND OF PLANNING

It is extremely important for transportation planning to be integrated more fully with other forms of community planning. Moreover, planning in general should be recognized as a life-enhancing process, not merely a regulatory procedure that imposes minimum standards.

But if this argument is accepted, there is still a major dilemma. Who formulates the policies? Who does the planning? Who is concerned about communities being functional for the everyday lives of residents? The answer is "everybody and nobody."

"Everybody," because decision-making on many aspects of temporal and spatial dimensions of communities is widely dispersed among firms, services, stores, bureaucracies, clinics, transit systems, and the other structures that comprise society. Each is guided by its own interests, lacking a comprehensive view of the whole picture. The authority of each imposes patterns of external constraints on the everyday lives of individuals.

"Nobody," because there is no clear, undivided jurisdiction over or responsibility for decisions about community time and space. The current form of disaggregated decision-making presents people in general, and employed mothers in particular, with unintended but real capability and authority constraints. It is dysfunctional insofar as it lags behind people's circumstances. In contrast, a more inclusive view of planning and public policy would create opportunities, thereby enhancing human liberties in everyday life as well as the individual's ability to optimize desired efficiencies.

Conventional planning seeks to avoid known dangers and achieve an economically rational infrastructure development. Expansions in the realm of planning may be liberating or constraining, depending in large part on how they are done. If the objectives of planning for everyday logistics are democratic and nondeterministic, reflecting a positive view of the individual and his or her needs, its procedures should be consistent and emphasize coordination rather than control.

A first step is recognition that many aspects of urban infrastructure have powerful influences on everyday behaviour. While this is particularly true for such population subgroups as employed mothers, who undertake non-traditional activities, it also applies to nearly everyone to some degree. There is a rational basis for measures to optimize opportunity and minimize unwanted constraints. Voluntary, well-informed coordination among the bodies and interests that can influence the logistics of everyday life would be a kind of democracy in action.

In any event, it is a legitimate matter of public concern when community patterns and infrastructure contribute to dramatic divergences in subjective experiences of employed spouses. Dealing with this calls for policy and action. That the policy sphere is relatively uncharted is more reason for its pursuit. The various sectors and actors must work together to rethink and coordinate the timing of urban functions. The "time of our lives" is not enhanced by a constant fight against time.

APPENDIX: NOTE ON METHODOLOGY

Interviewers in twenty randomly selected, representative census tracts called on households according to a random numbers table, screening them for eligibility, that is, whether one or more children up to 14 years of age lived there with one or more parents. Stratification procedures ensured that within each of the census tracts there were sufficient numbers of single-parent families and users of particular child care alternatives. Nineteen per cent of the families interviewed were headed by single mothers.[6] Among these single parents, 68 had outside employment, while 35 did not; the subsample of two-parent families included 247 women with jobs and 188 housewives. In most respects, the families chosen were diverse and representative of others in the metropolitan area.

Several data-gathering approaches were used to capture the complexity of everyday behaviour. A major tool was the time-budget. Everyone 10 years old and over in a household simultaneously filled in a chart, under an interviewer's supervision. Respondents detailed step-by-step what they had done the previous day (always a weekday). This included the starting and completion time of each activity, its location, and the persons involved. The information covered the period from the time each person arose, to the time they got up the following day (the day of the interview). Also included were less traditional, subjective aspects of each of the activities. Seven-point scales were used to indicate the degree to which an activity was perceived to involve choice and to record personal feelings of ease or tension. Trips were considered as activities and treated accordingly. The weekend time-use of family members was also assessed, but in less detail. The time-budget provides a quantitative measure of everyday behaviours, the various aspects of which can be analyzed simultaneously, permitting subpopulation and even cross-cultural comparisons (Szalai et al., 1973; Michelson and Reed, 1975; Michelson, 1979).

In addition, there were extensive interviews with each of the mothers in the primary household units, obtaining basic time-budget data for each of the children under 10, in consultation with the children as necessary. The mothers also provided information on the extent and sources of their own perceived time pressures, division of labour within the family, objective data on the family and its coping mechanisms, resources, and routines, and evaluations of the children, plus a variety of subjective assessments of life decisions.

The analyses were done at the University of California, Irvine, while I was Professor of Social Ecology there.[7] The Irvine branch of the university's Institute of

Transportation Studies stimulated my interest in the travel implications of the study data,[8] and a special substudy was carried out with the support of both the Institute of Transportation Studies and the United States Department of Transportation, Urban Mass Transportation Administration (Grant CA-11-0024).[9]

NOTES

1. A preliminary draft of this report was presented to the Canadian Urban Studies Conference, Institute of Urban Studies, University of Winnipeg, 16 August 1985. A revised draft was published as "Divergent Convergence: The Daily Routines of Employed Spouses as a Public Affairs Agenda," *Public Affairs Report, 26*(4) (August 1985) (Berkeley, California: Institute of Governmental Studies, University of California, Berkeley, 1986). The author is grateful for substantive and editorial suggestions by Robert Aldrich, Karen Altergott, Clair Brown, Tora Friberg, David Jones, Solveig Märtensson, Risa Palm, the editorial staff of the Institute of Governmental Studies, and to Beth Moore Milroy.

2. This view was also espoused, but operationalized in a different way than has the Lund school, by F. Stuart Chapin, Jr., and his colleagues at the University of North Carolina. In this regard, see Chapin (1965 and 1974).

3. This research was principally funded through a contribution by the Ministry of National Health and Welfare, National Welfare Grants Program. Basic funding for The Child in the City Programme came from Toronto's Hospital for Sick Children Foundation. Linda Hagarty, Susan Hodgson, and Suzanne Ziegler were co-investigators during various stages of the research and made substantial contributions to it, as did many interviewers, coders, and data processing personnel.

4. Sherry Ahrentzen took the initiative in formulating this analysis.

5. "The better way" is a slogan used by the Toronto Transit Commission.

6. Six families headed by single fathers were also interviewed. Because of their small number, they are not included in the findings.

7. The Program in Social Ecology helped support computer analyses. I am extremely grateful for extraordinary research assistance by Sherry Ahrentzen, Joan Campbell, Doug Levine, Linda Naiditch, and Danny Sun.

8. I am indebted in this regard to Gordon J. (Pete) Fielding, Al Hollinden, Will Recker, Genevieve Giuliano, and Lyn Long.

9. Nat Jasper and Judy Meade were interested and supportive research monitors.

REFERENCES

Carlstein, T. (1982). *Time Resources, Society and Ecology: On the Capacity for Human Interaction in Space and Time.* Boston, Mass.: Allen and Unwin.

Carp, F. M. (1974). *Employed Women as a Transportation-deprived and Transit Dependent Group.* Document No. TM-4-1-74. Berkeley, California: Metropolitan Transportation Commission, p. 6.

Chapin, F. Stuart, Jr. (1965). *Urban Land Use Planning.* Urbana, Illinois: University of Illinois Press.

Chapin, F. Stuart, Jr. (1974). *Human Activity Patterns in the City: Things People Do in Time and Space.* New York: John Wiley and Sons.

Commission of Inquiry into Part-time Work (1983). *Part-time Work in Canada.* Ottawa: Labour Canada.

Cullen, Ian (1978). "The Treatment of Time in the Explanation of Spatial Behaviour." In T. Carlstein, D. Parkes, and N. Thrift (Eds.), *Human Activity and Time Geography.* London: Edward Arnold.

Fox, Mary Frank and Hess-Biber, Sharlene (1984). *Women at Work.* Palo Alto, California: Mayfield Publishing Company.

Hägerstrand, Torsten (1969). "What About People in Regional Science?" *Papers of the Regional Science Association,* Vol. 24, European Congress, 1969, Philadelphia, Pennsylvania: Regional Science Association.

Hägerstrand, Torsten (1970). "Tidsanvändning och Omgivningsstruktur" ("Time-use and Environmental Structure"). *Statens Offentliga Utredningar 14,* part 4, pp. 1-46.

Hayghe, Howard (1982). "Dual-Earner Families: Their Economic and Demographic Characteristics." In Joan Aldous (Ed.), *Two Pay-Checks: Life in Dual-Earner Families* (pp. 27-40). Beverly Hills, California: Sage.

Jordan-Marsh, M. (1981). "Will Health Be the Day Care Child's Weekend Sandwich?" *The Networker: The Newsletter of the Bush Programs in Child Development and Social Policy, 2,* pp. 4-7.

Kamerman, Sheila B. (1980). *Parenting in an Unresponsive Society: Managing Work and Family Life.* New York: Free Press.

Koppelman, F. S., et al. (1978). "Role Influence in Transportation Decision Making." In S. Rosenbloom (Ed.), *Women's Travel Issues: Research Needs and Priorities* (pp. 309-53). Washington, D.C.: US Department of Transportation.

Lenntorp, Bo (1976). *Paths in Space-Time Environments: A Time-Geographic Study of Movement Possibilities of Individuals.* Lund Studies in Geography, No. 44. Lund, Sweden: C.W.K. Gleerup (Royal University of Lund).

Levine, E. P. (1980). "Travel Behavior and Transportation Needs of Women: A Case Study of San Diego, California." Master's Thesis, San Diego State University.

Märstensson, Solveig (1977). "Childhood Interaction and Temporal Organization." *Economic Geography, 53*(2), pp. 99-125.

Märtensson Solveig (1978). "Time Allocation and Daily Living Conditions: Comparing Regions." In T. Carlstein *et al.* (Eds.), *Human Activity and Time Geography* (pp. 181-97). London: Edward Arnold.

Märtensson, Solveig (1982). "Tidsbudjetstudier i Anslutning till Forsök med Anropstyrd Busstrafik" ("Time-Budget Studies in Connection with an Experiment with Dial-A-Bus"). Lund: Department of Geography, Royal University of Lund.

Meier, Gretl S. (1979). *Job Sharing: A New Pattern for Quality of Work and Life*. Kalamazoo, Michigan: W. E. Upjohn Institute for Employment Research.

Melbin, Murray (1978). "The Colonization of Time." In T. Carlstein et al. (Eds.), *Human Activity and Time Geography* (pp. 100-13). New York: Halstead Press.

Meltz, Noah et al. (1981). *Sharing the Work: An Analysis of the Issues in Worksharing and Jobsharing*. Toronto: University of Toronto Press.

Michelson, William (Ed.) (1979). *Public Policy in Temporal Perspective: Report on the Workshop on the Application of Time-Budget Research to Policy Questions in Urban and Regional Settings*. The Hague: Mouton Publishing.

Michelson, William (1983). *The Impact of Changing Women's Roles on Transportation Needs and Usage, Final Report*. Grant CA-11-0024, Urban Mass Transportation Administration, US Department of Transportation. Springfield, Virginia: National Technical Information Service.

Michelson, William (1985). *From Sun to Sun: Daily Obligations and Community Structure in the Lives of Employed Women and Their Families*. Totowa, New Jersey: Rowman and Allanheld.

Michelson, William and Reed, Paul B. (1975). "The Time-Budget." In William Michelson (Ed.), *Behavioral Research Methods in Environmental Design* (Ch. 5). New York: Van Nostrand Reinhold Company.

Mortimer, J. T. and London, J. (1984). "The Varying Linkages of Work and Family." In Patricia Voydanoff (Ed.), *Work and Family: Changing Roles of Men and Women*. Palo Alto, California: Mayfield Publishing Company.

Nollen, Stanley D., et al. (1978). *Permanent Part-time Employment: An Interpretive Review*. Vol. 1. New York: Praeger Publishing.

Ogburn, William (1964). *On Culture and Social Change: Selected Papers*. Chicago, Illinois: University of Chicago Press.

Oppenheimer, Valerie K. (1982). *Work and the Family: A Study in Social Demography*. New York: Academic Press.

Palm, Risa (1981). "Women in Non-Metropolitan Areas: A Time-Budget Survey." *Environment and Planning* A, *13*(3), pp. 373-78.

Palm, Risa and Pred, Allen (1974). *A Time-Geographic Perspective on Problems of Inequality for Women*. Working Paper No. 236, Berkeley, California: Institute of Urban and Regional Development, University of California.

Pickup, L. (1981). *Housewives' Mobility and Travel Patterns*. TRRL Laboratory Report 971, Crowthorne, Berkshire, England: Transport and Road Research Laboratory.

Pred, Allen (1977). "The Choreography of Existence: Comments on Hägerstrand's Time-Geography and Its Usefulness." *Economic Geography, 53*(2), pp. 207-21.

Ross, Catherine; Mirowsky, John; and Huber, Joan (1983). "Dividing Work, Sharing Work, and in Between: Marriage Patterns and Depression." *American Sociological Review, 48*(6), pp. 809-23.

Sen, L. (1978). "Travel Patterns and Behavior of Women in Urban Areas." In

S. Rosenbloom (Ed.), *Women's Travel Issues: Research Needs and Priorities* (pp. 417-36). Washington, D.C.: US Department of Transportation.

Staikov, Zahari (1973). "Modelling and Programming of Time-Budgets." *Society and Leisure, 5*(1), pp. 31-47.

Studenmund, A.H., et al. (1978). "Women's Travel Behavior and Attitudes: An Empirical Analysis." In S. Rosenbloom (Ed.), *Women's Travel Issues: Research Needs and Priorities* (pp. 355-79). Washington, D.C.: US Department of Transportation.

Szalai, Alexander, et al. (1973). *The Use of Time: Daily Activities of Urban and Suburban Populations in Twelve Countries.* The Hague: Mouton Publishing.

van Paasen, C. (1981). "The Philosophy of Geography: From Vidal to Hägerstrand." In Allen Pred (Ed.), *Space and Time Geography: Essays Dedicated to Torsten Hägerstrand* (pp. 17-29). Lund, Sweden: C.W.K. Gleerup (Royal University of Lund).

Ziegler, Suzanne and Michelson, William (1981). "Complementary Methods of Data Gathering in Literate, Urban Populations." *Human Organization, 40*(4), pp. 323-29.

5

Canadian Women's Housing Cooperatives: Case Studies in Physical and Social Innovation[1]

GERDA R. WEKERLE

Throughout Canada, women have been responding to the current crisis in affordable housing by developing their own non-profit cooperative housing projets. Women's groups have participated in federal non-profit housing programmes either through constructing new housing or by renovating existing buildings. Women are the focus of these projects, making them not only primary housing consumers but also, in some instances, the developers of the housing. Although there are fewer than twenty such projects nationally and they are all relatively small (averaging only thirty residents), an examination of these "aberrations" in the housing market highlights the circumstances under which women can be more actively involved in the creation and management of housing that is responsive to their needs.

Just as feminist services have resulted in questioning the conventional institutions of health care and family violence programmes (Dale and Foster, 1986), so feminist and women-dominated housing projects might challenge the traditional ways of delivering and managing housing. Because much of the housing literature portrays women as victims—unable to afford market costs, and, increasingly, homeless (McClain and Doyle, 1984)—these Canadian women's housing projects are important demonstration projects: living laboratories of what happens when women take charge of their own housing.

OUR STUDY

Between September 1985 and October 1986, Joan Simon, a Toronto architect, and I conducted in-depth case studies of ten women's housing projects in eight Canadian cities. We had two objectives: first, to document how each project was developed; second, to learn the residents' experience of living in a housing project specifically for women. Both objectives were carried out through in-depth interviews. In each city we also met with municipal, provincial, and federal housing officials to discuss housing conditions; we talked with directors of battered women's shelters and visited single parent centres. We generally tried to obtain some insight into women's housing needs and how they were being met in different regions of the country.

Our greatest initial difficulty was finding projects. We wanted to include all the women's housing projects in the country in our study. But even though all received some funding from CMHC, there was no list of projects. To find them, we followed up leads from newsletters, unpublished reports, and chance meetings with other women from across the country.

Our original sample included eight projects; two more were added later. When we visited cities, we learned of other women's housing not included in our study. For instance, in Vancouver, two women's housing projects, Sitka and Entre Nous Femmes, were starting construction in the fall of 1985; in Toronto, a third women's housing coop, the Perth Avenue Coop, was in the planning stages. One project, non-profit housing for native women on Manitoulin Island in Ontario, could not be included in the study because residents felt that they had already been over-studied. Women's housing projects have been proposed in New Brunswick, Prince Edward Island, and Quebec.

As projects have been completed in the larger centres, their success and the attendant publicity have encouraged women in other parts of the country to try to obtain funding to build housing for single parents or for other groups of women. By providing information about existing projects, we hoped to encourage other women's groups to consider housing projects developed by women. By increasing the visibility of women's housing issues, we hoped to increase support for women's housing projects from funding agencies and within the housing cooperative movement.

Diversity characterizes Canadian women's housing projects. There is great variety in their origins and sponsorship, in their physical design, and in their social objectives. They include new construction such as the Constance Hamilton Coop and the Beguinage in Toronto and renovations of existing buildings such as Grandir en Ville in Quebec City. There are small projects of only six units (Munroe House in Vancouver), while the newest coop in

Toronto—Perth Avenue Coop—has 109 units. Some of the projects are concentrated in one building, while a couple are on scattered sites.

There are three types of sponsorship: non-profit housing cooperatives; second stage housing for battered women and their children run by a non-profit group; and projects for single parents run by a non-profit group or a public housing authority. We were particularly interested in issues of empowerment and how different forms of tenure, the length of residence, and the presence or absence of a feminist philosophy affected women's opportunities for involvement in their housing.

This chapter examines the similarities and differences among five non-profit housing cooperatives. The coops span the country, with one each in Regina, Quebec City, and Halifax, and two in Toronto. Ethnic groups, religious groups, unions, and even groups of artists have long used the ·non-profit coop programme to create what the coop sector calls a "thematic coop": a living environment which reinforces group values and builds on existing social networks. Only recently, however, have women viewed the non-profit cooperative housing programme as a way to obtain appropriate housing. These five cases are the first examples of how women have used the programme to meet their housing needs and support their social objectives.

WOMEN FACE HOUSING CRISIS ACROSS CANADA

Reports of housing officials and social agencies across Canada portray an acute crisis in affordable housing—a crisis that primarily affects women. In all the cities we visited, agencies working with women reported that women's lower incomes and responsibility for children make them one of the most vulnerable and needy groups in today's housing market. In 1980, more that 64 per cent of Canadian women had incomes under $12,000, with 18 per cent under $4,000 (McClain and Doyle, 1984). Single parents fared worse. The poverty rate nationally for female-headed single-parent families was 44 per cent (Ross, 1983, p. 70). Because women are predominantly renters rather than homeowners, the majority of low-income women live in some of the worst accommodation: the oldest dwellings and the least adequate in terms of size and amenities (McClain and Doyle, 1984, p. 11). To compound the problem further, in the largest Canadian cities such as Vancouver, Toronto and Halifax, where vacancy rates for rental housing are less than 1 per cent, interviews with workers dealing with women in crisis revealed that landlords practise widespread discrimination against women heads of families, especially if they are on social assistance.

In every city, housing officials reported that single parents face severe problems in obtaining affordable housing. Single parents make up the majority of applicants for assisted and rent-geared-to-income housing; they comprise 58.5 per cent of all families in public housing and rent-supplemented units (CMHC, 1983); and they are the majority of families on waiting lists for assisted housing in major Canadian cities. Yet the chance of obtaining such housing is low. For example, Cityhome, the City of Toronto's housing agency, reported 12,000 persons on its waiting list in May 1984 (City of Toronto, Department of Pubic Health, 1984). The situation is no better in other cities. In Ottawa-Carleton, 18.9 per cent of families are headed by single parents; the majority of applicants for subsidized units are single mothers, many of them recently separated, with children. Yet appropriate housing can be found for only about 10 per cent of these families (Duvall, 1985). In Halifax-Dartmouth, an increasing number of women with children in serious housing crisis has been noted since the early 1980's. Social service agencies report that the largest number of calls came from single parents with children who were on social assistance or other fixed incomes. Around 15 per cent of these were homeless, the majority of them with children (Mellett, 1983).

NON-PROFIT HOUSING COOPERATIVES AS A RESPONSE TO WOMEN'S HOUSING CRISIS

In the mid-1970's both Canada and the United States re-examined their affordable housing strategies. The United States turned to cash assistance for targeted households, while Canada greatly expanded its non-profit and cooperative housing programmes. Both strategies represented a shift from a centralized housing programme to one that increased control at the local level.

In 1973, Canadian federal legislation established the non-profit cooperative housing programme. Amendments to the Canadian National Housing Act in 1978 placed responsibility for the actual development of housing projects in the hands of local community groups and municipalities. The federal government did not provide direct lending. Coops were financed by the private sector, with the federal government providing assistance to cover the gap between the economic costs of a project and its market potential at a time of double-digit inflation (Hannley, 1986). Approximately 30,000 coop units were developed between 1979 and 1985 in almost every region of the country.

Non-profit cooperatives were eligible for 100 per cent mortgage financing, with National Housing Act (NHA) insurance from Canada Mortgage and Housing Corporation (CMHC). CMHC covered the total operating costs up to the difference between monthly amortization costs at the market rate of interest and an interest rate of 2 per cent. Rents were set at the "low end of market" compared with market rents in the adjacent neighbourhood. It was a requirement of the program that at least 25 per cent of units be assisted housing for low-income residents.

The purpose of the non-profit cooperative housing programme was to extend the social status benefits of quasi-homeownership to two groups: first, a moderate income group which probably could not afford to purchase a dwelling; and second, low-income residents who received further assistance to reduce housing charges to a maximum of 30 per cent of adjusted family incomes. This programme had the intention of creating a social mix in coops, thereby avoiding the ghettos of the poor which had plagued the public housing programme.

Housing subsidies for low-income residents were decentralized by creating a subsidy pool for each cooperative to be distributed by members. While there was no theoretical or legal limit to the number of units that a coop subsidized, there was a limit to the amount of money for subsidy. CMHC gave the coop monthly cheques equal to the difference between a market-rate mortgage and a 2 per cent mortgage. This amount, plus rents, must cover the mortgage, all bills, and any subsidy to tenants. If rents are high, there is more money for subsidy; if rents are low, there is less money available. Coops have a fair degree of flexibility in how they use their subsidy pool. Some coops elect to give a large number of residents a small amount of subsidy, while others provide what they call "deep subsidies" which lower the rent of a few residents to 30 per cent of adjusted income. In addition, some provinces have provincial rent supplement programmes, which can be used in addition to the CMHC subsidy to lower housing costs for residents who pass an eligibility test.

The Canadian programme has two imaginative provisions to facilitate the creation of community-based initiatives. First, start-up funds are a fundamental part of the Section 56.1 delivery process and a key to the programme's success. The programme recognized that community groups require assistance in the planning and development of proposals to construct or rehabilitate dwellings for low-income individuals and families. If the project does not proceed, the funds provided to undertake assessment studies and pay for other preliminary professional assistance are treated as a grant; if the project does proceed, the development costs are included as part of the capital costs (CMHC, 1983, pp. 22-23).

In addition, the Community Resource Organization Program (CROP) helped to organize resource people who would take projects from the idea stage to final completion. The CROP groups quickly developed the expertise needed to deal with government officials, lawyers, architects, and bankers. They understood the steps involved in the development process and assisted the local coop groups in making applications or hiring consultants; they were also skilled in working in the participatory manner typical of volunteer groups. The CROP groups were paid by the coops from start-up funds. After the first three to five years, the resource groups became self-sufficient from the revenues received, and their funding was withdrawn (CMHC, 1983, p. 23).

Women are attracted to non-profit cooperative housing by the low membership fee (often less than $100) and by housing costs which are assisted or lower than market rents. The drawbacks of coop housing are implicit in its structure: with as much as three-fourths of units charging market rents, this housing can provide only a limited solution to the affordability problem facing many women.

Nationally, 25 per cent of residents living in non-profit and cooperative projects are single parents (Klodawsky, Spector, and Hendrix, 1983). A recent study of households living in thirty-seven non-profit cooperatives in Metropolitan Toronto found 20.4 per cent are single parents (Schiff, 1982). In the Ottawa-Carleton region, women living alone are attracted to coops far more than single men (21 per cent of residents are female singles compared with 13.5 per cent males) (Barton, 1983). Single parents are also attracted to coops because the mix of incomes avoids the stigma of public housing. Further, with their emphasis on equality, equity, and mutual self-help, housing coops do not appear to practise the discrimination against women heads of families so prevalent elsewhere.

Since women housing consumers are more likely to rent housing than to be homeowners (McClain and Doyle, 1984), they are also more likely to benefit from the positive aspects of collective ownership, such as greater housing security and freedom from worries of being evicted for housing conversions or demolitions. Over the long term, coop housing remains appealing because its housing charges are not expected to rise as quickly as costs in the private market and because women on low or stable incomes do not anticipate ever owning their own home. In our interviews, non-profit coops were described as the housing of first choice to which many women with children aspired.

WOMEN RESPOND TO THE NEED: THE DEVELOPMENT PROCESS

Women's coop housing has been developed by people who perceive that women have unique housing needs. But these people have come from diverse groups: professionals, social service workers, politicians, and the women themselves. Not surprisingly, several of the coops were initiated by single parents who had experienced difficulty in obtaining affordable housing for themselves and their children. According to Cathy Mellett, the Halifax Women's Cooperative was founded in 1981 by four single mothers who had not been able to find suitable affordable housing (personal correspondence with Cathy Mellett, 1985). They shared similar political ideals and wanted to share a household for mutual support. Their solution was to renovate existing housing on four sites close to downtown Halifax to create a coop of twelve units.

Similarly, Marie Leclerc, one of the founders of the Grandir en Ville Non-Profit Housing Cooperative in Quebec City, was motivated by the difficulties she experienced in living alone with a child. Her solution was to join with three other women who were also single parents. "I thought that if I was living with similar people to me, it would be easier. We did research to see what kind of project would suit us. It did not take long to figure out that cooperative housing was the way to go. To share responsibilities, rights, democracy—it was a good model for us" (personal interview with Marie Leclerc, 1986).

As part of a plan to save a heritage building, the Bon Pasteur Convent in Quebec City's financial district, the four women proposed to renovate it and use the space for seven non-profit cooperatives. Grandir en Ville gives priority to single parents but it does not limit members to this family type. To maintain diversity, the coop distributes its thirty units among singles, nuclear families, and single parents.

The Joint Action Coop in Regina, Canada's oldest women's housing cooperative, was incorporated in 1972 by a board comprised of professionals, academics, and persons in the housing and social service fields. The board members saw the need for low-cost housing for single parents, and the coop bought four existing low-rise buildings with a total of forty-eight units. Basing its exclusion criteria on stage of the life cycle, this coop is exclusively for single parents with children.

The Constance Hamilton coop in Toronto was spearheaded by women's hostel organizers and a municipal politician. In 1979, at a series of meetings, representatives of various women's hostels working on the Metro Toronto Social Services Long-Term Housing Committee (1979) discussed the concept of forming a structure that could acquire and run long-term housing for women. City of Toronto alderman Janet Howard initiated the idea of using CMHC funding to form a housing cooperative for women. A voluntary board of women, many of them professionals in the social service field, incorporated the Constance Hamilton Coop, which opened for occupancy in 1982.

The Beguinage,[2] a second Toronto women's housing cooperative, followed closely with the completion of a twenty-eight-unit coop in 1984. Again the motivation was concern about the housing situation faced by women. Under the heading "Why a Women's Housing Co-op?" an initial flyer for the coop stated:

> The current crisis in housing inevitably has the greatest effect on the most vulnerable members of society. At a time when the proportion of women-headed households is on the increase, the availability of adequate affordable housing is declining. Sole-support women of all ages, with and without children, are faced with serious housing problems. The Toronto Women's Housing Cooperative is *one* answer to the housing needs of women. (Toronto Women's Housing Cooperative, Inc., 1982)

Four of the coops—Constance Hamilton, the Beguinage, the Halifax Women's Cooperative, and Grandir en Ville—were feminist in their origins and objectives. The founders were active in the women's movement in each city, and their goals were to provide a supportive community to women and opportunities for empowerment. Selection procedures for new members in two of the coops, the Beguinage and the Halifax Women's Cooperative, give preference to women active in feminist activities or organizations. The Joint Action Cooperative (Regina), on the other hand, focused primarily on providing affordable housing to single parents without a specific ideology or set of social objectives.

GAINING ACCEPTANCE FOR A "WOMEN'S COOP"

The first obstacle for each group was gaining acceptance for a "women's coop," even though there were precedents in existing coops based on ties of ethnicity, religion, or trade union membership. According to Lynn Hannley, Director of Communitas, a coop housing resource group operating in Edmonton since 1972, "If you are using a responsive model, it attracts people who know each other. This was not a programme requirement but happened in various areas" (personal interview with Lynn Hannley, 1986). Within the coop housing sector, these "thematic" coops, as they are called, have aroused considerable debate because by their very nature there is some element of exclusion and segregation. At the same time, it is this ability to select members which also gives residents control over their community and the opportunity to build housing tailored to their particular needs.

The Constance Hamilton Coop illustrates how the concept of a women's coop was sold. According to Gay Alexander, the coop's project officer at the Toronto branch of CMHC:

The initial contact was very important. In the spring of 1980, Janet Howard approached CMHC and she was passed on with skepticism. Janet has some credibility at CMHC because she was involved with DACHI (Don Area Cooperative Homes Inc). The initial skepticism centered around comments that "we can't discriminate; we can't just house women to the exclusion of other groups." The women's coop idea was softened because of the hostel component. No one questions the need for hostels. The report from Metro Social Services carried some weight as did their recommendations for longer term hostel care. If it had been a straight women's housing coop, there would have been a lot more trouble. It would have gone through because they were persistent, but it could have been held up while management questioned whether there should be coops exclusively for women. They [the coop] modified the charter to get away from charges of discrimination.

The major concern of Constance Hamilton was that women be in charge of the project and that women sit on the Board. CMHC had no comment about that. Constance Hamilton obtained credibility from the hostel and from [the coordinators] who were cooperative and competent people. Some of the women on the Board are strong social worker types and known in the community. All that stability impresses. I felt I could support it because it was a very solid group of people. The reaction at CMHC was out of all proportion to the project. It has calmed down now and the project is seen as different because of the hostel and not because it is women. (personal interview with Gay Alexander, 1982)

One of the striking similarities in the stories about the development process of the various women's housing coops is the use founders made of women's networks and links among women active in the women's movement, women working in the coop movement, women professionals in the community, and women bureaucrats working at CMHC and in city housing departments. For instance, Gay Alexander was made project officer of the Constance Hamilton coop because she had been active in organizing a women's group within CMHC and was seen as an advocate for women. She subsequently became project officer for the Beguinage when it sought CMHC funding, and she later became development officer for the Perth Avenue Coop when she took a position with Lantana, a Toronto-based resource group. The project was inititated by women active in providing transition housing; it was carried forward by Janet Howard, a City of Toronto alderman active in housing and neighbourhood reform. Initial board members included Jean Woodsworth, former director of Victoria Daycare Services, who had prior experience with housing for sole-support mothers, Moira Armour, active in the Toronto feminist community and the

National Action Committee on the Status of Women, and Annette Salem, a feminist with experience in construction. Several board members of Constance Hamilton became founding members of the second Toronto women's housing coop, the Beguinage.

Commenting on her experiences with the government approval process for the Constance Hamilton Coop, architect Joan Simon said:

> Throughout we have found women who have been supportive of the project, some of whom had known that it was in the pipeline and were fostering it, some of whom just happened to be in the approval process and were intrigued by the idea. As women became aware of the coop and asked to be involved, they became so supportive it was hard to distinguish them from board members in terms of their attitude and concern. (personal interview with Joan Simon, 1982)

These examples illustrate that although few women have prior experience in developing housing, women have been successful in developing housing coops by drawing upon the sympathetic support of key women in the non-profit housing sector, government housing bureaucracies, and the voluntary sector.

HOUSING INNOVATIONS: THE PHYSICAL ENVIRONMENT

There has been much speculation about the form that housing responsive to women's needs should take (Hayden, 1981; 1984; Leavitt, 1985; Matrix, 1984). The few foreign examples of women's housing (all of which are transitional housing for single parents for a limited time period) have received considerable attention: Nina West Homes in London, England; the Mother's House in Amsterdam; and Warren Village in Denver (Hayden, 1984). However, there have been no detailed evaluations of how well they work from the residents' point of view.

Dolores Hayden argues for the need to provide physical space for communal sharing of household tasks, in particular meal preparation and dining. Her proposal for a non-sexist community includes space for the local provision of collective services and the creation of jobs for residents within the community (1981, 1984). Leavitt's (1985) plans for a new American home call for a flexible dwelling unit which would allow single parents to share housing with one another or with an elderly person or would provide space for working at home.

In a comprehensive summary and critique of the literature on the housing needs of single parents, Klodawsky, Spector and Rose (1985, pp. 8-13) conclude that eight non-physical and physical elements are critical in planning for housing for single parents. The most important is affordability. Two other non-physical elements are security of tenure, and procedures which ease the transition and the move in. Five elements of the physical environment are: accessibility based on the location of housing; the provision of appropriate facilities for children; minimal household maintenance; the creation of opportunities for sharing and support among residents; and privacy.

The women's housing cooperatives discussed in this chapter have incorporated these elements to varying degrees, based on the relative importance of physical design, services, and participation in management and decision-making.

Control of the Development Process

Founding members of several of the projects were familiar with the literature on women's needs in housing, and they spent considerable effort in defining how women's activities translated into design. A priority for the Constance Hamilton Board was to maintain control of the design and development process rather than allowing a resource group to make decisions on these matters. Janet Howard, the initiator of the coop, describes the early decision to maintain control:

> Early on the coop made the decision to maintain control of the development process and, in particular, to hire its own architect rather than giving over the building process to a resource group. It never would have entered our head to do a thing like that. *We* were developing a coop. We wanted to work with an architect and have a large say in how the units worked. We hired a resource group to save us time to free us to develop our membership. The Labour Council was hired and they were tactful enough not to send a man. Our priorities were in the software of this coop and the resource group could be very helpful with change orders, etc.
>
> We were looking for someone used to working with a group; someone experienced with a community setting, not just building beautiful isolated housing; someone experienced in working with CMHC. It was nice if it was a woman, but not mandatory; someone with sensitivity to a client group; someone aware that this was a development by and for women and realizing any special considerations this entailed. [When we interviewed her] Joan Simon had a certain amount of say about household traffic—who is where in a house and when. She showed slides illustrating the thinking behind that and is someone considering

the users of the architecture. Our experience with her has been excellent. She has never tried to bully us; she has concerns about the convenience of women. (personal interview with Janet Howard, 1982)

The Beguinage started with the ideal of restoring a stately downtown building. After half a dozen buildings were rejected by CMHC as uneconomic, the coop settled for new construction of stacked townhouses on two adjacent sites on the edge of skidrow near a large pubic housing complex. Although the coop had a commitment to working with a feminist architect in a participatory programming process, in order to have the housing built before the initial board burned out, it accepted a turnkey building where the architect and builder were preselected by the owner of the land. Despite these compromises, the coop feels itself fortunate to have found a sympathetic architect, Phil Goldsmith, and Rich Tyssen, a resource group project officer with extensive development experience. Both of them respected the group's concerns for how the small details of a project translated into livability. The end result was excellent, according to Kye Marshall, one of the founding members of the Beguinage: "When I first saw the project I was thrilled. I like it. It is well built. The women there feel it fills the function it was designed for. We quite liked the architects. They were nice guys and did a wonderful job on the outside. The developer and architect may have decided to make this their showpiece" (personal interview with Kye Marshall, 1986).

In all these women's housing cooperatives, the ultimate goal was to make affordable housing available quickly and within budget: design innovations or the expression of a women's culture and community through physical form were secondary. Although the design innovations are not striking, each group fought for certain features that it felt would contribute to members' quality of life.

Quality Materials, Long-term Maintenance, Privacy

The use of quality materials and long-term maintenance and durability were a key concern for the developers of the women's coops. Joan Simon discussed the attitude of the Constance Hamilton Coop Board: "The Board was very concerned with the habitability of the units. If we were working for a private developer, attention would have frequently been on gimmicks and trim rather than basic quality. The Board wanted to maximize living space and make houses better for people to actually live in" (personal interview with Simon, 1982). This involved attention to such aspects of the building as using concrete block walls, good quality wood windows that would not leak, more than a minimum amount of insulation, and construction that would

Halifax Women's Coop

ABOVE: The Beguinage, Toronto
BELOW: Grandir en Ville, Quebec City

allow residents to upgrade their housing and make additions in future.

Similarly, at the Beguinage, special attention was paid to sound and energy conservation. To eliminate sound transmission, a common problem in stacked townhouse projects, the architect stayed with simple forms and simple unit separation, designing special wall and floor treatment to buffer each unit. For energy conservation, external walls used 2x6 construction with extra insulation, sealing, and wood windows instead of cheaper aluminum windows.

At Grandir en Ville, the coop spent a lot of time considering the laundry room location. To save residents time, they debated having small laundries on each floor or a communal laundry room in the basement. Initially, they planned to have a walkup unit, but later an elevator was seen as necessary, adding $2,000 to the cost of each unit and making laundry rooms on each floor economically prohibitive. Another issue at Grandir en Ville was unconventional apartment layouts. Living rooms were located in the corners of the building to give them double exposures. As a consequence, in some of the apartments it was necessary to pass the bathroom and bedrooms to enter the living room. Although this was of concern to CMHC, residents chose this layout to get better living room space.

Design for Diversity

An objective of coop founders was to provide units which would meet the needs of a broad range of women. In the Constance Hamilton project, there are five different unit designs. Joan Simon commented:

> We designed units to suit a large number of lifestyles: 2-3 women sharing, multi-generational families, two single parents, etc. I split the living areas and put the living room on one floor and the dining room and kitchen on another so that both social spaces could be used at the same time. This meant the kitchen moved to the front of some units. The board wanted dining kitchens and not separate galley kitchens. The plan allows for a linear kitchen on one end of the dining room. The entrance to the units is often in the kitchen. Almost all the men in the approval process commented on this, while all the women who looked at the plan thought it was sensible. There is also a toilet in the laundry room for kids in the park, which had to be deliberately designed. (personal interview with Simon, 1982)

At the Beguinage, diverse unit sizes were created with different layouts of one-, two-, and three-bedroom units within the context of a simple form of stacking which facilitates servicing. The one-bedrooms are in mid-block; the three-bedrooms are in row houses at the end. The board insisted on same-size bedrooms rather than the conventional "master" and "junior" bedrooms since they assumed that some women would be sharing units. This small modification took considerable effort to convince both CMHC and the architect since conventional housing differentiates status within the family by size of bedroom.

At the Halifax Women's Coop, the response to the need for a diversity of units was the creation of a coop on four different sites in three different types of housing. There is a house with five bedrooms where women live communally, two duplexes, and a six-unit apartment building. Since members were involved in buying and renovating the buildings in which they were going to live, they determined details such as kitchen layouts and fixtures.

Because the Regina Joint Action Coop reduced costs by purchasing existing rental apartment buildings, where one-third of the units were one-bedroom apartments, this has built-in inflexibility and made it difficult to house single parents and their children comfortably over the long term.

Opportunities for Sharing

One of the requirements of non-profit cooperatives is that members participate in decision-making and managing their own project. Yet an ongoing complaint of coop residents is the lack of space within the projects for meetings and shared activities. One of the drawbacks of the women's housing coops and small non-profit coops is the lack of communal space. Joan Simon describes the dilemma faced by the Constance Hamilton Coop in Toronto:

> To make the coop work, we needed space for the coop members to get together. There is not much flexibility in a small coop to build a meeting space. We maximized the use of the laundry room as a community room by keeping it at ground level, so as to be able to supervise children in the park from there. The laundry room is also opposite the entrance to the women's hostel. (personal interview with Simon, 1982)

The coordinator's office is in a small dark office in the basement; the only inside communal space is a tiny basement room which would accommodate four people comfortably. A courtyard provides a large communal outdoor space which is heavily used for periodic coop celebrations, barbecuing and socializing, a communal herb garden, and a young children's play area. Jean Côté, architect of Grandir en Ville in Quebec City, discussed the issue of communal space:

GRANDIR EN VILLE CO-OP
QUEBEC, P.Q.

Noms des coopératives

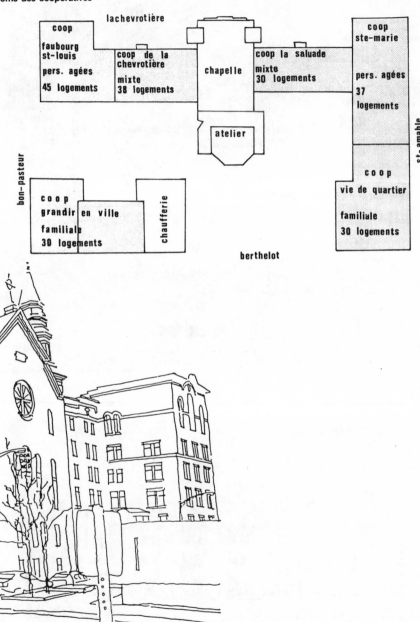

CONSTANCE HAMILTON CO-OP
Simon Architects

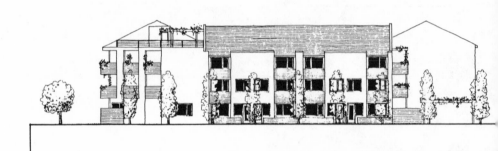

East Elevation

West Elevation

GRANDIR EN VILLE
THIRD FLOOR PLAN

GRANDIR EN VILLE
GROUND FLOOR

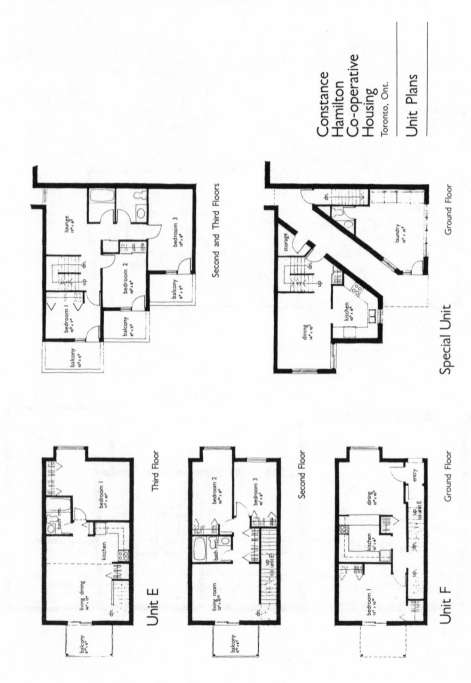

Constance
Hamilton
Co-operative
Housing
Toronto, Ont.

Unit Plans

Second and Third Floors

Ground Floor

Special Unit

Third Floor

Unit E

Second Floor

Ground Floor

Unit F

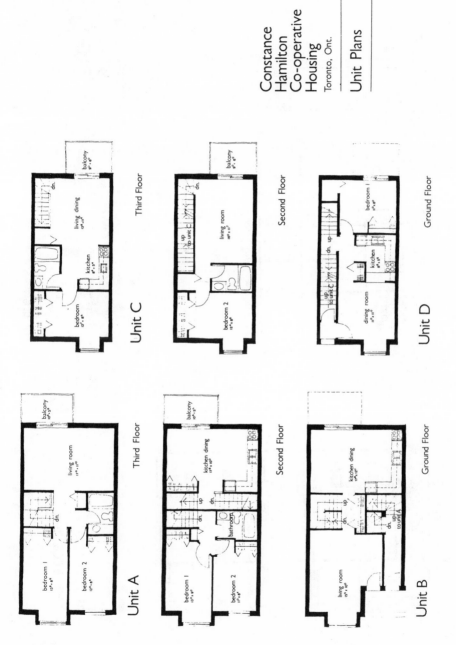

Constance
Hamilton
Co-operative
Housing
Toronto, Ont.

Unit Plans

Third Floor

Unit C

Second Floor

Ground Floor

Unit D

Third Floor

Unit A

Second Floor

Ground Floor

Unit B

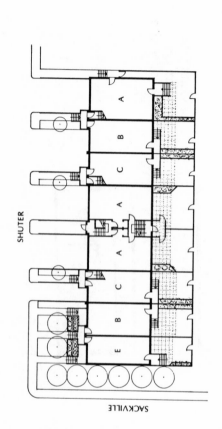

SACKVILLE

SHUTER

LANE

FRONT ELEVATION
415 SHUTER STREET   THE BEGUINAGE

SITE PLANS
THE BEGUINAGE

UNIT F (above units B & C)

CO-OP COMMON

MAIN FLOOR PLAN
UNIT B

SECOND FLOOR PLAN
UNIT B

UNIT A

THE BEGUINAGE

When the project started the group had an idealized vision of how they wanted to live which could not be translated into physical reality. On a practical level, one of the features that the group would have liked was an extra room on each floor to be used as a community space or when people have house guests. It might have even been possible to use this space as a temporary extension to an apartment. Under MUP's [Maximum Unit Prices] this sort of space was not economically feasible. There was constant pressure from CMHC to produce a "normal, conventional" apartment building. The coop did manage to get some communal space under the guise of a bachelor apartment that had to be squeezed in at the end to bring the unit costs in under $30,000 per unit. This has never been rented as an apartment and is used as an office and communal room. (personal interview with Jean Côté, 1986)

At the Beguinage, there is a small coop meeting room, a coordinator's office, and one laundry room for the whole project. Outdoor areas are private and attached to ground level units.

The Joint Action Coop has no communal space other than a ground level unit which has been taken over for the coordinator's office. There is no communal indoor space; outdoor shared space is the large backyards attached to each building which are used for children's play equipment.

Coop groups expressed their frustration with CMHC guidelines which did not allow funding for the meeting space essential to transacting normal coop business or developing a supportive community. Further, even the coop resource groups may not give communal space the priority it deserves. Commenting on this lack of support, Karen Macmillan of Lantana, a Toronto resource group, said:

In the coop sector, there has not been a lot of thought given to community space. What there is comes from notions of property management so that spaces provided include offices, space for meetings, a kitchen for socials, washrooms, and a laundry room. The coop sector approaches the mainstream model of privatized space. We do not have a model of community space. We fight with CMHC over community space; CMHC squeezes common space when the economics of a project dictate it. They argue this is less maintenance. It accords with the homeownership ethic, yet the norm of coop housing is that people are sharing. (personal interview with Karen Macmillan, 1986)

Halifax Women's Coop

Constance Hamilton Coop, Toronto

Appropriate Facilities for Children

It is uncommon for non-profit housing cooperatives to provide child care on-site. For example, 70 per cent of Toronto area coops do not provide any form of organized child care (Cooperative Housing Federation, 1985). All coops studied were concerned with the availability of child care, but only two were able to provide it. Grandir en Ville shared a child care centre with the project's six other coops and persons working in the adjacent financial district. The Joint Action Coop created child care space from three basement units. An outdoor play area was created in the common space shared by the four buildings. The Constance Hamilton Coop provides no formal child care; it is adjacent to a small park which provides play equipment and a wading pool; interior layouts were designed to facilitate supervison of small children. The Beguinage and Halifax Women's Coop have no child care facilities nor do they provide shared outdoor play space.

Accessibility

All of the coops chose locations which would provide good access to public transportation and other services. The Halifax Women's Coop is the best situated: its units are in two neighbourhoods within walking distance of downtown Halifax and with good access to bus service. The Joint Action Coop bought property in a stable suburban neighbourhood of family homes where recent construction has been luxury condominiums. The coop is located across the street from a major shopping mall, on a well-used bus line, close to the university, and in an area of good schools. Constance Hamilton is located in a community of other housing cooperatives, close to the subway line, in the west central part of Toronto. Major public recreation facilities are close by. The Beguinage also insisted on a downtown Toronto location. Although the location on the edge of skidrow and in a neighbourhood with a heavy concentration of public housing is not ideal, there is proximity to social services and transportation.

None of the projects described here will be written up in architectural journals as Aldo van Eyck's Mother's House in Amsterdam was (Hertzberger *et al.,* 1982), for there are few design innovations. Small concessions, such as Constance Hamilton's kitchens that blend into the living room or the same size bedrooms at the Beguinage, are considered major victories. The Section 56.1 non-profit cooperative housing programme limits the kind of construction, interior space, communal space, and amenities that can be provided through establishing Maximum Unit Price (MUP's) for each city and

Joint Action Coop, Regina

Grandir en Ville, Quebec City

region. Since MUP's are based on a combination of land and construction costs and are frequently not updated for several years, non-profit cooperatives are often severely constrained in where they can locate and what they can construct. Coops are often left with marginal housing sites which private developers consider undesirable: adjacent to railroad tracks, arterial roads, or on previous industrial lands. These are also the least desirable locations for families with children and for women living alone.

In addition, the focus on providing financing only for shelter and not for community services limits the ability of individual housing coops, and even larger communities of coops, to respond to many of the basic needs of single-parent households: child care, education and job training, opportunities for employment, and a supportive community (Social Planning Council for Metropolitan Toronto, 1984).

Lynn Hannley comments on the difficulties of achieving any design innovations under the coop housing programme:

> With low MUP's, it is difficult to do good quality anything. If you want to do anything innovative, the next step is to fight with CMHC. They are traditional and are reluctant to have things that are different. CMHC says innovations cost more and they get uptight. If something is unusual, they talk about this programme funding "modest housing" which is not seen to be innovative. (personal interview with Hannley, 1986)

Karen Macmillan of Lantana continues:

> The environment forces uniformity—the economic environment and the construction industry. The ideologies of resource groups are often business-oriented and it is hard to break through. The characteristics of user groups are such that only those which are particularly strong-willed and idiosyncratic get what they want. Women are not usually like that; they are often more compliant. We find that when we make innovations upfront, for users this is a one-time success; but the developer won't do any more coops. And so the resource group loses. (personal interview with Macmillan, 1986)

According to Macmillan, one reason that space for services such as child care is often left out of coops is the extra work required of the resource group. It is difficult to develop a housing project; adding social services of various types requires making connections with other funding agencies and piecing together different programmes. Resource groups need specialists in soft services who can integrate them with the physical environment.

SOCIAL INNOVATIONS

In the women's housing coops, it is the social innovations, not the physical innovations, that are impressive. These include responses to special needs, stratagems to keep housing affordable, a focus on the creation of community, and attention to management and decision-making structures that empower women.

Responding to Special Needs

While the coop housing sector is only now addressing its responsibility to provide housing for special needs groups such as the disabled, homeless singles, or single parents, women's coops have quietly responded to some of these needs. The Constance Hamilton Cooperative included a six-unit house to provide services to homeless women. These women may stay for as long as a year; the coop provides counselling and social supports. For three years, members of the cooperative took on the responsibility of managing the house, furnishing it, finding tenants, hiring and supervising a part-time staff person, and serving as volunteers to work with transition house residents. This year, for the first time, two women from the transition unit have moved into permanent housing within the cooperative. Since 1985, Nellie's Hostel for Women in Toronto has managed the hostel unit and provided full-time staff support: coop members found the hostel's operation too burdensome when added to their work managing the coop.

At the Beguinage there is a special concern for women with low incomes or special problems who cannot be accommodated in other coops. One unit is reserved for an ex-psychiatric patient and a deep subsidy is provided to reduce housing costs to less than 30 per cent of income. A new coop, the Sitka Coop in Vancouver, provides units for a new class of disabled persons: women with environmental allergies who need non-toxic housing. The leadership of single parents in developing the five housing projects described in this chapter has ensured that their needs and those of their children have been taken into account.

Affordability

All the women's coops are conscious of the relatively low incomes of women housing consumers and their pressing need for affordable housing. The coops employ various stratagems to reduce housing costs. The Joint Action Coop, where approximately half of the residents are on social assistance, has deliberately maintained rents at $275- $280 per month— substantially lower than market rents in the community. Giving priority to affordability has backfired, however, as the coop has neglected to maintain reserve funds and to perform necessary maintenance. As a result, the coop is viewed by the community as being rundown and a last resort for low-income single parents.

The Halifax Women's Coop looked for good housing available at less than the MUP's allowed by CMHC to keep housing costs affordable for members. This led to a major disagreement between the coop and its resource group:

> It was a conflict between their ideas of what our income potentials should be and a push to spend the maximum available under the programme with our evaluation of what our incomes were likely to remain at and the need to make the housing as affordable as possible. Some very astute purchases were made by the members and good housing at the lowest possible price was achieved by buying units in areas not yet "desirable" for renovations. The second way that quality and price were controlled was by putting an enormous amount of sweat equity into the renovations of the units. CMHC never allowed enough capital for extensive repair to these older buildings. So, in order to maximize the amount of renovations that could be done to the units, most of the labour was done by the women. The programme has not turned out to be as affordable as first expected. This does tend to change the longer we have the units, but repair costs, taxes, insurance, etc., all increase each year and this gets added to both the minimum and maximum housing charges. However, the coop has provided good quality housing and, more importantly, control over our housing which would not be possible for women who in no other way could ever consider owning housing in the inflated inner-city areas. (personal correspondence with Mellett, 1985)

Residents of Grandir en Ville have the best deal of all. The land was donated by the Quebec government: its cost is not part of the housing price. Thus, coop units rent for $225-$300 per month for studios to four-bedroom apartments in a renovated heritage building in the centre of Quebec City.

The dilemma for the coops which have chosen new construction is that high land prices, rising construction costs, and the requirement to set housing costs at the low end of market rents have made housing charges so high that often even founding members of the coop cannot afford to live there. At the Beguinage, housing charges are $430-$450 for a one-bedroom, $650 for a two-bedroom, and $720 for a three-bedroom unit. Heating costs and parking are extra. Of the twenty-eight units, eight are on permanent subsidy ranging from $100-$600 per month. In addition, the coop has found it necessary to provide two units with emergency subsidies as residents lose their jobs, are employed only part-time, or encounter unusual circumstances. In an effort to increase its subsidy pool, the Beguinage has even considered a special levy on residents whose housing costs are less than 30 per cent of income. This applied to only four units and was not considered a solution.

While the security of tenure offered by coops is an attractive feature to women residents, the relatively high cost of housing produced under the coop programme makes it inaccessible to most single-parent families and low-income women in general.

A Supportive Community

Creating a supportive community of women was the expressed goal of all the women's housing coops. According to Jean Woodsworth, chair of the founding board of directors of the Constance Hamilton Coop, one of the initial objectives was to create an environment where women might obtain support from other women to make changes in their lives, such as after divorce. It was to provide security of living arrangements and the possibility of community life. This has occurred: coop residents put out a monthly newsletter, sponsor workshops, and organize several yearly celebrations. Child care and exchanges of services are arranged informally.

Grandir en Ville was started by four single parents who viewed their status as an opportunity for personal and social transformation. They wanted to use housing to create an environment supportive of their way of life and favoured the coop model because they could control their own housing, solve common problems, and state their right to live as single parents.

In general, the women's coops provide a housing environment which is also a supportive community where residents know one another, friendships form, and a level of mutual aid develops that is more intense than is usually found even in other housing coops.

What Housing Does in Women's Lives: Empowerment Through Decision-making

Women's housing projects emphasize participation in management further than is typical in most coops. They view the potential resident control of coops in terms of feminist goals to empower women and allow them to take charge of their environment. Management in women's housing coops is seen as a learning experience where women can learn new skills from one another and develop new models of decision-making.

In his book, *Housing by People,* John Turner outlines how participation in management can empower residents:

> When dwellers control the major decisions and are free to make their own contribution to the design, construction or management of their housing, both the process and the environment produced stimulate individual and social well-being. When people have no control over, nor responsibility for key decisions in the housing process, on the other hand, dwelling environments may instead become a barrier to personal fulfillment and a burden on the economy. (1976, p. xxxiii)

One of the most important and least-noted advantages of living in cooperative housing is the opportunity for participating in policy-making and management of the housing environment. For residents, these "community" aspects are often more important than the shelter component. Schiff's (1982) study of Toronto coops found that 61 per cent of residents felt that the single most important reason for moving to a coop was the ability to manage their own housing. The image of a cooperative as fostering a sense of community was important to 52 per cent of residents. With these opportunities for involvement, two-thirds of residents may serve on a coop committee.

Recent studies show that women living in housing cooperatives place a higher value than male members on developing a supportive community and participating in coop decision-making (Farge, 1985a; Gerritsma, 1984; Leavitt and Saegert, 1984). Women also provide much of the on-going leadership in housing coops. Gerritsma's (1984) case study of a small Toronto coop demonstrates that women use coop positions to learn new skills in such areas as maintenance and finance and to develop and exercise leadership skills. However, even in housing coops, men are still more likely to be presidents and treasurers while women are secretaries and members who do the committee work (Farge, 1985b).

In women's housing coops, women do not "participate"; they are in control: women set up the coop, buy the land or buildings, hire the architect and resource groups, negotiate with CMHC for funding, and define how their needs might be met by the housing. Coop members have given careful thought to decision-making structures, to questions of participation and hierarchy, and to selection criteria for members. In the ongoing management of their coops, women are involved in hiring and supervising staff, financial planning, and maintenance.

Participation by members is typically higher in women's housing cooperatives than in other coops. At Constance Hamilton, 96 per cent of residents surveyed in 1983 served on at least one coop committee (Morrison and Payne, 1983). The Halifax Women's Coop rejected the hierarchical structure of president, vice-president, and so forth found in most coops; instead, it chose to run itself by consensus decision-making. The board of directors is all members and only members, and all major decisions are brought to a meeting of the full membership. The Beguinage decided to retain control of its own marketing rather than give over this function to a resource group. Although volunteers are inexperienced in marketing coop housing and thus may be slightly more inefficient, the coop wanted to target women who have a commitment to feminism and are identified with other women.

The question of who can be a coop member has been vital to these three coops. All have chosen to limit membership to women to ensure that control of the housing and the benefits remain with women. At Constance Hamilton, this means that men may live in the coop with a woman but they may not be voting members. This issue is not settled, especially concerning male children who are excluded from membership; it remains to be seen whether these bylaws will be retained.

The Joint Action Coop is the exception to the rule, and it has had enormous difficulties, many of which can be traced to management problems. In 1972, community professionals founded the coop, but they withdrew from active participation when the project was occupied. Over the years, a highly bureaucratized and punitive management structure evolved which pits resident against resident. As in all the women's coops, residents must share in certain maintenance tasks—snow clearing, yard work, cutting grass—and participate in the normal functions of the coop—serving on the selection committee or board of directors. However, unlike the other coops in our study, where residents participated willingly and according to their ability, at the Joint Action Coop there is a coercive system of verbal and written warnings for infringement of rules. Three written warnings result in eviction. Residents designated as block reps have the job of reporting on fellow residents. Not surprisingly, it is difficult to find residents willing to serve either as block reps or coop directors, and there is a high turnover in such positions. A 70 per cent yearly turnover of residents makes it impossible to develop either a supportive community or a stable management structure. In these circumstances, key budget and tenant selection decisions have been turned over to outside staff, exacerbating the problem.

Unlike the other coops in this study, the Joint Action Coop was not feminist in its origins. Regina feminists neither know nor identify with the Joint Action Coop. Because the coop was a pioneer with the concept of providing single-parent housing, it predated the 56.1 programme and did not benefit from the substantial start-up assistance and member education provided to later coops. Since its inception, this coop has been on a downward spiral, experiencing difficulties with financial management, decision-making, controlling staff, resolving disputes, and maintaining the buildings. One of the members of the board of directors said: "We're left alone; taboo in Regina. Residents are attracted by cheap housing. There is nothing for them here; no sense of companionship. Either your back is up against the wall, or you stay in your own apartment" (personal interview). Evidence of the reputation of the coop in the community are the comments of Diana Elias, Director of Regina's Transition House:

> Housing for single parents is theoretically a really good idea; women supporting women is very positive. At the Joint Action Coop, women receive mostly negative feedback, by and large. It is a tight hierarchical structure and especially for kids there is no structure. The Coop needs more objectivity and less bias; an environment where residents still have input and control. I would not refer any woman to Joint Action unless she was a very strong individual. When women come out of really destructive relationships, if they go into an environment where there is a lot of negativism, where power things are going on, they have to be fairly solid. I question whether our residents are ready for that. My dream has always been to incorporate a woman's place with housing and child care that provides a supportive environment for women. (personal interview with Diana Elias, 1986)

A positive development has been the interest taken in the coop by the Coop Housing Foundation of Canada which funded a feasibility study to examine needs for physical improvements and changes in management. As a result, residents approved taking on a $300,000 second mortgage to improve boilers, kitchens, and landscaping and pay for this through raising housing costs. This first contact with the larger coop sector through CHAS, a Saskatchewan resource group, has also highlighted the kinds of assistance available in member education and advice on management. There is some hope that social improvements will follow the physical ones.

CONCLUSIONS

The Joint Action Coop experience illustrates that women's housing coops need more than cheap housing in a good location to be successful. Residents seek, and in some cases need, a supportive community; they value the opportunities that coops provide for participation in decision-making and learning new skills.

To the disappointment of feminists, Canadian women's housing coops have no distinctly feminist design solutions. Their most striking aspect is that they have been built and are continuing to be built. Their innovation lies beyond the physical environment—an environment constrained by funding and bureaucratic hurdles—and in the realm of social innovations. The feminist approach has gone beyond housing as shelter, using it for the delivery of essential services, the creation of community, and the development of an economic base supporting on-site jobs for community residents (Simon 1986; Sprague, 1986). Using housing as a base for local economic development is a theme running through the feminist design literature (Hayden, 1984; Simon 1986; Sprague, 1986) and was part of the initial objectives of the Constance Hamilton Coop. However, CMHC guidelines generally preclude the design of residential units for home-based occupations, although the Perth Avenue Coop (Toronto) incorporates communal space which may be used either for child care or for enterprise space. The multi-dimensional view of housing held by founders and residents of the women's housing coops runs counter to current trends in the housing field to view housing as a commodity provided by the private market and the housing unit as a private sphere, isolated from the surrounding community. The very existence of housing developed, controlled, and managed by women provides an alternative paradigm to the market experience of women who are marginal housing consumers.

Since 1986, the Section 56.1 programme has been dramatically changed. The new coop programme will be funded by an indexed mortgage scheme which separates the construction of housing from the provision of subsidies to low-income residents; these residents will now be served by a rent supplement programme directed at households with "core need." It is still too early to say how these changes will affect women's housing coops still in the planning stages. Hannley (1986) suggests that there will be difficulties in matching persons eligible for subsidies with available housing and that this may pose problems for women's coops that insist upon additional criteria in their selection of members.

Within the context of the development of thematic housing cooperatives, defined by such characteristics as ethnicity, union affiliation, or artistic pursuits, it will be interesting to note how women's coops fare over time. Will they meet a short-term need for women at particular stages of the life cycle, or will members grow old together as some founders hoped? To what degree will feminist goals and objectives be maintained as the initial founders are no longer involved? Will there be pressures to admit as members men or male children raised within the coop, and will this inevitably lead to the dilution of women's control of the housing? Or will the development of a women's community be able to withstand these pressures and adapt to new realities? As the number of women's housing coops grows, will the initital isolation experienced by all these groups decline as networks of women's housing projects are developed and more linkages are made both with the wider housing cooperative movement and with the women's movement?

The small coops documented in this chapter cannot begin to serve the critical and massive housing needs of women across Canada. But their existence has called attention to housing as a women's issue and has highlighted an alternative solution. A recent development has been the emergence of grass roots organizations focusing solely on women's housing concerns. In Halifax, Mothers United for Metro Shelter (MUMS), whose leaders have lived in battered women's shelters and public housing, has mobilized the city in demonstrations and actions dramatizing poor women's housing plight. A new Toronto organization, Women Plan Toronto, has begun to lobby on behalf of women's shelter needs. During the International Year of Shelter for the Homeless in 1987, women's organizations across Canada are organizing to focus widespread attention on women's housing crisis. The experience of Canadian women's housing cooperatives shows that for women, adequate housing goes beyond shelter.

NOTES

1. This chapter is dedicated to Joan Simon, who was my partner in designing this study and visiting all the women's housing projects. Because of her untimely death, she could not participate in the creative task of making sense of the data; this study is the poorer for being without her insights and analyses. Claude André, a graduate student in the York University Faculty of Environmental Studies, contributed immeasurably to the study by his supervision of the coding of data and his knowledge of computer applications. He provided direction in the case study of Grandir en Ville. Sylvia Novac, a graduate student in the Faculty of Environmental Studies, participated in interviewing and in supervising other interviewers in Toronto. She generously shared her insights and experiences of living in coops. I am grateful to Gerald Daly and Slade Lander for their comments and queries which challenged me to sharpen my focus. Slade Lander deserves my continuing gratitude for his editorial assistance and advice. While the study was funded by grants from the Social Sciences and Humanities Research Council and Canada Mortgage and Housing Corporation, these agencies are not responsible for the views expressed here.

2. The coop explained its choice of name. "The building we purchase will be called the Beguinage. In seeking a name for the Co-op we discovered that during the 13th and 14th centuries, there were groups of women in various European countries called beguines. The beguines lived in communal houses called beguinages. The beguines were sole-support women who purchased their own

homes and shared their lives with other women. Our home, to be purchased by women, renovated (where possible) by women, maintained and sustained by women, will carry the name Beguinage, in honour and memory of those early beguines" (Toronto Women's Housing Cooperative Inc., 1982).

REFERENCES

Barton, Debbie (1983). *Housing in Ottawa-Carleton: A Women's Issue*. Ottawa: Elizabeth Fry Society.

Canada Mortgage and Housing Corporation (CMHC) (1983). *Section 56.1: Non-Profit and Cooperative Housing Program Evaluation*. Ottawa: CMHC.

City of Toronto, Department of Public Health, Social Environment Work Group (1984). *Housing and Health: Public Health Implications of the Affordable Housing Crisis*. Toronto: City of Toronto, Department of Public Health.

Cooperative Housing Federation (1985). *Preliminary Results of Survey of Members*. Toronto: Cooperative Housing Federation of Toronto.

Dale, Jennifer and Foster, Peggy (1986). *Feminists and State Welfare*. London: Routledge and Kegan Paul.

Duvall, Donna (1985). "Emergency Housing for Women in Canada." *Ekistics, 310* (January/February), pp. 56-61.

Farge, Brenda (1985a). "A Contribution to the Feminist Debate over Cooperative Housing." Toronto: OISE, Department of Community Psychology.

Farge, Brenda (1985b). "Survey of Cooperative Housing Foundation Annual Meeting." Toronto: OISE, Department of Community Psychology.

Gerritsma, Mary (1984). "Instead Housing Coop: Women's Second Chance to Lead and Learn." Toronto: OISE, Department of Adult Education.

Hannley, Lynn, (1986). "The New Federal Co-operative Housing Program." *Canadian Housing, 3*(1), pp. 14-17.

Hayden, Dolores (1981). "What Would a Non-sexist City Be Like?" In C. Stimpson et al. (Eds.), *Women and the American City* (pp. 167-84). Chicago: University of Chicago Press.

Hayden, Dolores (1984). *Redesigning the American Dream*. New York: Norton.

Herzberger, Herman, van Roijen-Wortmann, Addie, and Strauven, Francis (1982). *Aldo van Eyck*. Amsterdam: Stichting Wonen.

Klodawsky, Fran, Spector, Aron, and Hendrix, C. (1983). *The Housing Needs of Single Parent Families in Canada*. Ottawa: CMHC.

Klodawsky, Fran, Spector, Aron, and Rose, Damaris (1985). *Single Parent Families and Canadian Housing Policies: How Mothers Lose*. Ottawa: CMHC.

Leavitt, Jacqueline and Saegert, Susan (1984). "Women and Abandoned Buildings: A Feminist Approach to Housing." *Social Policy, 15*(1), pp. 32-39.

Leavitt, Jacqueline (1985). "A New American House." *Women and Environments, 7*(1), pp. 14-16.

Matrix (1984). *Making Space: Women and the Man-made Environment.* London: Pluto Press.

McClain, Janet and Doyle, Cassie (1984). *Women and Housing: Changing Needs and the Failure of Policy.* Toronto: James Lorimer and Company.

Mellett, Cathy (1983). *At the End of the Rope: Women's Emergency Housing Needs in the Halifax/Dartmouth Area.* Halifax: Women's Emergency Housing Coalition.

Morrison, Heather, and Payne, Margo (1983). "The Evolution, Implementation, and Initial Assessment of the Constance Hamilton Cooperative." Guelph: University of Guelph, Department of Consumer Studies.

Municipality of Metropolitan Toronto, Department of Social Services (1979). "Long Term Housing Needs of Women." Toronto: Municipality of Metropolitan Toronto, Department of Social Services.

Ross, David (1983). *The Canadian Fact Book on Poverty—1983.* Toronto: James Lorimer and Company.

Schiff, Myra (1982). *Housing Cooperatives in Metropolitan Toronto: A Survey of Members.* Ottawa: Cooperative Housing Foundation of Canada.

Simon, Joan (1986). "Women and the Canadian Co-op Experience: Integrating Housing and Economic Development." *Women and Environments,* 8(1), pp. 10-13.

Sprague, Joan Forrester, et al. (1986). *A Manual on Transitional Housing.* Boston: Women's Institute for Housing and Economic Development.

Toronto Women's Housing Cooperative, Inc., The Beguinage (1982). "What is the Toronto Women's Housing Cooperative Inc.?" Mimeo.

Turner, John F.C. (1976). *Housing by People.* New York: Pantheon.

6

New Families, New Housing Needs, New Urban Environments: The Case of Single-Parent Families[1]

FRAN KLODAWSKY and ARON SPECTOR[2]

INTRODUCTION

After the Second World War, government policies supported a large-scale housing industry in order to provide housing for veterans and their families, encourage their employment, and promote economic expansion (Klodawsky, 1985).

Between 1945 and 1966, most new housing took the form of single-family suburban dwellings. Private developers, influenced by building codes and mortgage insurance incentives, primarily built detached homes for traditional, two-parent nuclear families. Community support facilities were rarely emphasized; it was assumed that families would fill most of their own needs with the help of the neighbourhood school and district shopping centre. For families unable to buy into this dream, social housing programmes, including public housing, were developed to provide temporary shelter until they could afford to purchase homes.

By the early 1960's, various changes were starting to affect housing policy. Central urban commercial facilities and adult-centred, high-rise apartments emerged, and much low-cost housing was cleared to make way. Centrally located housing for the poor became costly and difficult to find. At the same time, the dominance of two-parent families began to decline, while elderly households and mother-led, one-parent families increased.

The number of single-parent families with children under 18 has been growing extremely rapidly since divorce legislation was reformed in 1968. In 1966, roughly 4 per cent of families with children under 18 were headed by a single parent. By 1981, this percentage had grown to over 9 per cent. The 1986 estimates, at the time of writing, are that roughly 11 per cent of families with children under 18, over 550,000 families, will be headed by a single parent.

Single-parent families headed by women are predominantly poor, with family incomes averaging 52 per cent of those with two parents. In single-parent families, particularly those with children too young to help, a single adult undertakes what is usually the work of two. Female-headed single-parent families are resource poor but require the housing and community resources necessary for rearing children. It is thus not surprising that female single-parent families spend a much higher percentage of their income on shelter, on average, than any other family group.

This essay starts with a discussion of how single-parent family housing has arisen as an issue in Canadian cities. Within this context, a number of specific criteria for assessing adequate and amenable family housing are identified. The magnitude and growth of single-parent families and the nature of their income and housing problems are then reviewed. Statements as to the nature of the housing needs of single-parent families are then developed using the identified housing criteria.

SINGLE-PARENT FAMILY HOUSING AS AN ISSUE

Contemporary housing design and the structure of the housing market itself are, to a great degree, a reflection of traditional views of the life cycle (Rossi, 1955, 1982). The majority of urban Canadian adults are assumed to move from the family home to a series of apartments, then to a single-family home designed for child rearing, then possibly back to a condominium or rental unit (Social Planning Council of Metropolitan Toronto, 1979). The design of much urban and housing policy in Canada is predicated upon the assumption that during the full extent of the life cycle, each household unit is occupied by either a single unattached individual or a single nuclear family headed by a husband and wife. Extended family households are increasingly uncommon. In addition, within the last two decades older children have more frequently left the family home, and older adults have joined separate communities away from younger adults raising children. An outcome of all of these trends has been increasing demand for separate housing units, each occupied by smaller numbers of people.

Households containing single-parent families reflect these trends. Most single-parent families are separate, nuclear families. In contrast, in the previous "bulge" of single parenting which occurred during and following the Second World War, families were much more likely to become extensions of existing households. Today, single-parent families search in housing markets where only part of the housing is geared towards family rearing (ibid.).

Implicit in the life-cycle housing model is the central role of home ownership as an investment opportunity. The early part of the adult life cycle is seen as a period of savings in the expectation of accumulating a sufficient down payment for entry into the ownership market. For the great majority of Canadian families, paying off the home mortgage has represented the principal source of investment and savings. The house is an asset useable by the mature family for such functions as financing higher education and sustaining an adequate standard of living during retirement (Fallis, 1983; Goldberg, 1983).

Single-parent families, with income levels well below those of other family types, are thus faced with a number of problems in the housing market, primarily related to their inability to buy single-family owner-occupied homes. For this reason, they are, by and large, unable to take advantage of those housing and neighbourhood forms designed for child rearing. In addition, they are unable to allocate funds to shelter and savings at the same time in order to accumulate a down payment. Finally, they face the dual responsibility of maintaining and sustaining a family in an environment where these functions are usually undertaken by two adults (Brandwein, 1977).

HOUSING AND THE FAMILY: ASSESSMENT CRITERIA

What criteria can be used in evaluating the adequacy of the living conditions of a particular type of family? In the following, emphasis is placed upon the requisites for effectively producing an adequate environment for the physical and psychological health of family members. These criteria are drawn from literature on women and environments,[3] from general discussions on contemporary families,[4] and from housing policy analyses.[5] The following discussion provides an overview of ten common assessment criteria. (For a more extensive discussion of why these criteria were selected, see Klodawsky, Spector, and Rose, 1985, Chs. 2 and 6.)

Affordability

Can a family afford sufficient housing, and is there then sufficient income left over for other needs such as food and clothing? The meeting of this criterion depends upon a composite of family income level and housing supply (Goldberg, 1983, p. 11). Most Canadian single-parent families are faced with low incomes and reside in relatively tight housing markets (Canadian Council on Social Development, 1984; Metropolitan Toronto Planning Department, 1983b; Ontario New Democratic Party Caucus, 1984; Social Planning Council of Metropolitan Toronto, 1979).

Accessibility

Are family members able to reach required services, schools, and employment opportunities easily and expeditiously? Location and proximity are related to such factors as access to public and private transportation and the concentration of destinations (Hayden, 1981, 1984; Michelson, 1983; Wekerle, 1979/80).

Availability

Is there a sufficient stock of units suitable for family rearing? If so, are there any forms of discrimination in the housing market which restrict access? Historically, there has been little incentive to provide housing for low- and moderate-income families in the private sector of the Canadian housing market (Canada Mortgage and Housing Corporation, 1984b, 1985; City of Toronto Housing Department, 1982; Dennis and Fish, 1972; Metropolitan Toronto Planning Department, 1983a, 1983b). Various levels of government have intermittently added to the existing supply, either through direct provision or through subsidy and incentive programmes. In the case of single-parent housing, supply problems may be aggravated by discrimination (Gurstein and Hood, 1975).

Security of Tenure

Are units secure or is there a threat of loss because of such factors as unit conversion? In terms of raising a family, stable homes, neighbourhoods, and schooling have been identified as important factors which contribute to positive child development and adult mental health (Dulude, 1984; Eichler, 1983; Leavitt, 1984). This is particularly important for single-parent families who are in the process of adjusting to significant events such as marriage dissolution, death of a spouse, or the responsibility of a newborn child (Anderson-Khlief, 1981; Schorr and Moen, 1979; Weiss, 1984).

Appropriateness of Facilities for Children

Are there adequate nearby neighbourhood facilities for children, such as school playgrounds and child care services? Does the housing unit itself provide sufficient and safe play areas and allow parents to supervise young children? Multi-unit apartment buildings with play areas well away from kitchen and other adult work areas are disadvantageous in terms of adults being able to supervise children casually while carrying on with other necessary activities (see, for example, Hayden, 1984; Leavitt, 1984).

Household Maintenance

Can the unit be maintained at a reasonable level of repair given the financial and time resources of family members? This is a particular concern in single-parent households where there is often a shortage of both income and person power (see, for example, Hayden, 1984).

Opportunities for Sharing and Support

Does the housing unit and its surrounding environment facilitate neighbourhood support and possibly sharing if required? Are there community-based support and information facilities nearby? Community resources can often provide a substitute for missing family resources. Is there the potential to substitute or augment community resources for insufficient family resources? (see, for example, Simon, 1983; Soper, 1980).

Privacy

Do the house and the neighbourhood provide sufficient privacy for families? Does the housing itself convey unsatisfactory images to others? A criticism of large public housing developments has been that their variance from surrounding housing designs often leads to stereotyping and stigmatizing their inhabitants. In addition, inadequacies in areas such as soundproofing, private living, and play space affect family privacy and its nurturing capacity (see, for example, Ontario Standing Committee on the Administration of Justice, 1982).

Suitability for Transition

How flexible are financial and housing arrangements to the needs of families in both the short and long run? Family life implies constant transition (Dulude, 1984; Duncan and Morgan, 1984; Eichler, 1983). For single parents there are often dramatic adjustments, such as during and shortly after separation or after the birth of a child. For most, there is a period of learning to get along under new, and often trying, circumstances. For others, single parenthood represents a phase ending in remarriage. For many, the ability to move two or three times in a short period, culminating in a new stable environment, is important in the process of adjusting to a new equilibrium.

Cost Effectiveness in the Use of Public and Private Funds

Is the housing unit a cost-effective way to invest private and/or public funds? Given scarce family and public resources, which options are most cost effective in achieving nurturing environments? What are the social costs of not producing a fully adequate environment? What mix of public, private, and third sector housing is most effective in providing an appropriate mix of environments for single-parent families? (see, for example, Hayden, 1984).

SINGLE-PARENT HOUSING PROBLEMS IN THE CANADIAN CONTEXT

How Many Single Parents are There?[6]

The single parent population has been growing rapidly in recent years. For 1986, the estimates are that there were approximately 550,000 single parents with children under 18, or close to 11 per cent of all families raising children. Of these, the great majority—just under 500,000 families—will be headed by women.

Single parents on the whole are younger now and a greater number are becoming single parents either without marrying or through divorce. Between 1976 and 1982, the average age of single parents declined by over two years, from 39 to 37. During this period, the number of never-married single parents grew at an annual rate of 11 per cent, and divorced single parents at an annual rate of 9 per cent. In contrast, the number of separated single parents increased at an annual rate of 3.6 per cent while the number of widows and widowers declined at a rate of 0.6 per cent, primarily because of better health care.

Many single-parent families are in transition. For example, recently widowed single parents, who tend to have more mature families, often have children who enter the labour force shortly after the death of the spouse. Among never-married women who bear children, only 16 per cent will form single-parent families.

Among divorced single parents, there is a fairly high probability of remarriage, although the average period of single parenthood is long. We have estimated that in 1982 the mean number of years before remarriage among divorced single parents was 11.6 years for women and 9.71 years for men. This is roughly the same amount of time that children under 18 live with a single parent.

What are the Income, Education, and Employment Characteristics of Single-Parent Heads?

In 1981, single-parent families had markedly lower incomes than did husband/wife families. Mother-led families have incomes which are dramatically lower than that of husband/wife families (60 per cent lower on average in 1981) whereas male-headed single families have incomes that are only slightly lower (15 per cent lower). In 1981, roughly 56 per cent of female single-parent families were below the low income cutoff line defined by Statistics Canada. Income varies by the gender of the single parent, his or her age, and any dependence on public assistance.

The reasons for these income variations can be partially traced to the degree and type of labour force participation of single mothers. Only 61 per cent of female heads were in the work force in 1981. Among these women, 54 per cent were employed in low-paid service and clerical occupations.

Single mothers experience discrimination in the work force as do other women. In 1981, within all major job classifications, full-time employed women earned less than men. However, holding type of occupation constant, full-time employed single mothers in 1981 earned even less on average than other women (derived from Statistics Canada 1984a and 1985). As well as discrimination, this trend may be related to the inability of single parents to exercise choice among job opportunities or to be flexible about work time because of the restrictions imposed by child rearing. Exacerbating wage issues is the greater number of single mothers who are employed part-time.

An important future concern for single parents raising children is the loss of experience and seniority in the job market. While income for both men and women generally increases with age, the wage gap between the sexes also dramatically increases.

Among mother-led families, this factor is somewhat exaggerated by the low family income levels of those headed by young mothers. Those under 25 have an average income that is 32 per cent of other families. This is in contrast to a high of 71 per cent for those over 55. Compounding these problems was the large increase after 1982 in unemployed single mothers, particularly those under 25. It is not surprising, then, that the major source of income for over 70 per cent of young single mothers are government transfer payments. For those chiefly dependent on government assistance, average incomes were only 18 per cent of the two-parent family average income.

A factor which is not significant in explaining income and occupation differences is education. The number of years and level of education completed by single mothers are quite similar to those of other married women. Single mothers are marginally more likely to have completed high school than single fathers, although, like other women, they are less likely to have completed university or other post-secondary education.

In What Types of Housing Do Single Parents Live?[7]

Single parents are predominantly renters. In 1982, approximately 68 per cent rented in contrast to just over 26 per cent of other families with children. Among those that own, just over one-third were widowed. A promising trend, probably related to reform in divorce settlements, has been a 4 per cent decrease from 1978 to 1982 in the number of female single parents who rent. Like other Canadian renters, most single-parent families reside in multiple family dwellings. However, among Canadians renting row housing and detached dwellings, single parents considerably outnumber other household types.

The homes of single-parent families, like those of most Canadians, are rarely without basic amenities such as baths, toilets, and hot water. Indications of variations in other aspects of quality are, however, apparent. In 1982, for example, an estimated 16 per cent of single parents lived in housing requiring major repairs, in contrast to 11 per cent of all families. Another indication of quality, overcrowding, shows a different trend. In surveys conducted by Statistics Canada between 1978 and 1982, single-parent housing is consistently less crowded, in terms of rooms or bedrooms per person. This is probably related to the loss of an adult as well as the smaller average family size of single parent families.

Thus, given available measures housing quality issues for single-parent families centre on the design of available units and the level of repair of these units.

THE HOUSING PROBLEMS OF SINGLE-PARENT FAMILIES

The ten criteria identified above serve as a basis for examining the inter-relationships among housing, the dynamics of single-parent family life cycles and family policy issues. What are the particularly pressing housing-related issues for this group?

Affordability[8]

Because single-parent families are predominantly female headed, income is an especially significant problem. In all single-parent households, a primary concern is that the principal roles of family sustainer and income earner are played by a single person. Among female single parents there may be a dramatic and sudden reduction in income, while among male single parents the phenomenon is less frequent or extreme. Because of their incomes, male family heads are usually better able to purchase household and child support services.

Nevertheless, for all single-parent families, the loss of the co-parent through death or divorce or the absence of a co-parent when a child is born are times of disruption marked by declining income and disinvestment. According to 1982 estimates, two-parent family assets grew at an annual rate of 9.2 per cent, female single-parent assets by 2.1 per cent, and male single-parent assets by 6.47 per cent.

For single mothers, shelter is the single largest expenditure. In 1982, an average of 26 per cent of their expenditures were allocated to shelter. Among female single parents, this varied by position in the life cycle and tenure. Expenditures ranged from an average of over 36 per cent of total budget allocations for those under 25 to 19.6 per cent for those over 55. Renters allocated an average of 29.1 per cent of expenditures to shelter; home owners without mortgages allocated 15.4 per cent.

Particularly among poorer mother-led families, shelter and food dominate expenditures. Based on 1982 expenditure data, we estimate that for an average mother-led family earning $17,692 in 1982, $48.46 of every $100 spent is allocated to food and shelter, leaving $51.54 for other expenditures. Reducing income by a $100/month leads to an average extra $1.00 or 4 per cent shift toward each of food and shelter and away from other expenditures such as transportation and health services. For those earning less than $10,000, over $64 of every $100 is committed to food and shelter. At this level, there is little left for anything over and above basic survival.

Accessibility

One area where expenditures are low, and where they decline sharply with decreasing income, is transportation. Mother-led single-parent families spend roughly one-third less of their income on transportation than do other families. The major reason of course is that these families are less likely to own cars. Roughly 47 per cent of these families have no access to an automobile, in comparison to 11 per cent of two-parent households. Car ownership varies with age; those least likely to own cars are families with a female head under 25.

Reduced mobility may influence income, since it limits both job choice and access to services. For example, the job of ferrying children to school and reaching work on time without an automobile is a difficult task for many parents. Lack of capital to purchase a car and the cash flow to maintain it limit choices for single parents in the labour market. In turn, these tend to limit residential choices to relatively expensive but accessible and service-rich downtown locations in larger Canadian cities.

In general, single parents have clustered in large cities over the last decade, primarily to be near support services. In 1982, an estimated 96 per cent of female single-parent families lived in cities with a population of over 25,000.

Availability

There is an increasing tendency for central-city, moderate-cost rental housing to be converted to other uses, such as condominiums and higher priced rental housing, reducing the overall supply of low- and moderate-income housing (City of Toronto Housing Department, 1982; Mellett, 1983; Regional Municipality of Ottawa-Carleton Planning Department, 1984). The growth of poor- and moderate-income single-parent families puts further pressure on the shrinking supply. Single parents are thus heavily concentrated in subsidized low- and moderate-income housing. For example, in Ontario the majority of rent-geared-to-income and public housing units now accommodate female single-parent households. In Manitoba, in 1984, roughly 65 per cent of participants in the Shelter Allowance Program were single parents. With respect to differential rents paid by male and female single parents, evidence from the 1978 and 1982 family expenditure data indicates that female heads tend to pay about 1 per cent more for comparable units.

Discrimination against single parents in market rental housing may accentuate availability problems. There is evidence of discrimination by landlords against female single parents (Gurstein and Hood, 1975).

Security of Tenure

As we have seen, single mothers are mainly low- and moderate-income renters. They are thus prone to the vagaries of particularly tight housing markets. In many parts of Canada, low- and moderate-rent units have increasingly been converted to luxury apartments and condominiums, particularly affecting this group's security of tenure.

There is another security of tenure problem. Because publicly funded housing is geared towards providing relatively short-term relief for the poorest of families, once a single parent increases her income through employment and/or through the earnings of teenage children, she may have her rent increased and eventually be required to vacate her unit. (In Ontario this is true when children are out of school and over 18 years of age.)

Appropriateness of Facilities for Children

There is no information available on the adequacy of low-income housing for child rearing generally, let alone for single-parent families. There is some evidence, however, that for the great majority of single-parent families, housing units have basic amenities and are in relatively good condition. The potential exists for further evaluation using available National Housing Act (NHA) design guidelines for play spaces and unit design appropriate for children of all ages in various types of housing units.

Approximately 46 per cent of young single parents (those under 35 in 1981) live in multiple-unit apartment complexes in large cities. These are not often designed with appropriate facilities for single-parent child-rearing. Aside from the conscious effort to provide supportive environments in specific circumstances, such as in the Constance Hamilton Coop in Toronto (Simon, 1983), the provision of safe play environments with areas for parental supervision is haphazard.

Household Maintenance

In 1982, mother-led families spent, on average, about 30 per cent more of their incomes on household maintenance, excluding child care, than did two-parent families. There is also a higher probability that single-parent homes require major repair. The loss of a parent puts an additional onus on the remaining adult, and sometimes on other family members, to provide the missing services either through purchase or additional effort. For women-headed single-parent families, there are shortages of both time and income. As a result, a great number of single-family detached houses, particularly units sheltering widowed and older, recently divorced single parents, have problems relating to irregular and inadequate maintenance. There has been little work in the area of housing design for single-parent families with respect to ongoing maintenance (Leavitt [1984] is a notable exception).

Opportunities for Sharing and Support

Alternatives to better design are shared living arrangements that permit pooling maintenance tasks among groups of single parents or between single parents and others.

Extended families, neighbours, and other community members may be prepared to help lone parents with some of their tasks, including child care, transportation, and sharing information.

A number of single parents, particularly those who have never married, become part of an extended family. In many cases, this can lead to conflicts over issues such as privacy and child rearing, as Anderson-Khleif notes (1981). Being part of an extended family, though, does seem to have the benefit of aiding short-term adjustments to single parenthood (MacKay and Austin, 1983).

Providing collective child care and car pooling are examples of activities that are easily organized when single-parent housing is clustered. Child care, however, may require space in community centres or schools.

There are indications that shared housing arrangements help reduce housing costs, distribute various household responsibilities such as maintenance and child rearing, and, in some case, encourage emotional support from empathetic peers. However, having appropriate private, public,and collective space in shared housing appears to be important to its success (Leavitt, 1984; Ontario Ministry of Muncipal Affairs and Housing, 1983).

Privacy

For many single parents, the wish to present themselves as "normal" families is important. In the past, large, badly designed and constructed public housing developments were built in part to prevent poor families from being able to satisfy this feeling (Dennis and Fish, 1972). While such families may wish, and require, enhanced support from the community and from neighbours, the appearance of normalcy is nonetheless crucial. "Privacy," in the sense of an environment that does not stigmatize the household, is thus a significant criterion for single-parent families.

In partial response to the "stigmatization" problem, the construction of large public housing projects was replaced during the 1970's by the building of social housing communities designed to "fit" within the surrounding community and suit tenants with a range of incomes. However, this income integration has, in some cases, resulted in isolation and the stigmatization of being obviously different than most of one's neighbours (Ontario Standing Committee on the Administration of Justice, 1982).

A potential alternative to traditional social housing options is to promote "intensification" strategies that encourage expanded use of housing stock that is too large for individual households. This approach encourages both the stabilization of population in older neighbourhoods and the continued viability of local services. Such strategies increase modest-cost housing opportunities for single-parent families in neighbourhoods with a variety of household types (see, for example, Ontario Ministry of Municipal Affairs and Housing, 1983).

Suitability for Transition

Housing needs vary for different single-parent families at different stages of transition. At one end of the spectrum could be a need for short-term emergency shelter. Somewhere "in the middle" is perhaps a need to start again, perhaps in rented accommodation without the encumbrance of long-term commitments. At the other end is a need for long-term housing in which to establish a stable, nurturing environment.

Housing options are needed which recognize that transition takes forms different from those experienced by nuclear families. Central to such options is mutual support, which might be achieved by mixing tenure forms and families in different stages of adjustment.

The case of older, widowed single parents is somewhat different. These women often have homes without mortgages, and loss of regular income becomes the main problem. Options that enhance mutual support could be encouraged, including having other single parents as boarders, and setting up mini cooperatives.

Cost-Effectiveness in the Use of Public and Private Funds

Fundamentally, effective use of public and private funds in the case of single parents must be judged by the overall ability to create nurturing environments for raising children. Several policy thrusts are needed. One is affordable housing units. Further thrusts should recognize the employment and wage prospects for women given their loss of experience in the labour force as a result of child rearing. There are special needs for job training and accessible child care.

CONCLUSION

Single-parent housing problems are income and resource problems. Because roughly 85 per cent of single parents are women, their problems relate to a differentiated labour market in which women's employment income is much less than men's. Moves towards resolving this general problem are also moves toward improving the housing and other living conditions of single-parent families.

The income problem is exacerbated by the "opportunity costs" of child rearing. Women lose experience and job opportunities when raising young children. When they do enter the labour market, they are often limited in the jobs they are able to take and the hours that they are able to work. Given their initial low income levels, they are often unable to afford cars which help them seek and choose jobs, housing, child care, shopping, and other opportunities. Single parents are thus often caught in a "web" of poverty aggravated by a general loss of experience and social and physical mobility.

In addition to inadequate income is the problem of lost adult resources. Housing and neighbourhoods have been designed to suit conventional life cycle patterns. The job of maintaining a household, of shopping, cleaning, and fixing, is onerous when combined with raising children and earning a living. Housing designed so that tasks such as cooking and child supervision cannot be easily shared with others or so that large amounts of maintenance are required increase the burden. In effect, the single parent lives as one adult in a world designed for nuclear families with two adults.

Lastly, the characteristics of single-parent families vary greatly and therefore call for varied solutions. Never-married single parents (often under 25, with infant children, and little job experience) is the group requiring the most comprehensive support. Divorced single parents, in contrast, often require short-term help to get through a traumatic adjustment period before re-entering the job market. Women between 25 and 44 make up the largest and fastest growing group of single parents. For these parents, part of the problem lies beyond income and maintenance in the areas of job retraining, more stringent definitions and enforcement policies regarding child support from absentee parents, and physical environments more compatible with doing both paid and domestic work.

Key policy questions in the context of lost income and human resources in single-parent families are the degree to which social and community services can complement the remaining store of family resources, and how these could be further developed and made more accessible.

Not addressing the housing and community needs of single-parent families can only lead to generations of destitute older women and children who have not been able to achieve their skill and aptitude potentials. The costs of refusing to deal with this problem are therefore enormous. Such a refusal would also indicate that Canadians were abandoning the tradition that has underpinned social policy since the 1930's, that is, using public resources for the effective development of Canada's social capital. Surely single-parent families deserve a continuation of this tradition of public support for the development of their potential.

NOTES

1. The report upon which this paper is based, *Single Parent Families and Canadian Housing Policies: How Mothers Lose* (1985), was carried out with the assistance of a grant from Canada Mortgage and Housing Corporation under the terms of the External Research Program (CR File No.: 6585 S8-2). The views expressed are those of the authors and do not represent the official views of the corporation.

2. The authors of this paper, listed alphabetically, accept full and equal responsibility for its contents.

3. See for example, Anderson-Khlief, 1981; Gerson, 1983; Gurstein and Hood, 1975; Hayden, 1981, 1984; Jordan, 1981; Leavitt, 1984; McClain and Doyle, 1983; Michelson, 1983; Netter and Price, 1983; Rose, 1984; Simon, 1983; Soper, 1980; Wekerle, 1979/80.

4. See for example, Armitage, 1978; Armstrong and Armstrong, 1982; Brandwein, 1977; Canadian Council on Social Development, 1984; Dulude, 1984; Duncan and Morgan, 1984; Eichler, 1984; MacKay and Austin, 1983; Ontario New Democratic Party Caucus, 1984; Priest, 1984; Schorr and Moen, 1979; Voluntary Children's Services Coordinating Committee of Ottawa-Carleton, 1984; Weiss, 1984; White, 1983.

5. Baer, 1979; British Columbia Housing Management Commission, 1983; Canada Housing and Mortgage Corporation, 1984a, 1984b, 1985; City of Toronto Housing Department, 1982; City of Vancouver Planning Department, 1983a, 1983b; Dennis and Fish, 1972; Dowler, 1983; Fallis, 1980, 1983; Goetze, 1983; Lapointe *et al.,* 1982; Metropolitan Toronto Planning Department, 1983a, 1983b; Ontario Ministry of Municipal Affairs and Housing, 1983; Ontario Standing Committee on the Administration of Justice, 1982; Regional Municipality of Ottawa-Carleton Planning Department, 1984; Schubert, 1982; Social Planning Council of Metropolitan Toronto, 1979; Zamprelli and Everett, 1982.

6. Data in the following sections concerning basic demography, income, labour force status and participation, tenure and income for single parents is derived by the authors from the 1981 Census Public Use Sample Tape family and household file (Statistics Canada, 1985) and from Vital Statistics published by Statistics Canada annually.

7. Housing quality and automobile access data in the following sections is derived from the micro data file compiled from the Statistics Canada Household Inventory, Fixtures and Equipment surveys of 1978, 1980, and 1982 (Statistics Canada, 1981, 1983, and 1984c).

8. Expenditure data in the following sections is derived or estimated from the micro data file of the Statistics Canada Family Expenditures Surveys of 1978 and 1982 (Statistics Canada 1982 and 1984b).

REFERENCES

Anderson-Khlief, S. (1981). "Housing Needs of Single Parent Mothers." In Suzanne Keller (Ed.), *Building for Women*. Lexington: Lexington Books.

Armitage, A. (1978). "Canada." In S. Kamerman and A. Kahn (Eds.), *Family Policy: Government and Families in Fourteen Countries*. New York: Columbia University Press.

Armstrong, Pat and Armstrong, Hugh (1982). *The Double Ghetto*. 2d ed. Toronto: McClelland and Stewart.

Baer, W.C. (1979). "Empty Housing Space: An Overlooked Resource." *Policy Studies Journal, 8*(2), pp. 220-27.

Brandwein, R. (1977). "After Divorce: A Focus on Single Parent Families. *The Urban and Social Change Review, 10.*

British Columbia Housing Management Commission (1983). *Canadian Social Housing Managed by Provincial and Territorial Housing Corporations: Comparative Characteristics*. Victoria: British Columbia Housing Management Commission.

Canada Mortgage and Housing Corporation (1984a). *Canadian Housing Statistics, 1983*. Ottawa: Statistical Services Division, Canada Mortgage and Housing Corporation.

Canada Mortgage and Housing Corporation (1984b). *Section 56.1 Non-Profit and Cooperative Housing Program Evaluation*. Ottawa: Program Evaluation Division, Canada Mortgage and Housing Corporation.

Canada Mortgage and Housing Corporation (1985). *Consultation Paper on Housing*. Ottawa: Canada Mortgage and Housing Corporation.

Canadian Council on Social Development (1984). *Not Enough: The Meaning and Measurement of Poverty*. Ottawa: Canadian Council on Social Development.

City of Toronto Housing Department (1982). *Shifting Foundations*. Toronto: City of Toronto.

City of Vancouver Planning Department (1983a). *Provision of Affordable Rental Housing through the Private Sector*. Vancouver: City of Vancouver.

City of Vancouver Planning Department (1983b). *Who Lives in Non-Market Housing?* Vancouver: City of Vancouver.

Dennis, M. and Fish, S. (1972). *Low Income Housing: Programs in Search of a Policy*. Ottawa: Canada Mortgage and Housing Corporation.

Dowler, Robert G. (1983). *Housing-Related Tax Expenditures: An Overview and Evaluation*. Major Report No. 22. Toronto: Centre for Urban and Community Studies.

Dulude, Louise (1984). *Love, Marriage and Money: An Analysis of Financial Relations Between the Spouses*. Ottawa: Canadian Advisory Council on the Status of Women.

Duncan, Greg and Morgan, James (1984). "An Overview of Family Economic Mobility." In *Years of Poverty, Years of Plenty*. Ann Arbor: Institute of Social Research, University of Michigan.

Eichler, Margrit (1983). *Families in Canada Today*. Toronto: Gage.

Fallis, George (1980). *Housing Programs and Income Distribution in Ontario*. Toronto: Ontario Economic Council.

Fallis, George (1983). *Housing Decisions in a Life Cycle Framework.* Ottawa: External Research Awards, Canada Mortgage and Housing Corporation.

Gerson, K. (1983). "Changing Family Structure and the Position of Women." *Journal of the American Planning Association, 49*(2), pp. 138-48.

Goetze, Rolf (1983). *Rescuing the American Dream: Public Policies and the Crisis in Housing.* New York: Holmes and Meier.

Goldberg, Michael (1983). *The Housing Problem: A Real Crisis?* Vancouver: University of British Columbia Press.

Gurstein, P. and Hood, N. (1975). *Housing Needs of One Parent Families.* Vancouver: YWCA.

Hayden, Dolores (1984). "What Would a Non-Sexist City Be Like?" In C. Stimpson et al. (Eds.), *Women and the North American City* (pp. 167-84). Chicago: University of Chicago Press.

Hayden, Dolores (1984). *Redesigning the American Dream.* New York: W. W. Norton.

Jordan, E. (1981). *The Housing Needs of Female-Led One Parent Families.* Ottawa: Canada Mortgage and Housing Corporation, External Research Awards.

Klodawsky, Fran. (1985). *Accumulation, the State, and Community Struggles: Impacts on Toronto's Built Environment, 1945 to 1972.* Ph.D. Diss., Queen's University.

Klodawsky, F., Spector, A., and Hendrix, C. (1983). *The Housing Needs of Single Parent Families in Canada.* Ottawa: Canada Mortgage and Housing Corporation, External Research Awards.

Klodawsky, F., Spector, A., and Rose, D. (1985). *Single Parent Families and Canadian Housing Policies: How Mothers Lose.* Ottawa: Canada Mortgage and Housing Corporation.

Lapointe, Yolande, Lenk, Anna, Meessen, Diane, and Milroy, Beth Moore (1982). *A Study of Tenant Displacement Associated with the Residential Rehabilitation Assistance Program in Ottawa.* Ottawa: School of Urban and Regional Planning, University of Ottawa.

Leavitt, J. (1984). "The Shelter Plus Issue for Single Parents." *Women and Environments, 6*(2), pp. 16-20.

MacKay, H. and Austin, C. (1983). *Single Adolescent Mothers in Ontario.* Ottawa: Canadian Council on Social Development.

McClain, Janet and Doyle, Cassie (1983). *Women as Housing Consumers.* Ottawa: Canadian Council on Social Development.

Mellett, Cathy (1983). *At the End of the Rope.* Halifax: Women's Emergency Housing Coalition.

Metropolitan Toronto Planning Department (1983a). *Program Evaluation and Five Year Targets: Metro Toronto Assisted Housing Study, Part II.* Toronto: Metropolitan Toronto Planning Department.

Metropolitan Toronto Planning Department (1983b). *Determination of the Need for Assisted Housing: Metro Toronto Assisted Housing Study, Part I.* Toronto: Metropolitan Toronto Planning Department.

Michelson, William (1983). "The Logistics of Maternal Employment: Implications for Women and Their Families." In *Child in the City Report no. 18.* Toronto: University of Toronto, Centre for Urban and Community Studies.

Netter, E. and Price, R. (1983). "Zoning and the Nouveau Poor." *Journal of the American Planning Association, 49*(2), pp. 171-89.

Ontario Ministry of Municipal Affairs and Housing (1983). *Study of Residential Intensification and Rental Housing Conservation Part I: Detailed Summary of Findings and Recommendations.* Toronto: The Ministry of Municipal Affairs and Housing.

Ontario New Democratic Party Caucus (1984). *The Other Ontario.* Toronto: Ontario New Democratic Party.

Ontario Standing Committee on the Administration of Justice (1982). *Report on the Ontario Housing Corporation and Local Housing Authorities.* Toronto: Committee on the Administration of Justice.

Priest, Gordon (1984). "The Family Life Cycle and Housing Consumption in Canada: A Review Based on 1981 Census Data." In *Canadian Statistical Review.* Ottawa: Statistics Canada.

Regional Municipality of Ottawa-Carleton Planning Department (1984). *Regional Housing Statement Update.* Ottawa: Regional Municipality of Ottawa-Carleton.

Rose, Damaris (1984). "Rethinking Gentrification: Beyond the Uneven Development of Marxist Urban Theory." *Environment and Planning D: Society and Space, 2*(1), pp. 47-74.

Rossi, Peter (1955). *Why Families Move.* Glencoe, Illinois: Free Press.

Rossi, Peter (1982). *Why Families Move Revisited.* Berkeley, California: Sage.

Schorr, Alvin and Moen, Phyllis (1979). "The Single Parent and Public Policy." *Social Policy, 9*(5), pp. 15-21.

Schubert, Saul (1982). "The Evaluation of Housing Allowance Programs." In Janet McClain (Ed.), *And Where Do We Go from Here?* Ottawa: Canadian Council on Social Development.

Simon, J. (1983). "Housing by and for Women: The Constance Hamilton Coop." In Judith Kjellberg (Ed.), *Women in/and Planning: Proceedings of a Conference.* Toronto: University of Toronto, Centre for Urban and Community Studies.

Social Planning Council of Metropolitan Toronto (1979). *Metro's Suburbs in Transition Part 1: Evolution and Overview* Background Report. Toronto: Social Planning Council of Metropolitan Toronto.

Soper, M. (1980). "Housing for Single Parents: A Women's Design." In G. Wekerle, R. Peterson, D. Morley (Eds.), *New Space for Women.* Boulder: Westview.

Voluntary Children's Services Coordinating Committee of Ottawa-Carleton (1984). *The Needs of Young Single Parents in Ottawa-Carleton.* Ottawa: Voluntary Children's Services Coordinating Committee of Ottawa-Carleton.

Weiss, Robert (1984). "The Impact of Marital Dissolution on Income and Consumption in Single-Parent Households." *Journal of Marriage and the Family, 46*(10), pp. 115-27.

Wekerle, G. (1979/80). "Urban Planning: Making It Work for Women." *Status of Women News, 6*(1).

White, Julie (1983). *Women and Part-Time Work.* Ottawa: Canadian Advisory Council on the Status of Women.

Zamprelli, Jim and Everett, Heide (1982). "Administering a Housing Allowance to Low-Income Families." In Janet McClain (Ed.), *And Where Do We Go from Here?* Ottawa: Canadian Council on Social Development.

7

Interacting with the Urban Environment: Two Case Studies of Women's and Female Adolescents' Leisure Activities

DENISE PICHÉ

In discussing theoretical and structural perspectives for the study of women and the urban environment, one could start by reviewing the work done since Lofland's "the thereness of women" (1975; see also Dagenais, 1980; Masson, 1984). Another approach, which is also appealing would be to look at urban studies in the light of the extremely valuable guidelines for non-sexist research put together by Margrit Eichler and Jeanne Lapointe for the Social Sciences and Humanities Research Council (1985). Further, how revealing an exercise it would be to examine the conscience of urban studies and urban planning with respect to what Eichler calls the deadly sins of sexist research (1985).[1] Would not such sins be plentiful, such as the sins of overextension of concepts when defining residential environments as private places and as rest areas for work done elsewhere? Would we not identify as sins of under specification the use of generic terms for such sex-specific situations as the typical car-driver in our transportation models or the reference to sex-indeterminate beneficiaries in urban plans and policies? Surely, we would not be surprised to find the sin of slothful slackness in the use of the stereotyped idea of the family.

However, my point of view here is more restricted, limited essentially to proposing and discussing one approach to the study of women's relationships with the environment: the study of women's experience of the city within the context of action research (Lewin, 1948), and what I would daringly call an interactive study of the feminization of urban culture.

Urban studies are at least partly aimed at producing more enlightened planning decisions, and planning is aimed at creating the world of tomorrow. Since these fields of investigation have generalized their view of urban society on the basis of only one sex, it is a priority to learn about women's experiences, representations, and aspirations to straighten out our biased knowledge and policies. As Hayden (1980) has tried to illustrate with her student projects for a non-sexist city, tomorrow could be planned differently if women are involved and taken into consideration.

However, it would be wrong to think that any interview with any woman would lead the planner to feminist Utopia.[2] Moreover, a feminist planner, even though conscious of the duality of urban experience, cannot give a ready-made answer to questions such as whether we should plan for women's needs as they are expressed in a sexually segregated society or plan for a changing society. The women's movement is carrying a major cultural change, but as with all major cultural transformations, its social projects are tried out, evaluated, and monitored in a dynamic process rather than having specific objectives from the beginning.

In this context, research for women, in the sense of "research that tries to take women's needs, interests and experiences into account and aims at being instrumental in improving women's lives in one way or another" (Duelli Klein, 1983, p. 90), raises questions about the nature and role of an appropriate methodology. On the other hand, learning about women's needs, interests and experiences calls for methods that will free our knowledge of all sexist assumptions and also free women's speech of its conditioned responses to the environment. It also calls for research projects that will take the form of "qualitative and descriptive studies, taxonomies of situations, systematic analysis of situations and just plain talking to people and observing them" (Reinharz, 1983, p. 173). Without a deep understanding of the experience of women, the stance for equality could result in the decline of their values and their integration into a world that they reject. On the other hand, the concern for the improvement of women's conditions often leads the researcher to opt for action research: an approach suited to supporting the actions and political aims of the women's movement and to documenting women's lives and strategies for change. (See, for example, Bowles and Duelli Klein, 1983; Dagenais, 1986; and Roberts, 1981.)

Feminist urban studies follow a similar pattern. For instance, many different women's projects in the city have been studied and reported. (See, for example, Keller, 1981; Wekerle et al., 1980, and the journals *Ekistics,* 1985; *International Journal of Urban and Regional Research,* 1978; *Signs: Journal of Women and Culture in Society,* 1980; and *Women and Environments,* 1976-87). Still another direction for research is investigating women's images and desires in a consciousness-raising approach that exposes the alienating effects of sexual oppression and liberates women's capacity to plan a non-sexist future.[3] Drawing upon two ongoing case studies, I shall try to illustrate that the latter approach can be fruitful with women who have not yet been at the forefront of urban projects.

One aim of these studies was to examine women's representations of their own leisure activities and leisure environment. Because leisure is defined by both its character of freedom and its socioeconomic range of activities, it was thought that the study of this area of human activity would facilitate a comprehension of both women's culture and their unequal condition. There is reason to believe that in spite of inequality of access to official leisure activities, women develop a form of leisure that remains invisible and undervalued on the fringe of the dominant world. This qualitative approach questions the unconscious sins of sexist planning such as the understated concept of family recreation, the apparently neutral investments in ice rinks and lighted baseball grounds, and the implicit assumption that a sports centre or an art centre are experienced similarly by men and women.

The first study here is at the stage of preliminary field work prior to action research. It consists of group interviews with married women with children, active in their homes and the community and as members of various women's or voluntary organizations, and of interviews with female adolescents from a public school. The women were interviewed about their urban experiences during their free time or leisure activities. These interviews focused on the social representation of these experiences rather than on the quantity and spatial range of their activities (see Szalai et al., 1972; Vandelac et al. 1984).[4] The study was done in a small town (5,000 inhabitants) and its rural vicinity, located in an economically depressed region which was, at the time, the object of major planning operations.[5]

The group interviews lasted for approximately two hours, and they brought together from four to seven persons. The participants in the four groups of women were selected by the various women's organizations in the community. The women varied greatly with regard to their age and their husbands' socioeconomic status, but they were all active in the community. The six groups of adolescents were selected by the public school's counsellor responsible for sociocultural activities: he was asked to organize groups of adolescents aged 13 and 14 years and others aged 15 to 17 years. The participants differed in terms of place of residence, family socioeconomic status, rate of participation in formal leisure activities, and favourite pastime.

The second study resulted from the demands of the tenants' association of the largest public housing development in Quebec City (1,400 residents; 446 apartments) for replanning and redesigning the whole site, paying special attention to adolescents' needs[6] and to those of women-headed families. In this case, we are still involved in participant observation and have completed a first proposal for the site. Here we have worked with the tenants' association, composed mainly of women, including many single parents and elderly widows. We also reached two groups of adolescents involved in organizing activities for youth. We have yet to reach women and female adolescents who do not participate in any community activity.

It must be said that, because of the state and nature of these case studies, the observations reported here cannot be applied to all women nor even to women sharing the same socioeconomic status as our respondents. They can only illustrate the importance of recognizing the sexual differentiation of environmental experience for the construction of unbiased urban theories and for the development of democratic planning processes.

WOMEN'S REPRESENTATIONS OF THEIR LEISURE TIME

The analysis here focuses on the nature of leisure for women, on how and where they seek leisure activities, on the constraints they feel, on their wants and desires in terms of leisure environments, and, to conclude, on their means to make these wants and desires known to planners and urban authorities.

As is the case with other workers, our respondents understood leisure time as the adverse of work. Since their unpaid work is domestic and entails organization and management of family life, and since their main work involves their homes, leisure for them is mainly getting away from home and from activities associated with it. This perspective clearly inverts their husbands' ideas of their own leisure, as they report it, which is often to take refuge in the home. Leisure is expressed by many as a way of preserving one's personal integrity and maintaining a balance with one's compulsory work load. The character of unpaid domestic work includes confinement, monotony, and continuous pressure from family demands (Friedan, 1963; Oakley, 1974; Vandelac et al., 1984). It is thus not surprising to find that leisure is conceived of in terms of meeting people, especially adults, getting away from home and child supervision, and/or resting alone.

Leisure time must be actively sought and set aside because women's work activities are endless and tied to the essentials of everyday life. In this context, free time is infrequently offered or given. Often, it seems that a special additional energy investment is required of our respondents to find free time and to occupy it with their own projects. Therefore, a profit must follow the extra investment. Whereas this profit could be sought in personal pleasure and gratification, our interviewees valued sociocultural activities; they have learned to forget themselves. Therefore, when their leisure activity is not strictly aimed at recuperating from fatigue, they turn to activities which offer social recognition. Their own physical fitness does not, in our investigation, appear as a motive; instead, it is treated as a hedonist achievement that is not meant for them.[7]

Family and domestic activities are hard work, and family members impose sharp limits on the chief homemaker's leisure time. Therefore, women often experience family leisure as work. Nevertheless, it can also become a valued leisure activity for them by permitting shifts both in work roles and in social life, providing that constant responsibility for children is relaxed, domestic tasks are reduced, and social relations are enhanced. These conditions account for the great success of permanent camping grounds during holiday periods. These places, at least on the surface, correspond to the dream of an idealized primitive or past society which is latent in some feminist thought:[8] a communal and integrated response to life requirements together with a "get away from it all" attitude in reaction to the regular demands of industrial and consumer society and, in the case of women, to the requirements of domesticity (see Cerullo and Ewen, 1984; Morville-Descolonges, 1978). Another way that domestic work can be experienced as leisure is when it requires special skills and competence and is socially recognized as an achievement of women's culture and traditions. An example is craftwork, an important activity among our respondents.

The home, although it is the work environment of our respondents, can become a place for leisure between periods of work when they can gain enough privacy to indulge in crafts, reading, seeing friends, or simply being by themselves. It is striking that television is not a valued leisure activity; it is rather a last resort to get away, especially in the restricted space of a public housing apartment.

Outside the home, our respondents seek public life and social contacts, often within the extended family, and they prefer unorganized, informal types of leisure activities, such as going to restaurants with friends, walking in the neighbourhood, or shopping. Even in sport and physical activity, they want to be able to go at their own rhythm. The only organized forms of leisure that are valued by these women are related to women's associations,[9] craft courses, and volunteer work. Although feminist studies tend to interpret these activities, especially community work, as unpaid work typical of women (Vandelac et al., 1984), women engaged in it see it as part of leisure. Their personal satisfaction emerging from these activities occurs because it is taking place in public life, in contrast to the majority of their activities which take place in the private and invisible domestic sphere. These means of association are important because they are the channels through which our respondents enjoy other activities such as local fairs, "days out," and facilities for craftwork. The craft courses in municipal recreational programmes are appreciated, but they are also criticized for being superficial and ill-equipped for practice after the sessions.

Constraints on leisure are numerous and were well-identified in the interviews. The main constraints are domestic and family tasks, with the responsibility for children being most demanding.

Financial constraints also limited access to leisure facilities, to services for replacing women's formal work, to transportation, and even to the required equipment for an activity. The women interviewed in the first study work out ingenious strategies to compensate for their economic dependency: they exchange books, travel with one another, or join women's associations where they can enjoy an inexpensive public life. However, to get organized like this, women must have minimum financial resources. In the public housing estate of the second study, poverty excludes them from most public and private services and activities and swells the burden of child care since the children also cannot get away. This poverty reinforces their feeling that they are segregated from the rest of the community. Few women feel in control of their environment in this case.

A third constraint perceived by our respondents is the instability of leisure programmes offered to them. They often mention activities that are not reliable or are cancelled for lack of participants. They also regret that their projects are not taken seriously by the municipal authorities. This lack of concern is interpreted by them as a devaluation of what they are and as a treatment of their leisure activities as superfluous pastimes. Women are here describing a subtle form of sexism that is detrimental to the development of new attitudes and behaviours.

These reality-based perceptions of constraints and lack of control over the environment can lead deprived women to social withdrawal. However, it does seem to bring many other women close together in informal social activities and structured women's associations. In this way, our respondents assert their belief in the power of their groups and in the autonomy they gain as members.

This overview of our respondents' perceptions of their leisure time leads us now to their perceptions of the urban environment. The places most often referred to are those accommodating informal activities and support-ive of a variety of uses. Women may refer here to the home if they have a space of their own and a neighbourhood supportive of the supervision of children. More often, they talk about a series of accessible and amenable urban places, like the street or the commercial centre, which provide a context for social interactions. They visit public places which are accessible, open, and friendly (see Lofland, 1984), especially when they are located in a natural or exceptional environment. However, women in our two studies differ on this point. Women in the public housing estate would need such resources close to their homes to use them with a feeling of security. It seems that they need to feel secure in proximate places before reaching out to a larger environment.

In contrast to places with informal rules, behaviour settings operating with a rigid organization and a fixed schedule, like the sports centre and the cultural centre, are not appealing to our respondents. These places do not belong to them.

A study of the characteristics of the local camping ground could be instructive for planners. What is appreciated about this setting? Is it the easy transition between privacy and community? The easy supervision of children? The sharing and visibility of domestic work? The provision of facilities and space for varied activities and games? The social mix of the users? Or simply the commercial Disneyland fiesta atmosphere?

However, on the whole, the greatest desire spelled out by the women who were interviewed is to find a roof for their shared activities and projects. They are constantly fighting for space: for their meetings; for handicrafts; for a municipal library; even for providing community services like support for the elderly, accommodation for women facing crises, and so on. In the same vein, just simply going out and about is a strong ambition of our respondents. This activity requires means of transportation that are flexible and under their control; the struggle for transportation might become another important issue for women.

The women in the first study express only two reservations about the future of their environment. First, they are fearful that the development of tourist facilities in their region might not be conceived of primarily as being for the needs of the local community. Second, they do not like large-scale festivals when the community loses control over the use of its environment to outsiders. In the second study, many women seem insecure in public environments, and they resent both the changes to their housing project imposed by the public housing corporation and the fact that their own demands are never taken into consideration.

In sum, the portrait of their leisure activities painted by the women interviewed is simple and clear. Is it read and understood by planners and urban authorities? If not, why not? Our respondents admit that they are consulted over recreational programmes and that they are aware of public hearings over planning objectives, but during the course of the group interviews, there was uneasiness over this topic. The participants felt something was wrong with their unwillingness to get involved, but they could not explain this. With further probing we discovered that, on the one hand, they are not really concerned by the questions asked or the object put forward for discussion during public hearings. On the other hand, they feel that their own priorities do not fit the general framework of the consultations and that they are often swept aside for their irrelevancy.

Many studies have shown the discrepancy between the understanding planners have of the environment and the way citizens experience it (for

French analysis, see Ledrut, 1973; Raymond, 1984; Ostrowetsky, 1983). We can see here that this is the case between planners and women. For instance, women are asked in surveys if they prefer to attend a lace-making course or physical fitness training when, in fact, they really want a women's centre or a well-equipped workshop where they could exercise their handicraft skills. In our first case study, social and health services were left off the agenda entirely when planners consulted citizens about priorities for the development of their region. Requests from the workshop organized by women concerning these particular subjects could not be fitted into the planning framework.

If these different representations of the environment and the lack of communication are to be over come, planners must begin searching for women's own terms of reference. For this purpose, research on women's social representations can be an important, although insufficient, support. These representations are modified with rapid social transformations, and women develop better strategies for the future as they become more conscious of their own interpretations of the environment; consequently research and action must become intermingled and carried on longitudinally. Planners and researchers experience the same situation: they simultaneously help create the conditions for change and study the process of that change.

ADOLESCENTS' REPRESENTATIONS OF THEIR LEISURE TIME

The mothers interviewed in the first study were very optimistic about the young generation in terms of its leisure activities. They believe their children are generally developing healthy leisure habits and do not see any discrimination working against their daughters. In the public housing estate, the situation is perceived differently: women see their children hanging around, and they blame the urban authorities for not offering proper services. But the mothers seem more sensitive to the effect of this situation on male adolescents than on female, most probably because male deviant behaviour is more noticeable.

In studies on adolescence, reality appears in a different light and it is far less comforting. Generally, it seems that the mechanisms of social reproduction are still efficient in modelling sexual differentiation in adolescence. For instance, surveys in Quebec show that female adolescents value family life more than careers and that they consequently continue to confine their career choices to traditional female sectors (Radio-Canada, 1979; Roberge et al., 1979). Unfortunately, there is a dearth of research on their spatial behaviour and strategies.[10] Hill's study of Toronto's ninth-graders is a rare source on the leisure time of adolescents (1980). Some of his findings are not surprising: girls show more social orientation in their leisure behaviour than boys, their involvement in sports is much less important, (de Koninck et al., 1983) and their spatial mobility is more limited. But Hill also found that males and females do not differ between them as much as individual adolescents differ from one another. Independently of their sex, some adolescents will be active in sports and some in cultural activities; others will spend most of their time just socializing. Girls involved in sports will behave much the same way as their male counterparts, although their numbers will be fewer.

The preliminary study presented here bears no comparison in scope with Hill's survey. Nonetheless, it is possible to draw from our interviews some observations on adolescents' concept of leisure, their leisure activities, their favourite environments, the constraints they feel, and some of their desires.

Unlike their mothers, female adolescents enjoy a lot of free time. Their leisure activities follow on from each other with much time devoted to socializing. As is the case for their mothers, domestic chores are not generally considered by them as leisure activities, although some specific domestic activities may be considered as leisure if the outcome is a sign of having a special skill. Also, unpaid or paid work outside the home is usually considered as leisure.

For the adolescents interviewed, having company is on the whole extremely important. However, their personalities seem to vary over a continuum between two poles. We find, at one end, adolescents who are self-willed and pursue their activities mainly to enjoy themselves and to achieve their goals and, at the other end, adolescents who are mainly looking for company and seeking the recognition of their peers. The variety of activities performed by the first group seems greater and these girls complain much less about having nothing to do, although they are not involved in many organized activities with scheduled meetings. The school orchestra and an informal softball league are the only exceptions mentioned. The second group of peer-oriented girls mostly participate in informal activities or watch the activities of other performers. Nevertheless, the lack of variety in female adolescents' activities by comparison with male adolescents is less related to the quantity of different activities open to them as to the quality of participation implied: female adolescents seldom participate with the aim of gaining in competence.

Explaining this situation is not an easy task. I would hypothesize that social recognition, reinforcement, and training are the weak "links" in the life of our respondents. These conditions are even worse in the public housing estate studies because the only support offered there is through organized sports which, according to male participants' own remarks, are a way out of delinquency. Female adolescents resent this lack of encouragement: they all mention the lack of training, support, or equipment as well as the instability of and unprofessional approach to programmes offered. Even in the area of traditional female handicrafts, they receive little encouragement to attain high skills: for instance, they are kept out of a women's association renowned for the achievements of its members.

Contrary to what we expected, female adolescents did not complain about being restricted in their access to the environment. In fact, they go wherever they can find peers and they seem to frequent all accessible places, except areas associated with groups of people with whom they do not identify. Places are differentiated according to life style, not sex. Adolescents enjoy each other's homes, the streets, outdoor sites, sports facilities, and commercial meeting places. At first glace, it seems that only lack of financial resources or transportation can prevent their access to a place. But their usage of places seems to be different from that of male adolescents: they are more often spectators or seeking social contacts, and they enjoy play activities rather than sports.

Female adolescents enjoy a privilege over their male counterparts: they can participate earlier in activities barred to them because of their ages. Indeed, they gain access to bars and to distant places because they go out with older males who have more money and access to cars. For all that, females envy male adolescents who can participate in wilderness excursions, an activity that is not seen as possible for them. Certainly, these facts show that female adolescents are not as autonomous as males, in spite of appearances.

Although they report being involved in many activities and going to many places, the majority of the girls interviewed complained that they have no space, that there is no place for them, and that there is not much to do in their town (this "no place to go, nothing to do" syndrome also exists for male adolescents; see Hill, 1980; Larkin, 1979). It is true that they are handicapped by having little money, which is not compensated for by memberships in clubs and leagues as is often the case for boys. But a stronger explanation for their complaints would appear to be the subtle sexism displayed, particularly through the lack of encouragement and recognition they get; the absence of models of innovative activities; and the generally unsupportive role of local organizations. It must be noted that male adolescents may suffer from the same deficiencies, but, according to the adolescents interviewed, males suffer less than females.

Being taken seriously, be it in sports or in arts and crafts, is our female adolescents' greatest desire. Their lack of deep and competent involvement may be assuaged by developing intimate affective bonds with a number of friends and meeting frequently at each other's homes, but these behaviours could also be interpreted as a compensation for the lack of opportunities offered to them in the public realm. Having no indoor space for such gatherings is another major problem for girls brought up in public housing estates because, in their case, they are often the object of sexual harassment while using outdoor space. Some female adolescents join males in their activities; this mixed participation seems to benefit the females. For instance, a few adolescents reported during the interviews that they could learn a sport or a skill with their boyfriends, or with males generally, that would otherwise have been inaccessible.

If insufficient encouragement is a main concern for female adolescents, what kinds of change would be meaningful to them? Certainly there are many positive measures that do not concern planners directly, such as those aimed at changing attitudes via education. However, city officers such as recreation specialists should be aware of and investigate the deep meaning of female adolescents' complaints and preferences. City authorities and planners must realize that they do not necessarily cater equally to girls' favourite activities, such as dancing, as they do to boys' participation in sports. Female leisure activities could be reinforced and recognized simply by being officially housed in a city's buildings. In questioning female adolescents, planners will also discover that they enjoy mixed social gatherings in the local camping grounds, in local events, in organized competitions. These androgynous recreational activities are positive when male and female adolescents learn to participate together. Therefore, there is a need for appropriate programmes and places. Public places should offer a variety of amusements, surfaces, and loose pieces of equipment for games and sports and proper facilities for handicrafts. Transportation should be offered in a flexible manner, since travelling, visiting, and going camping are all desires of adolescents. Another need that should be met is intimate private space for adolescents in residential settings, especially where housing density is high.

CREATING SPACE FOR WOMEN IN QUEBEC

The research we have been discussing was instigated by a new planning context in Quebec, starting at the beginning of the 1980's. The urbanization of Quebec and the modernization of its urban structure had taken place without any coherent planning. The 1,500 municipalities were each defining projects with no regard to the larger environment; not all had urban development or land-use plans or zoning by-laws. After fifteen years of argument and a few never-adopted draft bills, an *Act Respecting Land-Use Planning and Development* was finally adopted by parliament in 1979. This act establishes the general framework that will govern the development and application of regulations pertaining to land-use planning and development.

The 1979 Planning Act, together with various policies (such as a policy on leisure) that appeared during the same period, brought new hopes for involving people in the planning process. Previously, the ways citizens could express their concerns, such as through referenda on zoning amendments, proved quite insufficient for deciding the use value of the land (see, for example, Blary-Charles, 1981; Pilette, 1978). Apart from creating a new level of regional government through the formation of ninety-five regional county municipalities (RCM) responsible for the coordination of the choices and actions emanating from the various levels of decision making, the act has made statutory the preparation of a land-use development plan by each RCM as well as the preparation of a planning programme and bylaws affecting zoning, sub-division, and building. The citizens' hopes for this act rest on one of its main principles: "The citizen is involved in the various phases of the planning and revising procedure, through the vehicles of information, consultation and participation."

In theory, the domain that comes under the act's regulations is so broad that it calls on all citizens to participate. For instance, women would certainly have something to say about the general policies and planning objectives of their RCM, on the intermunicipal facilities and infrastructures to be installed, on the general aims of land development policy in their own municipality, and on a three-year schedule for the implementation of the projects proposed. Moreover, the compulsory framework defined by the act multiplies the opportunities for the citizen to get involved. For instance, citizens are to be informed of preliminary planning proposals, revised proposals, and the adopted land-use development plan and planning programmes. The act even specifies the means of pursuing this aim: in some circumstances, publication of the proposals in the local newspapers will satisfy the requirements of the act; in other cases, the municipal authorities are to mail an abstract of the plan to each civic address in its territory. Next, well-advertised public hearings must be held by the municipal authorities at various times during the planning process and whenever bylaws are to be adopted. The citizens may also require the Commission nationale de l'aménagement to prove the conformity of the bylaws to the planning programme; citizens may then vote to amend or repeal provisions contained in the bylaws.

Can this framework meet its ends? As Blary-Charles (1981) has shown, the institutionalization of participation may well discourage the ordinary citizen while the active urban agents (sellers) may well devise means of controlling the process. It is not enough to disseminate information about two or three views held by a municipality and to call for public hearings. The information must appeal to everyone by reflecting his or her life conditions. Unfortunately, the means of establishing a public dialogue and of translating people's voices into a plan have not been part of the planning tradition in Quebec. If women are to make an imprint on the urban plan and urban structure, a search for these aims must begin.

It must be reasserted that the data presented here are not representative of the whole population of women. They are the results of small group interviews with a number of women; therefore, they simply illustrate that people hold different representations of reality according to social status, age, and experience. However, the study shows that the social representations of the women and female adolescents interviewed are related to their sexual role. Women will not participate in the planning process unless it makes room for their views of the environment. Furthermore, because they have construed their wants in a social context that is based on the sexual division of labour, an adequate investigation of women's needs and desires cannot be limited to asking them directly what they want. As an example, when asked what they wanted, our adult respondents first expressed the needs of others, for instance the elderly and adolescents; later, they asked for leisure activities that would make them more competent in their domestic chores, like courses in home-decoration and child psychology. For their part, adolescents are so responsive to commercial influence that some would not hesitate to ask for horse-riding facilities simply because they have just visited a ranch. What should we do with such demands? Comply with them? Reject them? Work with them? Answering such questions will be the aim of a long-term research project directed primarily toward trying out new methods for listening to women.

The attempt to let women speak for themselves has to be a two-fold action. Reaching out for women is one aim. But women themselves should strive to take their place in public life. Confronted as they are with the urban environment, they are in a position to discuss its development with regard to their perceived needs. Therefore, they must develop a sense of the importance of their own views of the city, an ability to insert the answers to these needs in a planning programme and land-use development plan, and ways of expressing needs and solutions publicly. Further research should lead women to share their experience and to discuss their real priorities. It could consist of an exercise in planning conceived for women's groups aimed at helping the participants to state their choices for the environment, insert these proposals within the urban development scheme of their town, and evaluate means of implementing them. The whole idea is to create space for women in the planning process as well as space in the city. In this way, women will add their own knowledge and experience to our understanding of the city and our visions of its future. On the basis of preliminary studies, we foresee that women will express concerns over the physical planning and enhancement of all public spaces and the implementation of community facilities. However, it remains difficult to predict how, in the long term, women's ideas will evolve in interaction with the changing environment.

This proposal for women's participation is feasible on a large scale. the women's movement is well-enough structured with its many associations and interest groups to involve more women in the planning process. The interest of women is already there. Tapping this resource will therefore need little public investment in communications and support.[11] Reaching adolescents will be a more difficult task because they are less organized into formal groups. The school is the only reliable place to meet with them, and it is not a popular place. But, with a little imagination and an examination of many environmental education programmes, some progress could be made in planning for the needs of adolescents.

Nevertheless, the means of implementing and developing women's participation must themselves be objects of study in the framework of action research. It is necessary to study how women come to express themselves and what they express. Qualitative research into women's lives and actions to implicate them in decision-making about the city can therefore become one and the same approach, so that in addition to planning for women's changing social roles, we will construct a city where women have the power to create their own visions and plans.

NOTES

1. The author lists six main deadly sins: the overextension and underspecification of concepts, transforming a sociocultural difference into a biological one, the supposition that reality is experienced the same way by both sexes, the idea that there are appropriate roles and behaviours for each sex, the double-standard, and the extraction of social facts from their social context. She adds a seventh sin: the omnipresent stereotype of the family.

2. For instance, in several workshops I have organized for groups of women on their urban environment, I have never heard of any desire for the collectivization of domestic tasks that is often an aspect of Feminist Utopia.

3. The work of groups like the National Congress of Neighbourhood Women in the United States is an example here. They use consciousness-raising methods and develop education programmes in their work with women, because their experience taught them that it is the best way to induce change and support women in their actions to control their neighbourhood. Unfortunately, too little of the knowledge they have construed reaches the "scientific community."

4. As a whole, studies point at the limited spatial range of women's activities, their short periods of free time, their low rate of participation in sports and

physical activity, and the disregard of their favourite forms of leisure by officialdom.

5. The data presented here are extracted from group interviews with women. The case study also included analyses of the ongoing planning operation, the "schéma d'aménagement" of the region and the "plan directeur d'urbanisme" of the municipality, and a survey of women's organizations in the community.

6. The initial demand did not specify male adolescents, but it appeared with further examination that they were the main problem because of vandalism, noise, and so on. Invisible but known female behaviours like prostitution were more easily forgotten.

7. It must be emphasized that our respondents showed no trace of being preoccupied by glamour. The reproduction of the model of beauty without muscles has often been presented as an explanation of women's low rate of participation in sport. For instance, see de Koninck et al. (1983).

8. The yearning for a small, communal, and ecological society can be traced in radical feminist works such as D'Eaubonne (1974). Many feminist projects through American history can be likened to this search; many are related in Hayden (1981).

9. When I refer to women's organizations, I am not referring to feminist groups only. I am talking about a variety of women's groups, formal or informal, national or local, with varied objectives from health promotion to women's education. Their common characteristics are that they are instigated by women and that their membership is mainly female.

10. This contrasts with the numerous works on what is seen as youth problems: drug abuse, sexual behaviour, dropping-out of school, and so on.

11. In discussing women's strategies for sharing power in society, many thinkers have put forward the idea that local politics would be a good school where women could become initiated to politics, and that it is probably a suitable place for them to act on their own life conditions. The Council on the Status of Women in Quebec took such a stance a few years ago. For an interesting study of women in local politics, see Tardy (1982).

REFERENCES

Blary-Charles, R. (1981). "Participation: formalisme et réalité." In Corporation professionnelle des urbanistes du Québec, *La loi 125 et la participation* (pp. 57-64). Montréal: Corporation professionnelle des urbanistes du Québec, CPUQ.

Bowles, G. and Duelli Klein, R. (Eds.) (1983). *Theories of Women's Studies.* London: Routledge and Kegan Paul.

Cerullo, M. and Ewen, P. (1984). "The American Family Goes Camping: Gender,

Family and the Politics of Space." *Antipode, 16*(3), pp. 35-45.

Dagenais, H. (1980). "Les femmes dans la ville et la sociologie urbaine: Les multiples facettes d'une même oppression." *Anthropologie et sociétés, 4*(1), pp. 21-36.

Dagenais, H. (Ed.) (1986). *Approches et méthodes de la recherche féministe: Actes du colloque de mai 1985.* Québec: Groupe de recherches multidisciplinaires féministes, Université Laval.

D'Eaubonne, F. (1974). *Le féminisme ou la mort.* Paris: Pierre Horay Editeur.

de Koninck, M., Saillant, F., and Dunnigan, L. (1983). *Essai sur la santé des femmes.* Québec: Conseil du statut de la femme.

Duelli Klein, R. (1983). "How to Do What We Want to Do: Thoughts About Feminist Methodology." In G. Bowles and R. Duelli Klein (Eds.), *Theories of Women's Studies* (p. 90). London: Routledge and Kegan Paul.

Eichler, M. (1985). "Les six péchés capitaux sexistes." *Cahiers de recherche du GREMF, no. 6.* Québec: Université Laval (Groupe de recherches multidisciplinaires féministes).

Eichler, M. and Lapointe, J. (1985). *On the Treatment of the Sexes in Research.* Ottawa: Social Sciences and Humanities Research Council.

Ekistics (1985). Special issue: "Women and Space in Human Settlements," *52.*

Friedan, B. (1963). *The Feminine Mystique.* New York: Norton.

Hayden, D. (1980). "What Would a Non-Sexist City Be Like?: Speculations on Housing, Urban Design and Human Work." *Signs: Journal of Women in Culture and Society, 5*(3), pp. 170-87.

Hayden, D. (1981). *The Grand Domestic Revolution: A History of Feminist Designs for American Homes, Neighborhoods and Cities.* Cambridge, Mass.: MIT.

Hill, F. (1980). *The Lives and Times of Urban Adolescents: Activity Patterns and Neighborhood Perceptions.* Child in the City Report, Centre for Urban and Community Studies. Toronto: University of Toronto.

International Journal of Urban and Regional Research (1978). Special issue: "Women and the City," *2*(3).

Keller, Suzanne (Ed.) (1981). *Building for Women.* Lexington, Mass.: Lexington Books.

Larkin, R. W. (1979). *Suburban Youth in Cultural Crisis.* Oxford: Oxford University Press.

Ledrut, R. (1973). *Les images de la ville.* Paris: Anthropos.

Lewin, K. (1948). *Resolving Social Conflicts: Selected Papers on Group Dynamics.* New York: Harper.

Lofland, L. H. (1975). "The 'Thereness of Women': A Selective Review of Urban Sociology." In M. Millan and R. M. Kanter (Eds.), *Another Voice: Feminist Perspectives on Social Life and Social Science* (pp. 140-70). New York: Anchor Books.

Lofland, L. H. (1984). "Women and Urban Public Space." *Women and Environments, 6*(2), pp. 12-14.

Masson, D. (1984). "Les femmes dans les structures urbaines: aperçu d'un nouveau champ de recherche." *Revue canadienne de sciences politiques, 17*(4), pp. 754-82.

Morville-Descolonges, M. (1978). "A propos de la socialisation du travail domestique: l'analyse d'un village de vacances." *International Journal of Urban and Regional Research, 2*(3), pp. 482-98.

Oakley, A. (1974). *The Sociology of Housework*. New York: Pantheon.

Ostrowetsky, S. (1983). *L'imaginaire bâtisseur: les villes nouvelles françaises*. Paris: Librairie des Méridiens.

Pilette, D. (1978). "Les acteurs du zonage et leurs pratiques." *Cahiers de géographie du Québec, 22*(57), pp. 393-419.

Radio-Canada (1979). *Nous les 12 à 15 ans*. Montréal: Services des recherches, Radio-Canada.

Raymond, H. (1984). *L'Architecture: les aventures spatiales de la raison*. Paris: Centre du création industrielle, Centre Georges Pompidou.

Reinharz, S. (1983). "Experiential Analysis: A Contribution to Feminist Research." In G. Bowles and R. Duelli Klein (Eds.), *Theories of Women's Studies* pp. 162-91. London: Routledge and Kegan Paul.

Roberge, P., Belanger, P., and Rocher, G. (1979). *Aspirations scolaires et orientations professionnelles des étudiants*. Les Cahiers d'A.S.O.P.E. Québec: Université Laval.

Roberts, H. (Ed.) (1981). *Doing Feminist Research*. London: Routledge and Kegan Paul.

Signs: Journal of Women in Culture and Society (1980). Special issue: "Women and the American City," *5*(3).

Szalai, A. et al. (1972). *The Use of Time*. The Hague: Mouton.

Tardy, E. (1982). *La politique: un monde d'hommes?: Une étude sur les mairesses au Québec*. Montréal: Hurtubise HMH.

Vandelac, L., Belisle, D., Gauthier, A., and Pinard, Y (1984). *Du travail et de l'amour*. Montréal: Editions St-Martin.

Wekerle, G., Peterson, R., and Morley, D. (Eds). (1980). *New Space for Women*. Boulder: Westview.

8

Gender-Specific Approaches
to Theory and Method

BETH MOORE MILROY AND CAROLINE ANDREW

A principal issue raised in this book and central to the field of gender and urban environments is the desire by researchers both to understand and to change current affairs. In this concluding chapter we wish to explore some of the research consequences of this position.

Linking "understanding" and "changing" is not straightforward. The meaning of understanding is itself complex, although it is widely taken to include knowing from without, by way of observation, and also knowing from within, experientially, empathetically and intuitively. It entails both description and recognition of the context within which the description is proposed. Changing refers to physically rearranging the phenomena in our environment and the processes carried on there; to altering the concepts, methods, theories, and languages we use to investigate the world and ourselves; and to redefining criteria for what counts as knowledge. It means creating contexts in which women can act on their knowledge and understanding. Understanding and changing, then, as themes in feminist research embrace the desire to change values and world views rather than simply to make the existing male world accessible to women.

Insisting on the connection between understanding and changing is more than an act of research; it is also a political act. It brings scientific enterprise and politics face-to-face.

Feminists share this broad ground with many social scientists concerned to develop theories and methods that take human agency and purpose into account. Their projects are set apart from the tradition of basing theory and analysis on models of scientific inquiry originally designed to study non-human phenomena. Within the growing field of human-based theorists, a diversity of approaches is developing. Where feminists diverge from these is in explaining the categories of "woman" and "man," not assuming them to be givens. How this is done sets apart various lines of feminist thinking or "feminisms."[1]

The debate about theorizing in the research community at large reminds us to think about why we do research in the social sciences in the first place. Is it purely to acquire knowledge for its own sake? Or is it to change and improve something? Feminist researchers who are acutely aware of the pervasive androcentricity that has influenced the shape of urban environments cannot be disinterested inquirers removed from the prospect of creating a non-sexist environment. For that half of humankind which feels isolated from the social science explanations of its own experience, it would be shooting itself in the foot to settle simply for understanding. Acknowledging purposefulness in the research experience, in both researcher and researched, creates a dialectic between understanding and changing.

As we pursue this issue, referring first to theory in the field and later to research plans, we do so from the position that scientific investigation of social questions is never wholly divorced from political concerns: the entire enterprise from conceptualization to evidence is conducted within a framework saturated with conventions and values sanctioned by political discourse and actions. Further, we see inquiry as a "disciplined dialogue" between concept and evidence which captures the dynamic relationship between two indispensable facets grounded in theoretical and practical domains (Thompson, 1978, p. 43).

Suzanne Mackenzie has noted that little theorizing has been done as yet in the field of gender and environmental studies (1984a, 1984b). Feminists in these fields have had to make women visible as a relevant population subgroup, a task which required generating data about women's experience simply to permit issues concerning women to be raised. Considerable literature has been produced in Canada and elsewhere documenting the problems women encounter in existing urban environments.[2]

A second area which feminist researchers are developing is an understanding of the dynamic interaction between gender categories and built environments, in order to see how changes in one affect the other over time and space. This has entailed opening up the category "woman" (and, consequently, the category "man' also) to see what has constituted being a woman at different points in time. Clearly it is not a static category. One has sought to understand how such constructions come about, what set of social relations and activities contribute to setting and changing gender relations over time and space. A further undertaking has been a parallel opening up of the category "environments" seeing them as "sets of resources appropriated in historically variable ways, these modes of appropriation altering with societal space and time patterns" (Mackenzie, 1986, p. 269).

With gender and environment seen as historically contingent, one may then investigate how one influences the other at specific times and places. For example, in Mackenzie's empirical work we see that in central Canada from the turn of the century, the category "woman" increasingly specified a female who did not "work" but rather managed the home. The appropriation of the environment increasingly separated women from what was and still is conventionally construed as work: that is, activity in the formal economy (1980). There appeared, then, a coincidence between the full-time housewife, a new social model for masses of women, and suburban environments, also new to central Canada. Over the last couple of decades both the concept of woman and the appropriation of space have begun shifting in different directions again. Opening up the categories to inspection over time helps one grasp how specific gender relations and spatial forms develop in concert. Particular gender relations and spatial conditions are constructed in line with dominant interests; they are neither "natural" nor necessary in some absolute sense. If this is the case, each can in principle be shaped to suit women's as well as men's interests.

Now that research has begun to show the constraints of urban environments and the dynamic quality of gender relations, it is imperative to include a third task: shaping concepts and evidence into theories of gender and environment. Principles and empirical studies will not suffice to challenge the theories which currently underlie explanations in environmental fields until they are woven together conceptually (see Mackenzie, 1984a, pp. 16-17; Masson, 1984, pp. 769-70 and 781-82; Evans, 1983, pp. 219-28). Disconnected, they lend credence to pleas to recognize women, but they fall short of serving their full potential for understanding and creating environments where both women and men are recognized as actors. McDowell (1985) and Holcomb (1986) have noted that gender-sensitive work has had little impact as yet on geographic thought. But this fact should not discourage further efforts. The special contribution of this work is to highlight the tension between production and reproduction which have traditionally been linked activities for women only, and to challenge theories that value one to the disadvantage of the other. Inevitably feminists' work strikes at long-standard conceptualizations of work and economy and their location in space. Women, because they need to integrate reproductive and productive work, are inadequately placed into standard models. The convenient solution is to ignore the problem or make only minor adjustments. The more creative—and much more difficult to achieve— solution is to change the conceptualizations, theories, and practices. History would seem to indicate that the latter solution will have to be won; it will not come easily.

A range of descriptive and prescriptive mainstream theories from fields such as geography and planning merit re-examination given the evidence generated by making women and men problematic in analyses of urban phenomena. Probably the most encompassing of these are theoretical explanations of urban structure—how towns and cities acquire the forms they do. Conventional explanations depend on the classical economic principle of competition, reconceptualized in urban theory to account for constraints on land supply, or access to space. The greatest competition is for space located near economic activity (Women and Geography Study Group of the IBG, 1984, p. 45). Thus, the basis for explaining urban form is economic production and its category of land rent. Location theories show that activities "naturally" locate given their ability to pay the cost of land for the quantity of space required and given the spatial configuration already in place. To the extent that choice exists, it is exercised according to the traditional, rational, economic manner.

There is an associated, behavioural area of study in geography—also influential in planning—in which researchers examine people's actual rather than expected behaviour regarding decisions about locating activities and moving between them. Using concepts drawn more from sociology and psychology than economics (Johnston, 1983), this work permits a more complex interpretation of behaviour. Yet, like location theories, it does not theorize the implications of gender relations in the structure of decision making.

Against these dominant approaches, feminist theories are being developed based on concepts and research findings related in particular to the production/reproduction dynamic. These open up to investigation the possiblity that it is the interlinkage between productive and reproductive activity that structures cities, and that decisions are influenced by gender (Lewis and Foord, 1984; Klausner, 1986). Gradually the literature is showing how certain elements, such as conceptualizations of work, home, family, women, and so on, are related to one another in the creation of specific forms of gender relations. One feature of existing gender relations is that women's tasks, spaces, and images are devalued in relation to men's. Feminists argue that these differential valuations based on gender have material and theoretical implications for understanding the structuring of space. The challenge for feminists is to test the thesis that urban structures reflect the interplay of both productive and reproductive activities (themselves shaped by the historically constructed relations between women and men). Then they must attend to deconstructing and reconstructing the relations.

We also wish to make several observations about the research plan. If research is directed to understanding and changing, it follows that the preferred approaches will be those that link understanding and agency, a sense of how we are moved to act. This brings us back to the questions about research and politics that are currently exercising the research community and which influence the character of research plans.

Conventional social inquiry is frequently premised on the view that knowledge influences action, but not the other way round. Scientific research produces knowledge and politics acts on that knowledge; knowledge-creation and action are sequential and split. However, a different perspective is widely promoted in certain modes of research, including feminist research. Its premise is that knowledge and action are inter-related, the one affecting the nature of the other but neither necessarily taking precedence. As a consequence, investigation involves legitimizing experience and feelings in everyday action as sources of knowledge and understanding politics as a form of knowing-in-action whereby meanings are generated and reinforced by power.

Feminist methods broach another split in conventional inquiry, that between subject and object. Because women investigating gender relations are in some measure investigating themselves, they directly confront the issue posed in conventional research of determining an object for the researching subject. Social science methods have traditionally posited a subject/object split in order to claim that research results are objective. The researcher is detached from those whom one researches. Objectivity is a central criterion for reliable research in that tradition. Feminists and others have been developing research methods which specifically do not separate the researcher from the people who are the focus of research, nor from the data that is said to describe them (see Dagenais, 1981; Juteau-Lee, 1981; Laurin-Frenette, 1981; Morris, 1977; Smith, 1974; Vickers, 1982). Criteria other than objectivity are consequently used to assess the value of research results. In particular the value shifts from being able to make detached statements about some group to being able to speak in unison with it. These methods seek not only to heighten the researcher's understanding but also that of the people who are the centre of the research. In the process both the researcher and researched are subjects; no one is an object. This orientation proposes actions and solutions developed from within the group rather than developed by researchers and imposed by policy makers.

With these interpretations of the relationships between knowledge and action on the one hand and subject and object on the other, feminist researchers use at least two main avenues to link understanding and changing. One is via the qualities of the methods themselves, and the other relates to the use made of the research. The methods themselves can be clustered broadly into three categories (see Reinharz, Bombyk, and Wright, 1984, esp. pp. 448-50). In the first category are so called alternative methods which are qualitative and often characterized by contrasting them to quantitative methods. Different types of qualitative methods have been developed in various fields. ‡ In the discussion that follows, a few of these are mentioned in connection with studies in which they have been used, in order to demonstrate their translation to research related to women.

One method is action research, which is directed to contemporary situations. Fundamental to it is the act of bridging the gap between researcher and group members, a gap occasioned by differing experiences, knowledge, and perspectives. This idea of suspending preconceived notions about others in an effort to understand them on their terms generally underlies qualitative methods and is absent from quantitative ones. This principle can take several forms, but it always involves both field research and the participation by those studied in the description, if not analysis, of their experience. Documented and accessible accounts are found, for example, in the analysis of Munroe House in Vancouver (Women's Research Centre, 1980) and in Mies (1983, pp. 117-39) concerning establishing and running shelters for battered women. Another form of qualitative research is in-depth interviewing. One example is Luxton (1980). Finally in this category, one can mention the method for studying historical subjects which entails the researcher immersing herself in documented evidence of a period in order to understand what it was like to be a woman at that time. Using this approach, Wright (1980) has provided an historical study of American women and their houses, and Scott and Tilly (1982) have prepared an analysis of women's work and the family in nineteenth-century Europe.

In a second category are the hybrids which conjoin alternative methods with conventional ones. Armstrong and Armstrong (1983) have argued that this approach can be advantageous, pointing to the lacunae and distortions in the depictions of women's lives that can occur through dependence on quantitative data bases alone. As one corrective, they recommend that qualitative methods be used to complement quantitative data, to expand upon and to check the validity of data and implications drawn from qualitative surveys. These authors cite examples of how interviews with women about their work experiences have served to revise and enrich inferences drawn solely from quantitative data bases, such as those developed by Statistics Canada.

Finally, in a third category are conventional methods of quantitative data collection, including surveys and time-budgets. Some researchers have argued that these are useful for developing material that is sensitive to feminist concerns, provided they are corrected for possible sexist bias (for example, Eichler, 1983, ch. 3; Jayaratne, 1983). In addition, a number of

Canadian empirical studies, such as Klodawsky, Spector, and Rose (1985) and McClain and Doyle (1984) have analyzed existing statistics to establish how women's experience in the built environment differs from that of men.

Perhaps the most fruitful way to approach the choice of method is by thinking in terms of one's interests. The subject being studied, together with the interests and understanding of the researcher, should inform the choice of method. Questions along the line of "How many?" may be better handled using quantitative methods, while questions such as "What is it like to . . . ?" probably demand qualitative methods (Reinharz, 1983, p. 177).

The problems in choosing a research method are closely associated with those that emerge from the use of existing data. Caution is warranted when the research for women draws data from standard statistical data bases. Certain researchers have described how assumptions underlying data collection influence the questions that will and will not be asked (Armstrong and Armstrong, 1983; Oakley and Oakley, 1979; Allin and Hunt, 1982). They show that simply adopting non-sexist language and producing some tabulations by sex does not necessarily rid data of androcentric bias. The concepts and perspective one brings to the task of designing questionnaires and other data-gathering formats affects the types of questions asked and how they are presented to respondents (see, for example, Schuman and Presser, 1981). This poses serious difficulties for research projects concerning waged work and child care, for instance, since the prevailing view is to consider waged work as principally a male activity and child care a female activity.

An example drawn from Armstrong and Armstrong may illuminate the type of problem a researcher encounters. Statistics Canada's definition of work includes working for pay or without pay in any sort of business but excludes both work around the house and volunteer work. The authors note that:

> What Statistics Canada is interested in counting is not all the ways people spend their days or their energy, not how they survive on a daily basis, not how food gets to their tables, nor even how they improve their standard of living. On the other hand, interest is not limited to paid employment, to work that brings individuals money income. Rather, the focus of concern is work which results directly in profit and exchange. (Armstrong and Armstrong, 1983, pp. 4-5)

Hence the only things we can find out about what women (and men) do all day is that which is associated with a business. All of women's family and volunteer work—which is to say most of women's work—is disregarded. While the definition is not sexist in its language, it is sexist in its assumptions and thus in the data it brings to light. It is imperative therefore to keep in mind that the numbers that turn up in data bases are the results of certain choices about what it is important to know. Dominant theories about gender relations will invariably influence those choices.

A second avenue for integrating understanding and changing is to develop research plans that, apart from the methods used, incorporate specific commitments regarding dissemination and action to ensure that research findings are not left in obscurity. A helpful twelve-point strategy has been outlined by the International Exchange of Development Resources agency, a group that raises funds and gathers information to promote the exchange of resources among women worldwide (1982). Its position is that since policy-making is a political process, research should be taken to the people who elect the policy makers. Tasks include ensuring that research budgets allocate money for disseminating the results of studies, encouraging funding for women's groups rather than individuals so that skills and knowledge are developed more widely, and forming groups to monitor policies that run counter to research findings.

One concern particularly relevant in Canada relates to ensuring broader distribution of results. There is a tendency for important initiatives regarding women and environments to become known only locally because they are geographically specific. But in order to develop theories, policies, and actions rooted in the Canadian reality, we need the greatest possible understanding of this work. These locally specific studies are vital to producing the overall picture. *Women and Environments* is one publication designed to surmount the dissemination problem by bringing national and international attention to studies, experiences, and projects.

The commitment to develop methods sensitive to women and to ensure that findings reach those engaged in policy and practice can be characterized as a concern to do research *for* women rather than *about* them, to learn *with* women, not *from* them.

In conclusion, we reiterate the main point of this chapter: both theory and research must develop together. In combination they offer the likelihood of overcoming the sex biases of existing theory and research and of contributing to more positive gender relations in the future. In this pursuit feminist scholarship clearly must innovate. With greater understanding we may hope that communities can become life spaces that enable new relationships to flourish, and that planning them can be acts that make possible what we dare to dream.

NOTES

1. "Feminisms" is borrowed from Marks and de Courtivron's presentation of "new French feminisms" in which the pluralizing is intended to signify the attack against fixed categories and labels, including feminism, in recent French writings (1981). In the English-language literature of Britain and North America, distinctions are frequently made among radical, Marxist, liberal, socialist, psychoanalytic, phenomenological, and humanist feminism. Interpretations are not necessarily international because of the different political and theoretical traditions within which they have grown. Comparative treatments of various approaches are found in the Women and Geography Study Group of the IBG (1984, pp. 24-38); Elshtain (1981, pp. 201-353) and James (1982, pp. 233-38).

2. Much of the Canadian literature is documented in the annotated bibliography in this book, and the bibliographies of these sources provide guides to much of the American and British literature and some of the French.

3. In the area of community development, for instance, see the critical-emancipatory approaches of Freire (1972a, 1972b), Hall and Shirley (1982), and van Rensburg (1984), as well as the "empowerment" literature, including Gran (1983), and James (1982) on the relation between feminism and community action. For sociology a variety of interpretive methods exist: see Morris (1977), and Reinharz (1983) for her own form of experiential analysis designed for feminist research.

REFERENCES

Allin, Pat and Hunt, Audrey (1982). "Women in Official Statistics." In Elizabeth Whitelegg et al. (Eds.), *The Changing Experience of Women* (pp. 337-51). Oxford: Open University Press.

Armstrong, Pat and Armstrong, Hugh (1983). "Beyond Numbers: Problems with Quantitative Data." *Alternate Routes* (Carleton University) 6, pp. 1-40.

Dagenais, Huguette (1981). "Quand la sociologie devient action: l'impact du féminisme sur la pratique sociologique." *Sociologie et sociétés*, *13*(2).

Eichler, Margrit (1983). *Families in Canada Today*. Toronto: Gage.

Elshtain, Jean Bethke (1981). *Public Man, Private Woman: Women in Social and Political Thought*. Princeton: Princeton University Press.

Evans, Mary (1983). "In Praise of Theory." In Gloria Bowles and Renate Duelli Klein (Eds.), *Theories of Women's Studies* (pp. 219-28). London: Routledge and Kegan Paul.

Freire, Paulo (1972a). *Cultural Action for Freedom*. London: Penguin.

Freire, Paulo (1972b). *Pedagogy of the Oppressed*. London: Penguin.

Gran, Guy (1983). *Development by People*. New York: Praeger.
Hall, Trish and Shirley, Ian (1982). "Development as Methodology: Locality Development, Social Planning and Social Action." In Ian Shirley (Ed.), *Development Tracks: The Theory and Practice of Community Development*. Palmerston North, New Zealand: Dunmore Press.
Holcomb, Briavel (1986). "Geography and Urban Women." *Urban Geography*, 7(5).
International Exchange of Development Resources (1982). "Making Policy Responsible to Research." Reprinted in International Supplement, *Women's Studies Quarterly*, 1, p. 19.
James, Bev (1982). "Feminism: Making the Private World Public." In Ian Shirley (Ed.), *Development Tracks: The Theory and Practice of Community Development*. Palmerston North, New Zealand: Dunmore Press.
Jayaratne, Toby Epstein (1983). "The Value of Quantitative Methodology for Feminist Research." In Gloria Bowles and Renate Duelli Klein (Eds.), *Theories of Women's Studies* (pp. 140-61), London: Routlege and Kegan Paul.
Johnston, R. J. (1983). *Geography and Geographers*. 2d ed. London: Edward Arnold.
Juteau-Lee, Danielle (1981). "Visions partielles, visions partiales: visions (des) minoritaires en sociologie." *Sociologie et sociétés*, 13(2).
Klausner, D. (1986). "Beyond Separate Spheres: Linking Production with Social Reproduction and Consumption." *Environment and Planning D: Society and Space, 4*, pp. 29-40.
Klodawsky, Fran, Spector, Aron, and Rose, Damaris (1985). *Single Parent Families and Canadian Housing Policies: How Mothers Lose*. Ottawa: Canada Mortgage and Housing Corporation.
Laurin-Frenette, Nicole (1981). "Les femmes dans la sociologie." *Sociologie et sociétés, 13(2)*.
Lewis, Jane and Foord, Jo (1984). "New Towns and New Gender Relations in Old Industrial Regions: Women's Employment in Peterlee and East Kilbride." *Built Environment, 10(1)*, pp. 42-52
Luxton, Meg (1980). *More than a Labour of Love*. Toronto: Women's Educational Press.
Mackenzie, Suzanne (1980). "Women and the Reproduction of Labour Power in the Industrial City: A Case Study." Working Paper 23, Urban and Regional Planning, University of Sussex, Brighton, England.
Mackenzie, Suzanne (1984a). "Catching Up with Ourselves: Ideas on Developing Gender-Sensitive Theory in the Environmental Disciplines." *Women and Environments, 6(3)*.
Mackenzie, Suzanne (1984b). "Editorial Introduction." *Antipode, 16(3)*. Special issue: "Women and Environments."
Mackenzie, Suzanne (1986). "Feminist Geography." *The Canadian Geographer/Le géographe canadien, 30(3)*, pp. 268-70.
Marks, Elaine and de Courtivron, Isabelle (1981). *New French Feminisms*. New York: Schocken.
Masson, Dominique (1984). "Les femmes dans les structures urbaines: aperçu d'un

nouveau champ de recherche." *Canadian Journal of Political Science/Revue canadienne de science politique*, *17*(4).

McClain, Janet and Doyle, Cassie (1984). *Women and Housing*. Toronto: James Lorimer and the Canadian Council on Social Development.

McDowell, L. (1983). "Towards an Understanding of the Gender Division of Urban Space." *Environment and Planning D: Society and Space*, *1*, pp. 59-72.

McDowell, L. (1985). "Some Gloomy Thoughts from Britain: A Response to Suzanne Mackenzie on Developing Gender-Sensitive Theory." *Women and Environments*, *7*(1).

Mies, Maria (1983). "Towards a Methodolgy for Feminist Research." In Gloria Bowles and Renata Duelli Klein (Eds.), *Theories of Women's Studies* (pp. 117-39), London: Routledge and Kegan Paul.

Morris, Monica B. (1977). *An Excursion into Creative Sociology*. New York: Columbia University Press.

Oakley, Ann and Oakley, Robin (1979). "Sexism in Official Statistics." In John Irvine, Ian Miles, and Jeff Evans (Eds.), *Demystifying Social Statistics* (pp. 172-89). London: Pluto Press.

Reinharz, Shulamit (1983). "Experiential Analysis: A Contribution to Feminist Research." In Gloria Bowles and Renata Duelli Klein (Eds.), *Theories of Women's Studies* (pp. 162-91). London: Routledge and Kegan Paul.

Reinharz, Shulamit, Bombyk, Marti, and Wright, Janet (1984). "Methodological Issues in Feminist Research: A Bibliography of Literature on Women's Studies, Sociology and Psychology." *Women's Studies International*, *6*(4).

Schuman, Howard and Presser, Stanley (1981). *Questions and Answers in Attitude Surveys: Experiments on Question Form, Wording and Context*. New York: Academic Press.

Scott, Joan and Tilly, Louise (1982). "Women's Work and the Family in Nineteenth Century Europe." In Elizabeth Whitelegg et al. (Eds.), *The Changing Experience of Women* (pp. 45-70). Oxford: Open University Press.

Smith, Dorothy E. (1974). "Women's Perspective as a Radical Critique of Sociology." *Sociological Inquiry*, *44*(1), pp. 7-13.

Thompson, E. P. (1978). *The Poverty of Theory and Other Essays*. New York: Monthly Review Press.

van Rensburg, Patrick (1984). "Education and Culture for Liberation." *Development Dialogue*, *1*, pp. 138-50.

Vickers, Jill McCalla (1982). "Memoirs of an Ontological Exile." In Angela Miles and Geraldine Finn (Eds.), *Feminism in Canada* (pp. 27-46). Montreal: Black Rose Books.

Women and Geography Study Group of the IBG (1984). *Geography and Gender: An Introduction to Feminist Geography*. London: Hutchinson.

Women's Research Centre (1980). *A Review of Munroe House: Second Stage Housing for Battered Women*. Vancouver: Women's Research Centre.

Wright, Gwendolyn (1980). *Moralism and the Model Home: Domestic Architecture and Cultural Conflict in Chicago 1873-1913*. Chicago: University of Chicago Press.

Annotated Bibliography

BETH MOORE MILROY and CAROLINE ANDREW,
with the collaboration of SUSAN MONTONEN

This bibliography brings together the principal contributions in print relating to gender relations and the Canadian environment dating from the early 1970's. While we believe we have included the majority of titles, the bibliography falls short of being an exhaustive listing.

Our general criteria for selecting an item were that (1) it should be concerned both with gender relations (or women or sex) and with community environments; and (2) it should either be written about a Canadian situation or be written by someone working in Canada. More specifically, we have tried to identify works having to do with the location of goods and services in space and related design, policy, and programme considerations, and with gender-based relationships, including political, economic, and social as experienced in community space. Thus we have emphasized works on housing; transportation; child care; leisure; planning and design of urban environments; material on demography and labour linked to urban structure; and items written from the perspective of specific population groups such as single-parent households. Because we wished to retain a strong focus on the intersection of gender and environments, little material from the labour and family debates is included, even though we realize these are directly relevant and clearly have spatial implications.

Books, articles, and reports are annotated; theses and dissertations are not because we were unable to review these. Annotations include the general intent of the item, as well as specific information on the methods used, the period of time to which each refers, and the type of space. In the latter we sought to identify various scales in space from the urban-centred region or small community to the neighbourhood; and subsets of these include the block level, housing project, park, or building. Some entries are broadly applicable to a given city or country or are non-specific with respect to space.

Sources used to compile the bibliography of books, articles, and reports included the *Canadian Periodical Index* from 1974 to June 1987; *Women and Environments* and *Atlantis* until they began to be indexed in *CPI* in 1987 and the papers in this text. Items were searched in a rippling out process until no new titles were found. Sources searched for theses and dissertations were *Thèses universitaires québécoises sur les femmes, 1921-1981*, by Yolande Cohen, with the collaboration of Andrée Boucher (2d ed. Québec: Institut québécois de recherche sur la culture, 1983); *A Bibliography of Canadian Theses and Dissertations in Urban, Regional and Environmental*

Planning, 1974-1979, compiled by Helma Libick for the Canadian Association of Planning Students Bibliography Committee, 1980; and *Canadiana* (Ottawa: National Library), for the years 1980-85.

We would appreciate being made aware of missed or new titles. Please send these, preferably with annotations comparable to those found below, to *Women and Environments*, c/o Centre for Urban and Community Studies, 455 Spadina Avenue, Toronto, Ontario, M5S 2G8.

BOOKS/ARTICLES/REPORTS

AARONS, Rachel (1981). "Women and the Small Town Syndrome." Paper presented at the National Rural Mental Health Conference. (Available from *Women and Environments*, 455 Spadina, Toronto, M5S 2G8.) 18 pp.

Describes the reasons why women's resource centres are needed in small towns. Using the example of the founding of the Squamish, B.C., centre, concrete experience is tied to a philosophy of community development, a process, and actions to meet some of the women's expressed needs.

Method: Analysis of a case
Time: Circa 1980
Space: Small towns

ANDREW, Caroline (1985). "La gestion du local: un enjeu pour les femmes?" *Revue internationale d'action communautaire*, *13*(53): pp. 103-8.

Analysis of the role played by women in decision-making bodies at the local level. Women are much more present in structures dealing with questions of collective consumption (health, education) than in municipal structures.

Method: Case study, analysis
Time: 1980's
Space: Quebec — particularly the Outaouais region

ARMSTRONG, Pat and ARMSTRONG, Hugh (1983). "Beyond Numbers: Problems with Quantitative Data." *Alternate Routes* (Carleton University) *6*, pp. 1-40.

Begins from the position that data and data-gathering methods are neither neutral nor atheoretical and proceeds to argue for sex-specific statistical data collection as well as using qualitative data to complement it. The authors discuss the shortcomings of some major Statistics Canada data bases and the Census for doing research for women, showing how these sources can miss or distort women's experiences.

Method: Analysis of documents; interviews
Time: 1980's
Space: Canada

BARNSLEY, Jan and ELLIS, Diana (1987). *Action Research for Women's Groups.* Vancouver: Women's Research Centre.

Provides a 6-part kit on action research: (1) the Women's Research Centre and our assumptions about action research; (2) an introduction to action research; (3) making the decision to do a research project; (4) designing an action research project; (5) carrying out an action research project; (6) communicating the findings of an action research project.

— Method:
Time: 1980's
Space: non-specific

BARTON, Debbie. (1983). *Housing in Ottawa-Carleton: A Women's Issue.* Ottawa: Elizabeth Fry Society. 75 pp.

A study of housing programme needs of women in the Ottawa-Carleton area. Needs relate to the general problem of affordability and to the provision of specialized residential facilities for particular groups of women.

Method: Literature review, interviews with directors of residential facilities for
             women
Time: Early 1980's
Space: Ottawa-Carleton

BLACK, David M. (1980). *The Impact of CMHC Policies and Programs on Housing for Women.* Ottawa: Program Evaluation Unit, Policy Evaluation, CMHC.

Identifies the proportion of need represented by female-led households vis-à-vis total housing need and the extent to which the former are clients of CMHC programmes. Housing need is defined using affordability, suitability, and adequacy criteria. Data sets are from 1974 and 1976 HIFE, and 1977 to 1979 relating to non-profit, coop, rent supplement, public housing, rural, and native housing programmes. Author finds that female-led families represent approximately one-third of the housing need and 57 per cent of the CMHC client group. Pattern is similar across all five regions of Canada.

Method: Data analysis
Time: Late 1970's
Space: Canada

BOWLBY, S. R., FOORD, J., and MACKENZIE, S. (1982). "Feminism and Geography." *Area, 14*(1), pp. 19-25.

Suggests that successful development of geographic theory requires examining separation of women's and men's roles in light of current feminist theory. Some recent theoretical writing on geography and women is examined and its links with current feminist social analyses are explored.

Method: Literature review and analysis
Time: 1970-80
Space: Non-specific urban

BUREAU OF MUNICIPAL RESEARCH (September 1981). *Work-Related Day Care: Helping to Close the Gap*. Toronto: Bureau of Municipal Research. 50 pp.

Examines the question of work-place day care as a viable alternative to meet demand. Recommendations are made for action by the Province of Ontario, municipalities, the business community, employees, and labour unions.

Method:　　Case study, analyzing existing statistics, literature review
Time:　　　Early 1980's
Space:　　　Ontario

BUTLER, Diana (1975). "Women in Planning: Career Development." *Plan Canada*, *15*(2), pp. 62-67.

Provides data on enrolment of women in planning schools, membership of women in the Canadian Institute of Planners; discusses attitudes that present obstacles to hiring and promoting women planners; and suggests several measures needed to improve the status of women.

Method:　　Data analysis; observation and experience
Time:　　　1975
Space:　　　Canada

BUTLER, Richard W. and PHILLIPS, Susan (1980). "Women at City Hall." In G. R. Wekerle, R. Peterson, and D. Morley (Eds.), *New Space for Women* (pp. 273-86). Boulder: Westview.

Reports on an investigation into the concerns women in London, Ontario, have about the quality of life in urban environments and the role women play in the decision-making process. The results were later incorporated with the views of women in other cities to get a Canada-wide perspective. (See CANADA, Ministry of State for Urban Affairs, 1975.)

Method:　　Literature review; partially structured interviews
Time:　　　Mid 1970's
Space:　　　London, Ontario

CANADA. Ministry of State for Urban Affairs (1975). *Metropolitan Canada Women's Views of Urban Problems*. Ottawa: Ministry of State for Urban Affairs. 29 pp.

Provides a summary of nine separate reports on women's perceptions of the quality of the Canadian urban environment.

Method:　　Case study, various methods employed in each case study.
Time:　　　Mid-1970's
Space:　　　Canadian cities (Vancouver, Calgary, Winnipeg, London, Montreal, Quebec City, Saint John, Halifax, and St. John's), October 1971.

CANADIAN COUNCIL ON SOCIAL DEVELOPMENT (October 1971). *The One-Parent Family: Report of an Inquiry on One-Parent Families in Canada*.

Ottawa: Canadian Council on Social Development. 166 pp.

Inquiry into the problems of men and women who are raising their families alone, with particular reference to the social policy implications of these problems.

Method: Partially structured interviews; structured questionnaires; group discussions.
Time: Early 1970's
Space: Halifax/Dartmouth, Hull, London (Ontario), Grey County (Ontario), Winnipeg, Vancouver.

CICHOCKI, Mary K. (1980). "Women's Travel Patterns in a Suburban Development." In G. R. Wekerle, R. Peterson, and D. Morley (Eds.), *New Space for Women* (pp. 151-63). Boulder: Westview.

Examines the extent to which the physical form of the metropolis discriminates against the existing lifestyles and future opportunities for women.

Method: Time-budgets; partially-structured interviews
Time: Early 1970's?
Space: Suburban Toronto

CITY OF HALIFAX (1985). "Housing Halifax: A Symposium on Housing in Halifax, 1985. Submissions." Halifax: City of Halifax.

Compiles the briefs on housing issues presented to the City of Halifax including those relating to women and housing from: Women's Emergency Housing Coalition, Ad Sum House, One Parent Family Support Network, YWCA Halifax, M.U.M.S. (Mothers United for Metro Shelter), Nova Scotia Advisory Council on the Status of Women.

Method: —
Time: 1985
Space: Halifax

COMMUNITY PLANNING ASSOCIATION OF CANADA, NOVA SCOTIA DIVISION (1985). "Women and Community — Dartmouth Project." Dartmouth, Nova Scotia: CPAC/Nova Scotia. (Available from CPAC/NS, 2015 Gottingen Street, Halifax, N.S., B3K 3B1.)

Series of publications. Presents material related to this funded project's goals, which were to obtain the views of women on a range of community planning and related issues; and to inform and facilitate the participation of women in the municipal planning review process. Method and results of a systematic survey of Dartmouth women on community issues are available together with publications designed to facilitate women's participation in planning.

Method: Questionnaire Survey; multi-cluster sampling; Community development
Time: 1984-85
Space: Dartmouth, Nova Scotia

COMMUNITY PLANNING ASSOCIATION OF CANADA, NOVA SCOTIA DIVISION (1985). "Women and Community Action." Halifax, Nova Scotia CPAC/Nova Scotia. (Available from CPAC/NS, 2015 Gottingen Street, Halifax, N.S., B3K 3B1.)

Series of publications. Continues community development around municipal affairs, child care and housing, which were issues of immediate concern identified in the survey project noted above. Actions and publications were funded by a 1985 CEIC Canada Works grant, with supplementary funds from the Secretary of State Women's Programme.

Method: Community Development
Time: 1985
Space: Halifax-Dartmouth

COOK, Ramsay and MITCHINSON, Wendy (Eds.) (1976). *The Proper Sphere: Woman's Place in Canadian Society*. Toronto: Oxford University Press. 335 pp.

Collection of documents which provides an historical record of the changes in the roles of women in Canadian society.

Method: Historical research
Time: Mainly 1870-1918
Space: Canada

COOLS, Anne (1980). "Emergency Shelter: The Development of an Innovative Women's Environment." In G. R. Wekerle, R. Peterson, and D. Morley (Eds.), *New Space for Women* (pp. 311-18). Boulder: Westview.

Describes the structure and philosophy behind the operations of an emergency shelter for women and their children.

Method: Case study
Time: Early 1970's
Space: Special purpose home — emergency shelter in Toronto

CORBETT, Ron (May 1986). "The Incidence of Single Parent Families by Settlement Type in Atlantic Canada." Sackville, New Brunswick: Rural & Small Town Research and Studies Programme, Dept. of Geography, Mount Allison University. 33 pp., bibliography, tables, maps, figures.

Reports findings of first of three phases of a project examining one-parent families and their housing needs. Phase One looks at spatial location and concentration, Phase Two at profiles of those families, and Phase Three at relevance of existing government housing policies and programmes. First phase findings include showing that there is not a strong relationship between the incidence of one-parent families and urban centres in Atlantic Canada, which contrasts with some central Canada findings; and that many small towns and villages have incidence rates higher than most of the larger urban centres. In absolute numbers, over 60 per cent of single-parent families live in small towns and villages.

Method: Analysis of 1981 census data, using census divisions and subdivisions
Time: 1981-86
Space: Newfoundland, New Brunswick, Nova Scotia, Prince Edward Island

CROSS, D. Suzanne (1984). "The Neglected Majority: The Changing Role of Women in Nineteenth Century Montreal." In Gilbert A. Stelter and Alan F. J. Artibise (Eds.), *The Canadian City: Essays in Urban and Social History* (pp. 304-27). Ottawa: Carleton University Press.

Examines the growth in female population and employment opportunities for women in nineteenth-century Montreal and indicates some sources for the study of women in the field of social and urban history.

Method: Historical research
Time: 1850-1900
Space: Montreal

CSIERNIK, Rick et al. (1985). *An Overview of the Impact of the Recession on Women in Hamiton-Wentworth*. Hamilton: Social Planning and Research Council. 133 pp.

Documents changes in the economic situation for women in Hamilton-Wentworth 1981 to 1984 using data on demographics, various aspects of work (full-time, part-time, unionized, volunteer, house) and lack of work outside the home, together with training and education opportunities, day care, housing, and mental health. Four subgroups receive special attention: native women, immigrant women, women in conflict with the law, and senior women.

Method: Analysis of existing statistics
Time: 1981-84
Space: Regional Municipality of Hamilton-Wentworth, Ontario

DAGENAIS, Huguette (1980). "Les femmes dans la ville et dans la sociologie urbaine: les multiples facettes d'une même oppression." *Anthropologie et Sociétés*, *4*(1), pp. 21-35.

A study of the subordinate place of women in cities and in urban sociology. The specific nature of women's oppression must be recognized if conditions and analyses are to change.

Method: Literature survey, analysis
Time: Current
Space: —

DELGATTY, Margaret (1977). *Report on the YWCA Single Parent Housing Survey*. Winnipeg: YWCA, 60 pp.

Investigates the housing and support service needs of families who have recently become single-parent families.

Method: Partially-structured interviews
Time: Late 1970's
Space: Winnipeg

DOYLE, Cassie and McCLAIN, Janet (1984). "Women, the Forgotten Housing Consumers." In Jill McCalla Vickers (Ed.), *Taking Sex into Account: The Policy Consequences of Sexist Research* (pp. 219-42). Ottawa: Carleton University Press.

Demonstrates that the current position of women as consumers, and their specific housing needs, were not identified in the analysis, planning, and programme development that preceded housing policy changes in Canada in the 1970's.

Method: Literature review; analyzing existing statistics
Time: 1970's
Space: Canada

DUVALL, Donna (January-February 1985). "Emergency Housing for Women in Canada." *Ekistics*, *52*, pp. 56-61.

Describes the type of help and different shelters available for women in Canada.

Method: Literature review
Time: 1980's
Space: Special purpose homes — emergency shelters

EVANS, J. and COOPERSTOCK, R. (Winter 1983). "Psycho-Social Problems of Women in Primary Resource Communities." *Canadian Journal of Community Mental Health*, Special supplement no. 1, "Psycho-Social Impacts of Resource Development in Canada: Research Strategies and Applications," pp. 55-66.

Reviews forty-three studies related to the psychosocial impacts of resource development upon women resident in isolated single-industry communities. Identifies the indicators that ideally would be used in such studies and discusses the reports' findings against these indicators. Argues that sufficient community case reports have been developed which both establish the need to quantify data and provide the heuristic tools for this next stage of study.

Method: Literature review
Time: 1970's and early 1980's
Space: Mainly Canadian resource communities

FARGE, Brenda Doyle (Winter 1986). "Women's Leadership in Co-ops: Some Questions." *Women and Environments*, *8*(1), pp. 13-15.

Reports on survey conducted at the Co-operative Housing Foundation of Canada's 1985 annual meeting. Designed to learn if existing findings on women's involvement in co-ops in Toronto could be generalized across Canada and what the motives are and gains derived from involvement.

Method: Structured questionnaire; literature review
Time: 1985
Space: Housing co-operatives; Canada

FLETCHER, Susan and STONE, Leroy O. (1982). *The Living Arrangements of Canada's Older Women*. Ottawa: Statistics Canada. 74 pp.

Provides a review of the living arrangements of Canada's older female population focusing in particular on the differences in living arrangements between older men and older women, and between different age groups of older women. The relationship between living arrangements and ease of accessibility to services is also discussed.

Method: Analyzing existing statistics
Time: Mainly 1970's with projections to 2021
Space: Canada

FOWLER, Pauline (Fall 1985). "Reclaiming Architecture: Women's Cultural Building." *Women and Environments*, 7, pp. 14-17.

Describes an architect's proposal for a women's cultural building, highlighting the differences between women's and men's architecture.

Method: Observations by author
Time: 1985
Space: Community Centre

GILBERT, Anne and ROSE, Damaris (Eds.) (1987). "Espaces et femmes." *Cahiers de géographie du Québec*, *31*(83). Special issue.

Whole issue looks at women and built environments. Articles in both French and English.

Method: —
Time: 1980's
Space: International, with an emphasis on Quebec

GILL, A. M. (1984). "Women in Northern Resource Towns." In *Social Science in the North*, Association of Canadian Universities for Northern Studies, Occasional Publications No. 9. pp. 61-73.

Examines role of women in northern communities, including as "stabilizers" of the male work force, and their responses to these environments. Findings from research in Thompson and Leaf Rapids, Manitoba, show among other things that women have more negative images of northern communities than men.

Method: Literature review; structures questionnaire survey using rating scales
Time: Early 1980's
Space: Thompson and Leaf Rapids, Manitoba

GOLIGER, Gabriella (1983). "Constance Hamilton Co-op: Housing by Women for Women." *Habitat*, *26*, pp. 22-26.

Describes the first housing co-operative in Canada created by and for women, located in Toronto.

Method: Case study
Time: Early 1980's
Space: Co-operative housing

GOOD, D. B. (Lin) (1975). "Women in Planning: A Citizen's View." *Plan Canada*, *15*(2), pp. 68-71.

Compares role of women in planning in 1925 and 1975 and suggests that progress has been less than breathtaking. Describes attitudes towards women in the field and the usual spheres in which women contribute.

Method: Personal observation
Time: 1925-75
Space: Canada

GRIFFITHS, Nan (Editor and Workshop Coordinator of the NCC Women's Task Force) (1975). *Women in the Urban Environment: Proceedings of a National Workshop*. Ottawa: National Capital Commission. 41 pp.

Proceedings of a national workshop on the concerns of women in shaping the urban environment. The proceedings cover the identification of the specific needs of women, planning recommendations and proposals to meet these needs and, finally, strategies for ways of improving women's input into the planning process.

Method: Position papers and reports prepared by participants; discussion among the participants
Time: Mid-1970's
Space: Canada

GURSTEIN, Penny and HOOD, Nancy (1975). *Housing Needs of One-Parent Families*. Vancouver: YWCA, 65 pp., Appendices A to I, 31 pp., and videotape (available at CMHC Canadian Housing Information Centre, Head Office, Ottawa).

Aims to determine user needs for these families with a view to improving the adequacy of housing itself and housing-related programmes and services.

Method: Questionnaire survey, personal and telephone interviews, group discussions, information exchange sessions, video
Time: Mid-1970's
Space: Vancouver

HALE, Sylvia M. (Fall 1985). "Integrating Women in Development Models and Theories." *Atlantis*, *11*(1), pp. 45-63.

Addresses the critique posed by feminist theory that women's issues have been left out of macro analyses of national development. Attempts to integrate women's issues into contemporary development models while considering mechanisms to promote change. Five models are considered: (a) the social welfare approach; (b) the grass roots networking and participatory democracy approach; (c) the culture of poverty thesis; (d) entrepreneurship; and (e) neo-imperialism. Draws on data gathered during fieldwork in villages in North India.

Method: Field research; argumentation
Time: 1980's
Space: Developing areas

HARRISON, Brian R. (1981). *Living Alone in Canada: Demographic and Economic Perspectives 1951-1976*. Ottawa: Statistics Canada. 60 pp.

Analyzes the increase, from 1951 to 1976, in one-person households and determines some of the fundamental causes for the increase.

Method: Analyzing existing statistics
Time: 1951-76
Space: Canada

HARVEY, Andrew S. and CLARK, Susan (1975). *Descriptive Analysis of Halifax Time-Budget Data*. Halifax: Dalhousie University, Institute of Public Affairs, Regional and Urban Studies Centre. 37 pp.

Determines the factors affecting participation in, and duration of, activities, for married men and women.

Method: Analysis of time-budget data
Time: 1971-72
Space: Halifax

HOBBS, Margaret and PIERSON, Ruth Roach (Winter 1986). " 'When Is a Kitchen Not a Kitchen?' " *Canadian Woman Studies/Les cahiers de la femme*, 7(4), pp. 71-76.

Examines the Canadian Home Improvement Plan introduced by the federal government in 1937 as a remedial programme to ease unemployment by encouraging especially working-class homeowners to do improvements. Authors look at importance of this programme in defining and reinforcing appropriate sex-typed roles in society.

Method: Historical research
Time: 1936-40
Space: Houses; Canada

JACOBSON, Helga E. (1977). *How to Study Your Own Community: Research from the Perspective of Women*. Vancouver: Women's Research Centre.

JACOBSON, Helga E. (1978). *Women's Perspectives in Research*. Vancouver: Women's Research Centre.

JOHNSON, Laura Climenko (1977). *Who Cares?: A Report of the Project Child Care Survey of Parents and Their Child Care Arrangements*. Toronto: Social

Planning Council of Metro Toronto, 287 pp. and appendices.

Aims to provide the empirical data needed to recommend policies on day care provision, including whether it should be provided through the private or public sector or in combination. Surveys the child care arrangements that parents of children up to six years of age used over a one-year period.

Method: Questionnaire survey
Time: 1976
Space: Metro Toronto

JORDAN, Elizabeth (November 1981). *The Housing Needs of Female Led One Parent Families.* Ottawa: Canada Mortgage and Housing Corporation. 42 pp.

Looks at the housing needs of female-led one-parent families, highlighting the problems and making recommendations for further study. The Canadian situation is compared with that in the United States, Great Britain, and Scandinavia.

Method: Literature review
Time: Early 1980's
Space: Canada, and other countries.

KJELLBERG, Judith (Ed.) (1983). *Women and Planning: Proceedings of a Conference, Toronto, May 1982.* Edited by Judith Kjellberg. Toronto: Women in/and Planning. 73 pp.

Proceedings of a conference on the professional issues for women in planning, architecture, and related professions and academic disciplines, and on the environmental issues for women generally.

Method: —
Time: 1982
Space: Canada

KLODAWSKY, Fran and ROSE, Damaris (1985). *Employment Opportunities for Women in Architecture and Urban Planning: Problems and Prospects.* Ottawa: Labour Canada, Women's Bureau. 65 pp. (English), 67 pp. (French).

Describes the employment opportunities for women in the fields of architecture and urban planning and assesses the prospects for the future for women and for the fields.

Method: Analyzing existing statistics; partially structured interviews
Time: 1980's
Space: Canada

KLODAWSKY, Fran, SPECTOR, Aron N., and HENDRIX, Catrina (January 1984). *Housing and Single Parents: An Overview of the Literature.* Bibliographic Studies No. 15. Toronto: Centre for Urban and Community Studies, University of Toronto. 48 pp.

Reviews the Canadian literature on housing and single parents and compares this research with recent American and British work. An annotated bibliography makes up half of the document.

Method: Literature review
Time: 1980's
Space: Canada, United States, Britain

KLODAWSKY, Fran, SPECTOR, Aron N., and ROSE, Damaris (1985). *Single Parent Families and Canadian Housing Policies: How Mothers Lose.* Ottawa: Canada Mortgage and Housing Corporation, External Research Program. 348 pp.

Deduces the housing and demographic characteristics of single parents, and examines some existing Canadian housing programmes in terms of the needs of single parent families and in comparison with programmes in other countries.

Method: Analyzing existing statistics; policy analysis; literature review
Time: 1980's
Space: Canada, United States, Europe

LEACH, Belinda, LESIUK, Ellen, and MORTON, Penny E. (Spring 1986). "Perceptions of Fear in the Urban Environment." *Women and Environments*, *8*(2), pp. 10-12.

Describes a representative survey of women students at Carleton University who were asked to identify locations on the campus that they perceived as fearful and to explain why. Links this study to others regarding women's perceptions of danger in urban environments and proposes recommendations.

Method: Structured questionnaire survey
Time: Circa 1985
Space: University campus

LETTRE, Solange (1985-86). "Des coopératrices du secteur coopératif d'habitation et leur participation au mouvement des femmes." *Coop'eratives et d'eveloppement*, *17*(1), pp. 159-73.

Studies the links between cooperative housing and the women's movement by studying a group of residents of cooperative housing. Concludes that the influence of feminism can be seen not only in the social involvement of the women but also in their day-to-day life and that cooperative housing can represent a feminist model of development.

Method: Interviews
Time: 1980's
Space: Sherbrooke, Quebec

LI, Selina (1978). *Options for Single Mothers.* Project Child Care. Working Paper No. 4. Toronto: Social Planning Council of Metropolitan Toronto. 44 pp.

Conducts secondary analysis of data gathered by Project Child Care in order to understand why some single mothers work outside the home while others do not; what the sociodemographic differences are between employed and welfare-recipient single mothers; and some of the problems encountered by employed single mothers.

Method:	Sub-sample of eighty-seven employed mothers with children under seven years drawn from larger project Child Care sample; data is from structured in-depth interviews; not statistically generalizable
Time:	Late 1970's
Space:	Metropolitan Toronto

LIGHTMAN, Ernie S. and JOHNSON, Laura C. (1977). *Child Care Patterns in Metropolitan Toronto*. Toronto: Social Planning Council of Metro Toronto, Project Child Care Working Paper No. 2. 48 pp.

Locates and identifies various types of informal child care arrangements and their frequency and patterns of use. Draws on a statistically representative sample.

Method:	Questionnaire survey — stratified cluster sampling. (Detailed description of sample design available in Project Child Care. Sample Design Report, March 1976 from SPC — Metro Toronto.)
Time:	Mid-1970's
Space:	Metro Toronto

LUXTON, Meg (1980). *More than a Labour of Love: Three Generations of Women's Work in the Home*. Toronto: Women's Press. 260 pp.

Describes the work that women do in the home, shows how their work has changed over three generations, and isolates the various forces that shape and change domestic labour.

Method:	Interviews, participant observation
Time:	1920-70
Space:	Flin Flon, Manitoba

MACKENZIE, Suzanne (1981). *Women and the Reproduction of Labour Power in the Industrial City*. Working paper 23. Brighton: Urban and Regional Studies, University of Sussex. (Available for £3.00 from Urban and Regional Studies, Arts Building, University of Sussex, Falmer, Brighton, England, BN1 9QN.)

Tries to understand the relationship between women's social position and the processes of urban landscape transformation, examining the change in womens' position which arose with industrialization and the way in which women's response to this change influenced and was articulated in the transformation of Toronto's landscape between 1880-1910.

Method:	Historical analysis
Time:	1880-1910
Space:	Toronto

MACKENZIE, Suzanne (1984). "Editorial Introduction." *Antipode, 16*, pp. 3-10.

Provides an historical and conceptual context for the papers presented in this special issue of the journal on the theme women and the environment. The focus of the special issue is on socialist-feminist perspectives.

Method: Literature review; argumentation
Time: Historical; and 1980's
Space: Non-specific

MACKENZIE, Suzanne (Fall 1984). "Catching Up With Ourselves: Ideas on Developing Gender-Sensitive Theory in the Environmental Disciplines." *Women and Environments, 6*, pp. 16-18.

Argues that we must assimilate social changes involving the changing roles of women into the theory and methodology of the environmental disciplines rather than merely empirically acknowledging women as a population subgroup.

Method: Argumentation
Time: Mid-1980's
Space: —

MACKENZIE, Suzanne (1985). "'No One Seems to Go to Work Anymore': Women Redesignating and Redesigning the City." *Canadian Woman Studies/Les cahiers de la femme, 6*(2), pp. 5-8.

Speculates on neighbourhood spaces and homes that women might create which are sufficiently flexible to accommodate both domestic and salaried activities.

Method: Imaginative essay
Time: Future
Space: Non-specific urban

MACKENZIE, Suzanne (1986). "Feminist Geography." *The Canadian Geographer/Le géographe canadien, 30*(3), pp. 268-70.

Describes the transition from the special interest field of the "geography of women" to a feminist geography, with an independent theoretical and method-ological basis. The latter, she argues, involved breaking down the categories "women" and "environment" so as to be able to ask these types of questions: how do changes in modes of appropriating the environment alter the activities defined as appropriate to "women" and "men" and therefore alter gender categories? How do changes in gender affect modes of environmental appropriation?

Method: Argumentation
Time: 1980's
Space: —

MACKENZIE, Suzanne (1987). "Women's Responses to Economic Restructuring: Changing Gender, Changing Space." In Roberta Hamilton and Michèle Barrett (Eds.), *The Politics of Diversity* (pp. 81-100). Montreal: Book Centre.

Argues that changes in the use of environments and changes in gender relations are inextricably connected and cannot be fully understood in isolation from each other. Examines relation between gender and environment in Canadian cities over time, focusing especially on current period of economic restructuring and evidence of changes in women's use of home and community space. Uses data from interviews with homeworkers in Trail-Nelson and Kingston.

Method: Argumentation; questionnaire survey
Time: 1980's
Space: Communities in Trail-Nelson, B.C., area and Kingston, Ontario; Canada generally

MACKENZIE, Suzanne and ROSE, Damaris (1982). "On the Necessity for Feminist Scholarship in Human Geography." *Professional Geographer*, *34*(2), pp. 220-23.

Explains that geographers concerned with built environments must bring an understanding of changing gender roles to bear on traditional views of separated spheres of waged work and domestic work in order to inquire into the ways women are meeting the conflicts of dual roles.

Method: Literature review and analysis
Time: 1980's
Space: Non-Specific

MACKENZIE, Suzanne and ROSE, Damaris (1983). "Industrial Change, the Domestic Economy and Home Life." In J. Anderson, S. Duncan, and R. Hudson (Eds.), *Redundant Spaces in Cities and Regions?: Studies in Industrial Decline and Social Change* (p. 155-200). London: Academic Press.

Attempts a synthesis of the analytical separation between the spheres of production and reproduction by outlining the historical relationships between the major activities that go on in the work place and in the home. The historical information is European in origin.

Method: Historical research
Time: Historical; and 1980's
Space: Britain

MASSON, Dominique (December 1984). "Les femmes dans les structures urbaines: aperçu d'un nouveau champ de recherche." In *Canadian Journal of Political Science*, *17*, pp. 755-82.

Reviews the literature on women and the city in the field of urban politics, showing the trends toward theory-building in the area of gender politics, and of continuing investigations of this question in the context of more traditional approaches to urban politics.

Method: Literature review
Time: 1980's
Space: Canada, United States, Europe

MCCLAIN, Janet and DOYLE, Cassie (1984). *Women and Housing: Changing Needs and the Failure of Policy*. Toronto: James Lorimer and Company and Canadian Council on Social Development. 82 pp.

Analyzes the housing needs of Canadian women and reviews previous housing policies, confirming that women as housing consumers were not considered in pre-1980's policy and programme development.

Method: Literature review; analyzing existing statistics
Time: 1970's
Space: Canada

MCINNIS, Pat (Winter 1986). "Cabin Fever: Northern Women and Mental Health." *Women and Environments*, *8*(1), pp. 4-6.

Reports on research on women's health needs in fifteen northern Ontario communities which identified common mental health problems across the communities. These findings emerged while conducting workshops not specifically designed to focus on mental health.

Method: Workshops
Time: 1983-85
Space: Northern Ontario communities

MEDJUCK, Sheva (Fall 1985). "Women's Response to Economic and Social Change in the Nineteenth Century: Moncton Parish 1851 to 1871." *Atlantis*, *11*(1), pp. 7-21.

Attempts to document the everyday lives of the ordinary women of Moncton Parish and to show from the records how women dealt with the economic and social conditions of their times. Includes analysis of marriage and fertility rates, participation in paid work (which shifts from decade to decade), and women heads of households. Argues for an approach to historical analysis that attempts to understand how women affect historical conditions.

Method: Analysis of census records 1851, 1861, 1871
Time: 1851-71
Space: Moncton, New Brunswick

MELLETT, Cathy J. (1982). *At the End of the Rope: A Study of Women's Emergency Housing Needs in the Halifax/Dartmouth Area*. Ottawa: Canada Mortgage and Housing Corporation. 53 pp.

Provides information on the numbers of women contacting area agencies with serious housing needs and determines the need for emergency shelters.

Method: Structured questionnaire (mail); partially structured interviews; needs assessment
Time: Early 1980's
Space: Halifax/Dartmouth, Nova Scotia

MENZIES, S. June (April 1976). *New Directions for Public Policy: A Position Paper on the One-Parent Family*. Ottawa: Advisory Council on the Status of Women. 29 pp.

Suggests new directions in public policy which assist the one-parent family to become an economically viable family unit.

Method: Analyzing existing statistics
Time: Mid-1970's
Space: Canada

MICHELSON, William (1973). *The Price of Time in the Longitudinal Evaluation of Spatial Structures by Women*. Toronto: Centre for Urban and Community Studies, University of Toronto, Research Paper No. 61. 39 pp.

Explores the extent that behavioural expectations in housing choice are confirmed by subsequent experience and whether the time-budget is sufficiently versatile to measure this. Included in the findings is that women know they are making a major compromise in moving to suburban homes and they are least satisfied in the way they spend their time of all movers studied.

Method: Time-budgets
Time: Early 1970's
Space: Toronto inner city and suburbs

MICHELSON, William (October 1983). *The Logistics of Maternal Employment: Implications for Women and Their Families*. Toronto: University of Toronto, Centre for Urban and Community Studies. Child in the City Report No. 18. 155 + pp.

Assesses from individual level data on families' daily conditions and experiences what logistical differences, reflecting extra-familial factors, are found in the everyday lives of employed and single mothers. Also assesses the implications of these additional responsibilities for children, and for policies and practices relating to employment, women, and families.

Method: Stratified representation sample; structured questionnaire survey;
            time-budgets
Time: 1980
Space: Metro Toronto

MICHELSON, William (1985). *From Sun to Sun: Daily Obligations and Community Structure in the Lives of Employed Women and Their Families*. Totowa, New Jersey: Rowman and Allanheld. 208 pp.

Presents the problems and outcomes which can arise for families when mothers are employed outside the home and assesses the implications for policies and practices relating to employment, women, and families.

Method: Time-budgets; field research; structured questionnaire (personal interview)
Time: 1980
Space: Toronto

MICHELSON, William, LEVINE, Saul, and MICHELSON, Ellen (1979). *The Child in the City: Today and Tomorrow.* Toronto: University of Toronto Press. 272 pp.

Elaborated and expanded proceedings of a lecture series based around the Child in the City Project and exploring various aspects of urban life in industrialized countries for children.

Method: —
Time: 1970's
Space: Cities; non-specific

MICHELSON, William, LEVINE, Saul V., SPINA, Anna-Rose et al. (1979). *The Child in the City: Changes and Challenges.* Toronto: University of Toronto Press. 520 pp.

Provides eight research papers on aspects of children's lives in urban environments including community services, shared child-rearing and urban physical form and content.

Method: —
Time: 1970's
Space: Cities; non-specific

MICHELSON, William and MICHELSON, Ellen (Eds.) (1980). *Managing Urban Space in the Interest of Children.* Toronto: Child in the City Programme, University of Toronto. Canada/MAB Committee. 255 pp. (English), 262 pp. (French).

Method: —
Time: 1970's
Space: Cities; non-specific

MILROY, Beth Moore (1984). *Women and Housing: Policy Statement.* Prepared for the Social Planning Council of Ottawa-Carleton. Ottawa: Social Planning Council of Ottawa-Carleton. 11 pp. (Available from The Council, 256 King Edward, Ottawa, K1N 7M1.)

Draws on empirical evidence to provide the rationale for insisting on gender specificity in matters relating to housing. Argument is based on the principle that women's and men's housing experience differs with respect to (a) acquiring and paying for it, (b) living in it on a daily basis, (c) moving between it and jobs and services, and (d) gaining access to emergency housing.

Method: Policy development
Time: 1980's
Space: Ottawa-Carleton area

MOMSEN, Janet Henshall (August 1980). "Women in Canadian Geography." *Professional Geographer*, *32*, pp. 365-69.

Compares the status of women in geography departments, as students and faculty, in Canada and the United States.

Method: Questionnaire survey
Time: 1978-79
Space: Canada, United States

MOMSEN, Janet Henshall (Summer 1980). "Women in Canadian Geography." *Canadian Geographer*, *24*, pp. 177-83.

Discusses the status of women in geography departments of Canadian universities.

Method: Questionnaire survey
Time: 1978-79
Space: Canada

MORRISON, Carolyn (Winter 1982). "Options for Women in Geography: Some Experiences Shared." *Canadian Geographer*, *26*, pp. 360-66.

Studies the non-academic career fields chosen by female M.A. students of geography, gauging their attitudes about geography as a discipline and as preparation for a career.

Method: Unstructured interviews
Time: Circa 1981
Space: Canada

NADEAU, D. (March 1982). "Women and Self-Help in Resource-Based Communities." *Resources for Feminist Research, 11*(1), pp. 65-67.

Assesses the programming and organizational structure of a northern B.C. initiative, the Women's Self-Help Network, which functions in rural and resource-based communities.

Method: Observation
Time: Early 1980's
Space: Northern B.C. communities

NATIONAL COUNCIL OF WELFARE (April 1976). *One in a World of Two's: A Report by the National Council of Welfare on One-Parent Families in Canada.* Ottawa: National Council of Welfare. 41 pp.

Exposes the hardships faced by one-parent families.

Method: Analyzing existing statistics
Time: Mid-1970's
Space: Canada

NORTHERN BRITISH COLUMBIA WOMEN'S TASK FORCE (1977). *Report on Single Industry Resource Communities*. Vancouver: Women's Research Centre. 100 pp. (Available for $3.00 from Women's Research Centre, Ste. 301, 2515 Burrard Street, Vancouver, V6J 3J6.)

Uses case studies to describe everyday problems of women in resource towns designed primarily for male workers. Kitimat, Fraser Lake, and MacKenzie are covered. Argues that women should be involved in planning and design because, as currently built, these towns reinforce marginal roles for women.

Method: Case studies
Time: Mid-1970's
Space: Northern Canadian communities

NOVAC, Sylvia (October 1986). *Women and Housing: An Annotated Bibliography*. CPL Bibliography 178. 26 pp. Chicago: Council of Planning Librarians. (Available for $9.00 from 1313 East 60th Street, Chicago, Illinios, 60637.)

Covers five years prior to publication of literature on housing for women from a feminist perspective. Restricted to Western nations and does not cover specific issues such as housing for the elderly, emergency, or transitional housing.

Method: —
Time: 1980-85
Space: Houses

NOZICK, Marcia (Winter 1986-87) "Women Embrace Their Own Economic Development." *City Magazine*, 9(1), pp. 7-9.

Describes two community economic development initiatives for and by women. One is "Community Economic Options," a project of the Women's Skills Development Society of British Columbia, which is engaged in consciousness-raising workshops and helping to identify skills and start projects. The other is "Women's Economic Development Corporation" of St. Paul, Minnesota—a non-profit organization which helped launch 546 businesses owned and run by women. Draws out the contrasting features of the two approaches.

Method: Mini case studies
Time: 1980's
Space: Communities in British Columbia and Minnesota

PEDERSEN, Diana (Winter 1986). " 'Keeping Our Good Girls Good': The YWCA and the 'Girl Problem,' 1870-1930." *Canadian Woman Studies/Les cahiers de la femme*, 7(4), pp. 20-24.

Examines the YWCA movement, in which thirty-nine branches were established in Canadian communities between 1870 and 1930, as early attempts to create public space for women. Focuses on efforts to protect young women from the insalubrious city as they acquired some independence. Argues that the approach to gaining public support for YWCAs helped to reinforce views that women were temporary workers; that women's sexuality, not men's, needed supervision; and reproduced both the oppressive and positive features of the mother-daughter relationship among women of different classes.

Method: Historical research
Time: 1870-1930
Space: YWCA buildings; Canada

PEDERSEN, Diana (February 1987). " 'Building Today for the Womanhood of Tomorrow': Businessmen, Boosters, and the YWCA, 1890-1930." *Urban History Review/Revue d'histoire urbaine, 15*(3), pp. 225-42.

Argues that women reformers had their own distinct perception of the city and definition of urban reform but, lacking capital and political power, had to depend on support of male reformers. Study examines relationship between the YWCA and Canadian businessmen as manifested in fund-raising campaigns.

Method: Historical research
Time: 1890-1930
Space: YWCA buildings; Canada

PETERSON, Rebecca (1986). "Women as a Special User Group in a Changing North American Cultural Context." *Environments, 18*(3), pp. 64-73.

Reviews changing family form and work roles of North American women since 1950's and links this to a critique of built environments from the perspective of women as a special user group.

Method: Literature review
Time: 1950-86
Space: North America

PETERSON, Rebecca, WEKERLE, Gerda R., and MORLEY, David (December 1978). "Women and Environments: An Overview of an Emerging Field." *Environment and Behaviour,10*, pp. 511-34.

Discusses how changes in women's sense of themselves, in their relations with men, and in their social roles are expressed in the relationship between women and their environments. A broad organizing framework is developed for study in this area.

Method: Literature review
Time: 1970's
Space: Canada, United States

PICHE, Denise (Summer 1979). "L'appropriation de l'espace par les femmes." *Atlantis, 4*(2), part 2, pp. 189-99.

The author discusses the question of women's appropriation of their environment and arrives at the conclusion — after discussing the little and probably diminishing control women have over their environment and the reasons for wanting to appropriate space — that it is urgent for women to work towards a feminization of the planning process in order to work for a better environment.

Method: Analysis, literature review
Time: 1970's
Space: non-specific

PINARD, Yolande (1983). "Les débats du mouvement des femmes à Montréal, 1893-1902." In Marie Lavigne and Yolande Pinard (Eds.), *Travailleuses et féministes: les femmes dans la société québécoise* (pp. 177-98). Montreal: Boréal Express.

A study of the first women's movement in Montreal, focusing particularly on the Montreal Local Council of Women (MLCW). The study looks at the work of the MLCW in the context of the urbanization of Montreal in the early twentieth century and the social problems arising from the rapid urbanization.

Method: Literature survey, archival material
Time: 1893-1902
Space: Montreal

ST. MARTIN, I. (1981). "Women in Schefferville: Research Notes." In J. Bradbury and J. Wolfe (Eds.), *Perspectives on Social and Economic Change in the Iron-Ore Mining Region of Quebec-Labrador*, McGill Subarctic Research Paper No. 35. Montreal: Centre for Northern Studies and Research, McGill University.

Discusses some aspects of the experience of women in Schefferville as wage earners, mothers, and homemakers at the point when the mining company was winding down its operation.

Method: Questionnaire survey; analysis of existing data
Time: Late 1970's
Space: Schefferville, Quebec

SIMON, Joan C. (Winter 1986). "Integrating Housing and Economic Development." *Women and Environments*, *8*(1), pp. 10-12.

Identifies the opportunities for women afforded by housing cooperatives. From a secure home base, women are learning management and housing sector skills that can be used in seeking paid work beyond the cooperative.

Method: Field research
Time: 1980's
Space: Canada, United States

SOCIAL PLANNING COUNCIL OF METROPOLITAN TORONTO (April 1984). "Lone Parent Families in Metropolitan Toronto." In *Social Infopac*, *3*. 7 pp.

Examines the characteristics of one-parent families and discusses the implications for policies, benefits, and programs in meeting the families' needs.

Method: Analyzing existing statistics
Time: 1980's
Space: Toronto

SOPER, Mary (1980). "Housing for Single-Parent Families: A Women's Design." In G. R. Wekerle, R. Peterson, and D. Morley (Eds.), *New Space for Women* (pp. 319-32). Boulder: Westview.

Describes an experiment to involve women in the planning of a federal demonstration housing project for women who are sole-support mothers.

Method: Case study
Time: 1975
Space: Special purpose homes; single-parent families

STAMP, Judy (1980). "Toward Supportive Neighborhoods: Women's Role in Changing the Segregated City." In G. R. Wekerle, R. Peterson, and D. Morley (Eds.), *New Space for Women* (pp. 189-98). Boulder: Westview.

Explores how women are changing neighbourhoods to meet the needs of their changing lifestyles.

Method: Informal observation by author
Time: 1970's
Space: Suburbs; inner-city residential areas

TARDY, Evelyne (1982). *La politique: un monde d'hommes?* *Une étude sur les mairesses au Québec.* Montreal: Hurtubise HMH. 111 pp.

A survey of women mayors in Quebec, using a control group of men mayors, in order to compare socioeconomic factors, prior social and political experience and attitudes. Emphasis is put on the obstacles to women's political participation.

Method: Interviews
Time: 1970's and early 1980's
Space: Quebec

TRUELOVE, Marie (Fall 1984). "Constraints for Subsidized Daycare Users." *Women and Environments*, 6, pp. 12-13.

Examines the distance to, and choice in, subsidized day care for approximately 5,000 children and suggests the appropriate roles for municipal governments.

Method: Case study
Time: 1980's
Space: Metro Toronto

WEKERLE, Gerda R. (1981). "Women in the Urban Environment." In Catherine R. Stimpson et al. (Eds.), *Women and the American City* (pp. 185-211). Chicago: University of Chicago Press.

Provides a review of the literature in the women and urban environment field, grouping these works into three major categories: those exploring the private-public dichotomy; those examining the fit between the urban environment and women's changing roles; and those focusing on environmental equity in the sense of women's right to equal access to public goods and services.

Method: Literature review
Time: Mainly 1970's
Space: Canada, United States, Europe

WEKERLE, Gerda R. (1984). "A Woman's Place Is in the City." *Antipode*, *16*(3), pp. 11-19.

Discusses some of the recent research on women's urban experience, highlighting work in the areas of transportation, housing, supportive neighbourhoods, and women's activism around urban issues.

Method: Literature review
Time: 1970's and early 1980's
Space: United States, Canada

WEKERLE, Gerda R. (April 1985). "From Refuge to Service Center: Neighborhoods that Support Women." *Sociological Focus*, *18*(2), pp. 79-95.

Focuses on recent research into women's needs in the urban environment which criticizes the images of the neighbourhood as refuge or as non-place network, and suggests that the appropriate focus for research and urban policy is the image of the neighbourhood as service centre.

Method: Literature review
Time: Contemporary
Space: Urban neighbourhoods; Canada, United States, Europe

WEKERLE, Gerda R. and CARTER, Novia (1978). "Urban Sprawl: The Price Women Pay." In *Branching Out*, *3*, pp. 12-14.

Discusses research showing how women are inconvenienced living in suburbs.

Method: Literature review
Time: 1970's
Space: Canada

WEKERLE, Gerda R. and MACKENZIE, Suzanne (1985). "Reshaping the Neighbourhood of the Future as We Age in Place." *Canadian Woman Studies/Les cahiers de la femme*, *6*(2), pp. 69-72.

From a review of demographics of age, incomes, and current dwellings, considers future housing and neighbourhood needs of older women.

Method: Literature review; interpretation
Time: 1985 and beyond
Space: Canada

WEKERLE, Gerda R., PETERSON, Rebecca, and MORLEY, David (Eds.) (1980). *New Space for Women*. Boulder: Westview. 332 pp.

Brings together papers which address specific problems encountered in homes and office buildings, in urban and suburban areas, and in neighbourhoods, and which assess the institutional barriers to change that have prevented women's needs from being adequately addressed in the environmental decision-making process.

Method: —
Time: 1970's
Space: Canada, United States

WELLMAN, Barry (1984). *Domestic Work, Paid Work and Network*. Research Paper No. 149. Toronto: Centre for Urban and Community Studies, University of Toronto. 63 pp.

Analyses the community networks of a large sample of individuals in a Toronto borough according to their involvement in paid and domestic labour. Compares mainly producers ("working men"), reproducers ("housewives"), and double loaders ("working women") with further comparisons to singles and retired people.

Method: Questionnaire survey; small set of in-depth interviews
Time: Early 1980's
Space: Toronto

WOMEN'S RESEARCH CENTRE (1979). *Beyond the Pipeline: A Study of the Lives of Women and Families in Fort Nelson, B.C. and Whitehorse, Y.T.* Vancouver. Women's Research Centre. 251 pp. ^a 5 appendices ^a 17 pp. bibliography. (Available for $5.00 from Women's Research Centre, Ste. 301, 2515 Burrard Street, Vancouver V6J 3J6.)

Outlines how women view their lives and how they expect them to change because of resource development, specifically the Alaska Highway gas pipeline. Gives descriptions of the two communities, the community's planning and housing, and women's work from the perspective of the women who live in Fort Nelson and Whitehorse.

Method: Modified participant observation; in-depth interviews
Time: 1979
Space: Fort Nelson, British Columbia; Whitehorse, Yukon

WOMEN'S RESEARCH CENTRE (1980). *A Review of Munroe House*. Vancouver: Women's Research Centre. 35 pp. ^a 5 appendices and bibliography. (Available for $3.00 from Women's Research Centre, Ste. 301, 2515 Burrard Street, Vancouver V6J 3J6.)

Documents the development and operation of a second stage house for battered women, including its policies; gives a description of Munroe House from perspective of residents; and assesses its benefits and limitations. Appendices provide instruments for data collection, eight case histories, policy statements, and composite profile of residents.

Method: Modified participant observation; open-ended interviews
Time: 1980
Space: Housing for battered women

WOOD, Diane (April 1976). "Women in the Urban Environment." *Community Planning Review*, *26*, pp. 3-6.

Provides a summary of the National Capital Commission's 1975 conference on women in the urban environment.

Method: —
Time: 1975
Space: Canada

THESES/DISSERTATIONS

ATKINS, J. Louise (1979). "The Status of Female Planning Practitioners in Canada." Master's Thesis, University of Waterloo.

AULD, Catherine Margaret (1980). "The Self-Help Potential of Single Parent Housing Tenants." Master's Thesis, Community Planning Department, University of Manitoba.

BEATTY-GUENTER, Patricia P. (1980). "Women's Roles and the Urban-Rural Continuum." Master's Thesis, University of Victoria.

BENNET, Judith Mackenzie (1981). "Gender, Family and Community: A Comparative Study of the English Peasantry, 1287-1349." Ph.D. Diss., University of Toronto.

BERNIER, Jean-Marie (1976). "Etude descriptive des usagers de quatre garderies à but non lucratif." Thèse de maîtrise, Service Social, Université de Montréal.

BOURGEOIS, Manon (1977). "Aspects sociaux de l'évaluation d'un centre d'hébergement pour femmes." Thèse de maîtrise, Sociologie, Université de Montréal.

DESCARRIES-BELANGER, Francine (1978). "La production de la division sociale des sexes." Thèse de maîtrise, Sociologie, Université de Montréal.

ELIAS, Brenda Mary (1978). "Residential Environment and Social Adjustment among Older Widows." Master's Thesis, University of Guelph.

GILL, Alison M. (1982). "Residents' Images of Northern Canadian Resource Communities." Ph.D. Diss., University of Manitoba.

HARRISON, Brian Reginald (1979). "Living Alone in Canada: A Sociodemographic Analysis." Master's Thesis, Carleton University.

HOOD, Nancy Elizabeth (1976). "One-Parent Families: Their Housing Needs." Master's Thesis, University of British Columbia.

JOO, Andrew (1977). "Characteristics of Families Using Child Day Care Centres." Master's Thesis, University of Calgary.

LANGIN, Susan Esther (1981). "Resource Development and New Towns: A Women's Perspective." Master's Thesis, University of British Columbia.

LEWIS, Elaine (1978). "Conjugal Roles in Urban Environments: A Selected

Comparison." Master's Thesis, McGill University.

LUXTON, Margaret Joan (1978). "Why Women's Work Is Never Done: A Case Study from Flin Flon, Manitoba, of Domestic Labour in Industrial Capitalist Society." Ph.D. Diss., University of Toronto.

MACKENZIE, Suzanne (1983). "Gender and Environment: The Reproduction of Labour in Postwar Brighton." D.Phil. Thesis, University of Sussex, Brighton, England.

MARRA, Glenna Lee (1977). "When Mothers Work: Their Needs for Child Care Services." Master's Thesis, Department of Education, Dalhousie University.

MARTINEAU, Diane (1980). "La personne âgée et l'environnement construit." Thèse de maîtrise, Psychologie, Université de Montréal.

McINTYRE, Eileen Lifsha (1979). "The Provision of Day Care in Ontario: Responsiveness of Provincial Policy to Children at Risk Because Their Mothers Work." Ph.D. Diss., Department of Social Work, University of Toronto.

MEADOWS, Mary Lea (1981). "Adaptation to Urban Life by Native Canadian Women." Master's Thesis, University of Calgary.

MITCHINSON, Wendy Lynn (1977). "Aspects of Reform: Four Women's Organizations in 19th Century Canada." Ph.D. Diss., York University.

MOSOFF, Fern (1978). "A Feminist Appraisal of the Organization of Residential Environments." Master's Thesis, Department of Urban and Regional Planning, University of Toronto.

RADIO, Vera Nadya (1974). "Community Development, Social Movements and Feminism." Master's Thesis, University of Alberta.

RIDINGTON, Jillian Botham (1978). "Women in Transition: A Study of a Vancouver Transition House as Agent of Change." Master's Thesis, University of British Columbia.

SANGADASA, A. (1981). "Married Female Labour Force Participation and Fertility in Canada." Ph.D. Diss., University of Alberta.

SHAPIRO, Lorraine, (1978). "The Housing Needs of Working Women." Master's Thesis, University of Waterloo.

SHAW, Susan M. (1983). "The Sexual Division of Leisure: Meanings, Perceptions and the Distribution of Time." Ph.D. Diss., Carleton University.

SIDDIQUE, C. Muhammad (1980). "Work and Family in a Contemporary Urban-Industrial Society: An Analysis of Canadian Data." Ph.D. Diss., University of Toronto.

VAN VLIET, Willem (1980). "Use, Evaluation, and Knowledge of City and Suburban Environments by Children of Employed and Non-Employed Mothers." Ph.D. Diss., University of Toronto.

WARNER, Nancy (1976). "Planning Implications of Women's Increased Participation in the Work Force." Master's Thesis, Department of Urban and Regional Planning, University of Toronto.

WENSEL, Joan Marlene (1977). "The Alberta Women's Bureau: A Community Development." Master's Thesis, University of Alberta.

YOUNG, James (1978). "An Exploratory Study of the Relative Convenience of City and Suburban Public Housing Projects for Sole Support Mothers." Master's Thesis, Department of Urban and Regional Planning, University of Toronto.